OUR WORLD IN PICTURES

BUGS, BUTTERFLIES, BEETLES & BEES

OUR WORLD IN PICTURES

BUGS, BUTTERFLIES, BEETLES & BEES

CONSULTANT **PROFESSOR ADAM HART**
WRITTEN BY **BEN FFRANCON DOWDS, ANDREA MILLS, LIZZIE MUNSEY**

Fact checker Steve Hoffman

Project Editor Bipasha Roy
Project Art Editors Revati Anand, Noopur Dalal
Editors Zaina Budaly, Vandana Likhmania, Aashirwad Jain
Art Editors Prateek Maurya, Anna Pond, Aparajita Sen
Senior Picture Researcher Nishwan Rasool
Project Jackets Art Editor Vidushi Chaudhry
Deputy Managing Editor Sreshtha Bhattacharya
Managing Editors Rachel Fox, Kingshuk Ghoshal
Managing Art Editors Govind Mittal, Owen Peyton Jones
Pre-Production Team Vishal Bhatia, Vijay Kandwal
Production Editor Gillian Reid
Production Controller John Casey
India Creative Head Malavika Talukder
Publisher Andrew Macintyre   **Art Director** Mabel Chan

First published in Great Britain in 2026 by
Dorling Kindersley Limited
20 Vauxhall Bridge Road,
London SW1V 2SA

The authorised representative in the EEA is
Dorling Kindersley Verlag GmbH. Arnulfstr. 124,
80636 Munich, Germany

Copyright © 2026 Dorling Kindersley Limited
A Penguin Random House Company
10 9 8 7 6 5 4 3 2 1
001–352658–March/2026

All rights reserved.
No part of this publication may be reproduced, stored in or introduced into a retrieval system, or transmitted, in any form, or by any means (electronic, mechanical, photocopying, recording, or otherwise), without the prior written permission of the copyright owner.

DK values and supports copyright. Thank you for respecting intellectual property laws by not reproducing, scanning or distributing any part of this publication by any means without permission. By purchasing an authorised edition, you are supporting writers and artists and enabling DK to continue to publish books that inform and inspire readers. No part of this publication may be used or reproduced in any manner for the purpose of training artificial intelligence technologies or systems. In accordance with Article 4(3) of the DSM Directive 2019/790, DK expressly reserves this work from the text and data mining exception.

A CIP catalogue record for this book
is available from the British Library.
ISBN: 978-0-2417-7218-8

Printed and bound in China

www.dk.com

This book was made with Forest Stewardship Council™ certified paper—one small step in DK's commitment to a sustainable future. Learn more at www.dk.com/uk/information/sustainability

CONTENTS

Brilliant bugs	6
Bug groups	8

Body basics 10

Anatomy of an insect	12
Big and small	14
Super senses	16
Extraordinary eyes	18
Supreme sight	20
Little but loud	22
Fabulous antennae	24
Prehistoric bugs	26
Leggy crawlers	28
Little speedsters	30
Colours and patterns	32
Don't eat me!	34
Brilliant butterflies	36
Life of a butterfly	40
Magnificent moths	42
Bright beetles	44
Dragonflies and damselflies	48
Life of a dragonfly	50
Distinct pairs	52

Where bugs live 54

Habitats	56
Underground creatures	58
Insect architects	60
Safe haven	62
Desert dwellers	64
Up in the mountains	66
Rainforest bugs	68
Super spiders	70
Foamy hideaway	72
Urban insects	74
Aquatic bugs	76

A bug's life — 78

Bug behaviour	80
Pollinators	82
Eating pollen	84
Buzzing bees	86
Social insects	88
Active ants	90
Protective patrollers	92
Wasps and sawflies	94
Parental care	96
Faking it	98
Masked moth	100
Nocturnal bugs	102
Light lovers	104
Night lights	106
Great gatherings	108
Migratory insects	110
Migrating monarchs	112
Bug talk	114
Crickets and grasshoppers	116

Finding food — 118

Hunting and feeding	120
Plant lovers	122
True bugs	124
Hungry hunters	126
Sneaky spider	128
Lacewings and relatives	130
Deadly weapons	132
Mighty mantises	134
Formidable fly	136
Wonderful webs	138
Stinging scorpions	140
Venomous insects	142
Ant attack	144
Incredible interactions	146
Unique diets	148
Parasitic bugs	150

Living with bugs — 152

Why we need bugs	154
Backyard bugs	156
House bugs	158
Swarming mayflies	160
Little helpers	162
Bugs in danger	166
Helping bugs	168
Glossary	170
Index	172
Acknowledgments	174

> This book encourages you to explore the fascinating world of bugs. When observing them, remember to treat all insects and their habitats with care. Avoid trapping them inside nets or jars, and do not harm them. If you catch any bugs, release them as soon as possible.

Brilliant bugs

No matter where you are in the world, you're near a bug – from a fly whizzing about the house or a butterfly fluttering around the garden to a spider making its web on a tree or a beetle climbing up a plant in a forest. More than 80 per cent of all animals on Earth are bugs.

AROUND THE WORLD
Bugs can be found on every continent on Earth other than Antarctica. Almost any habitat plays host to these tiny creatures, including forests, woodlands, wetlands, deserts, mountains, and polar regions. Wherever you live, you won't have to go far to spot a bug. Look in the corners of ceilings, venture outside in the garden, or go for a walk in nature – and you'll be rewarded. You might want to take a picture of a bug and see if you can find it in the pages of this book.

How bugs help

Bugs are living proof that good things come in small packages. They are absolutely essential to a diverse range of environments because they keep habitats healthy, ensure the growth of new plants, and provide a reliable food source for many animals. Many bugs play their part in regulating the population of other bugs and limiting the spread of disease.

Pollinating plants
Many bugs, including bees, carry pollen from one flower to another while looking for food, helping plants reproduce.

Providing a food source
Invertebrates are a major food source that animals such as birds, bats, reptiles, and even other invertebrates depend on.

INCREDIBLE INVERTEBRATES

Invertebrates are creatures without a backbone. One group of invertebrates is called the arthropods. They have a hard external skeleton and legs with joints. When you say "bug", you are talking about members of this group. In the pages of this book you will find many examples of three types of arthropod – insects, arachnids, and myriapods.

Striped bug, an insect

Lobed argiope, an arachnid

Pacific giant centipede, a myriapod

BE A BUG EXPERT!

Bug experts pack an essential tool kit before they step out to observe bugs. They might use a transparent container with air holes in the lid to hold bugs when studying them. Magnifying glasses help them see a bug's body in greater detail, while apps on a tablet might let them identify one easily. They might even draw the bug to keep a record. You will learn most about bugs by watching them – what tools will you use on your own bug adventure?

See-through jar

Magnifying glass

Smart phone or tablet

Notebook and pen or pencil

Controlling disease
Some bugs eat other disease-spreading bugs. Dragonflies devour mosquitoes and flies that may carry deadly germs.

Limiting numbers
Many bugs eat other bugs, often helping to keep their numbers in check. For example, wasps hunt the larvae of certain species.

Improving soil health
Dung beetles have a habit of digging burrows and breaking down dung (animal waste). This adds air and nutrients to the soil.

Bug groups

There are well over a million species of bugs on Earth. With so many varieties, scientists find it helpful to arrange them in a structured and organized way. This "bug" tree classifies bugs into related groups, much like a family tree. Each branch categorizes bugs that share similar characteristics.

Widespread creatures

Arthropods form the largest group of animals in the world. About 900,000 of the 1.2 million arthropod species are insects, with thousands more being discovered every year. This sounds like a lot, but there could be as many as 10 million insect species in total. This is nothing compared to the number of insects alive at any one time – around 10 quintillion (10 followed by 18 zeroes). Nearly 38 per cent of all insects are beetles.

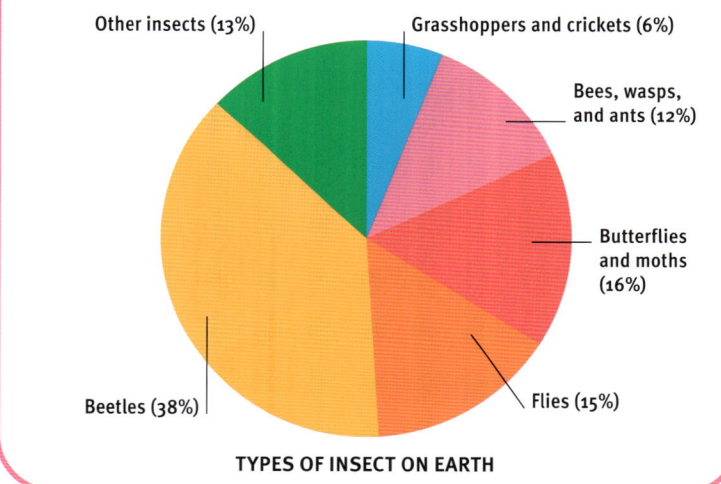

TYPES OF INSECT ON EARTH

- Other insects (13%)
- Grasshoppers and crickets (6%)
- Bees, wasps, and ants (12%)
- Butterflies and moths (16%)
- Flies (15%)
- Beetles (38%)

Arachnids
Members of this land-based group of arthropods have a two-part body and eight legs, but no antennae or wings.

Spiders
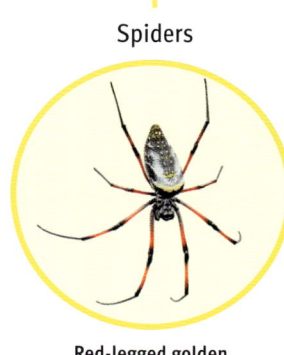
Red-legged golden orb-weaver spider

Scorpions

Tanzanian red clawed scorpion

Beetles

Seven-spot ladybird

Butterflies and moths

Rajah Brooke's birdwing

Flies and mosquitoes
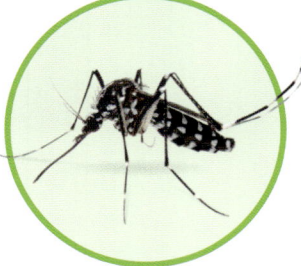
Asian tiger mosquito

Bees, wasps, and ants

European honeybee

TYPES OF ARTHROPOD
Most major types of arthropod are shown here on this tree, with an example given of each type.

ARTHROPODS
They all have jointed legs, segmented bodies, and hard exoskeletons (external skeletons) that are shed periodically as they grow.

Myriapods
The name myriapod translates as "many feet" in Greek, and this group includes creatures with lots of legs and long, segmented bodies.

Insects
The most diverse group of arthropods is the insects. They have three body parts – the head, thorax, and abdomen – as well as six legs. Some have wings.

Centipedes

Megarian banded centipede

Millipedes

Yellow-spotted millipede

Harvestmen

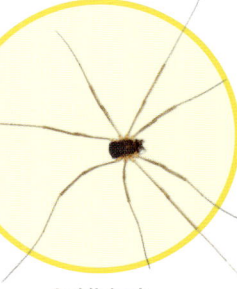

Saddleback harvestman

Mites

Red velvet mite

Ticks and relatives

Castor bean tick

Other arachnids

Hooded tick spider

Grasshoppers, crickets, and katydids

Common green grasshopper

Dragonflies and damselflies

Scarlet dragonfly

True bugs

Oleander aphid

Other insects

Green lacewing

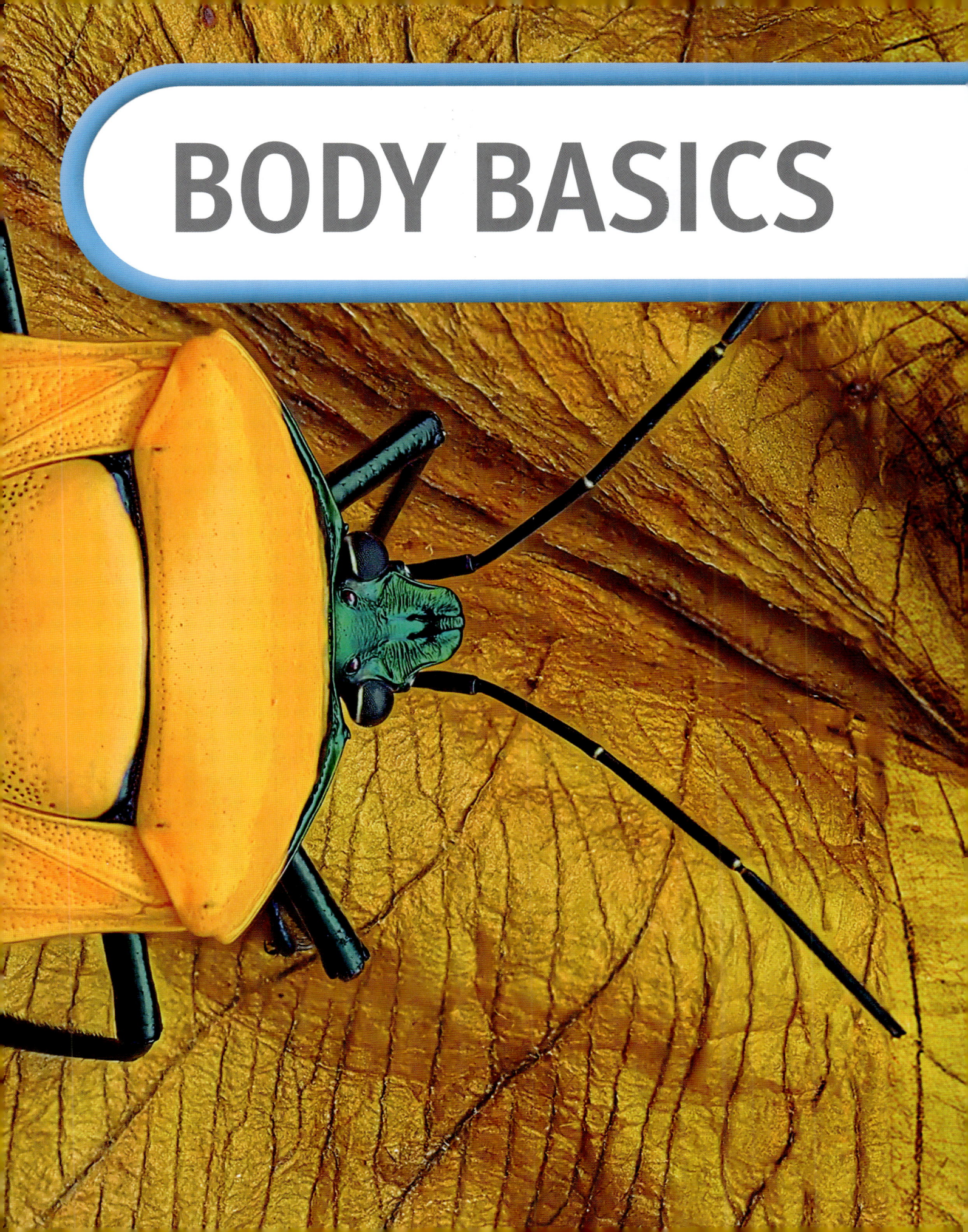

BODY BASICS

Body basics

Anatomy of an insect

Every bug belongs to a huge group of invertebrates called arthropods – which are the most widespread creatures on Earth. Insects form one group of bugs. They have three body parts, consisting of a head, thorax, and abdomen, as well as a hard, protective exoskeleton and three pairs of jointed legs. Many insects have wings, too.

Arachnid bodies

Some bugs, including spiders, scorpions, and mites, are known as arachnids. Unlike insects, arachnids don't have three distinct body parts. Spiders have a fused head and thorax (called the cephalothorax), and a separate abdomen, while all three body sections are joined in a mite.

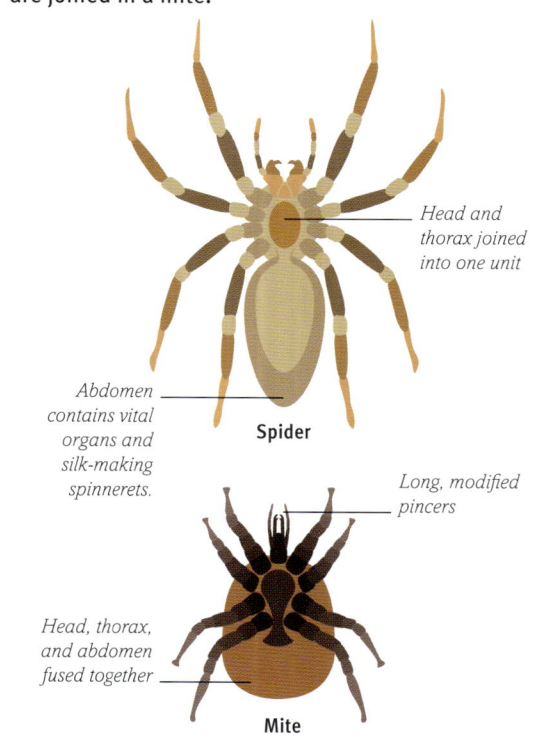

Head and thorax joined into one unit

Abdomen contains vital organs and silk-making spinnerets.

Spider

Long, modified pincers

Head, thorax, and abdomen fused together

Mite

Compound eyes provide a clear view in all directions, enabling the insect to detect the slightest movement near it.

Thorax ❯ The central section of the body is the thorax. Six legs and one or two pairs of wings are attached to it, while strong muscles line the inside. This is the insect's engine room, providing the power to walk, jump, or fly.

Strong joints on each leg add flexibility to the insect's movements.

Abdomen ❯ The rear section is the abdomen, which houses vital organs such as the heart and guts. Many insects also have small openings called spiracles along their sides, which let them breathe.

African jewel beetle

Each long antenna contains sensors that detect chemicals released by food, mates, or threats.

Head › The head contains sensory organs, including eyes to see, mouthparts to taste and feed, and antennae to sense sounds, scents, and other changes in the bug's surroundings. Its brain uses the information collected by these organs to decide how it should react to its environment.

African jewel beetle in flight

Double wings › Many insects have two pairs of wings, which sometimes serve different functions. In beetles, for example, the front pair of wings is tough and hard, and forms wing cases called elytra. These protect the delicate hindwings underneath that are actually used for flying.

Types of leg

Insects have developed different types of leg over time to suit their needs. Most have walking legs to easily move through a diverse range of habitats. But some have legs for more specific purposes, such as digging, grabbing, or jumping.

Shovel-like legs push aside soil.

Digging legs The mole cricket is an insect with digging legs. Its muscular front legs end in sharp claws to tear through soil, while searching for plant roots and insects to eat.

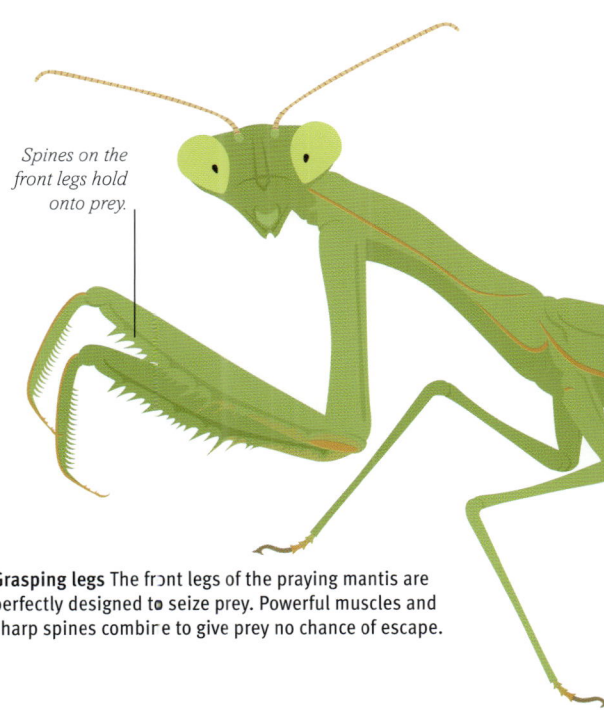

Spines on the front legs hold onto prey.

Grasping legs The front legs of the praying mantis are perfectly designed to seize prey. Powerful muscles and sharp spines combine to give prey no chance of escape.

Back legs are packed with the most muscles.

Jumping legs The impressive jumps of the grasshopper come from its long back legs. These powerful limbs push the insect forwards at high speed to leap through the air.

Body basics

Big and small

Bugs come in all shapes and sizes, from miniature mites to mighty millipedes. Some of them are so small they can only be seen under a microscope, while others can grow to be the size of small birds. Few other kinds of animal have this range of sizes. In most insect and spider species, females are bigger than males, often much greater in size.

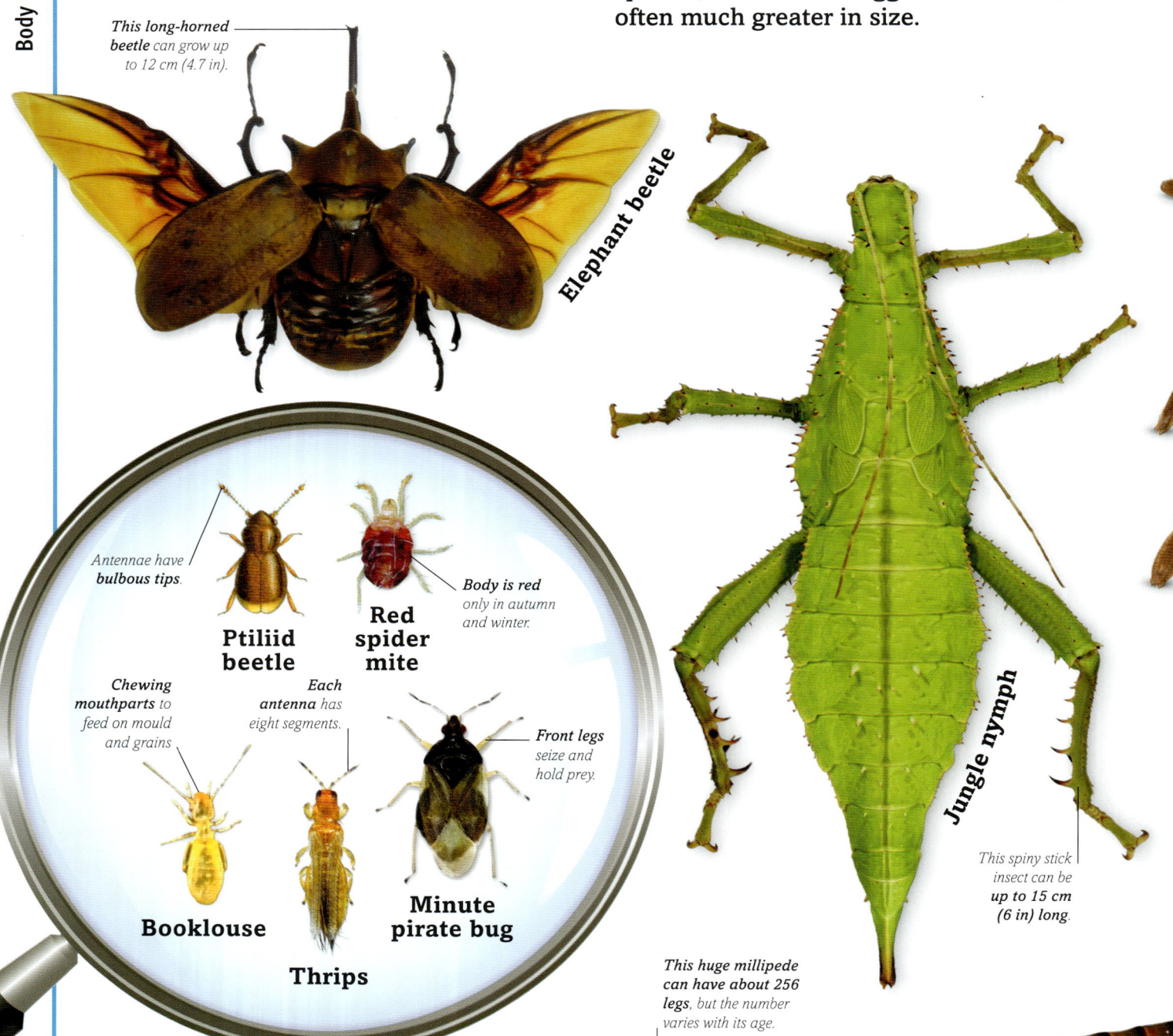

This long-horned beetle can grow up to 12 cm (4.7 in).

Elephant beetle

Antennae have bulbous tips.

Ptiliid beetle

Body is red only in autumn and winter.

Red spider mite

Chewing mouthparts to feed on mould and grains

Booklouse

Each antenna has eight segments.

Thrips

Front legs seize and hold prey.

Minute pirate bug

Jungle nymph

This spiny stick insect can be up to 15 cm (6 in) long.

This huge millipede can have about 256 legs, but the number varies with its age.

The truly tiny are almost invisible to the naked eye. **Spider mites** and **ptiliid beetles** can be less than 0.5 mm (0.02 in) long – smaller than a grain of sand. Small bugs can still have a big impact, though. Some **thrips**, for example, eat other insects and mites, keeping their population in control. At the other end of the size spectrum are some remarkable record holders. The world's largest spider, the **Goliath birdeater**, is the size of a dinner plate. The 35-g (1.2-oz) **Australian giant burrowing cockroach** is the world's heaviest cockroach. The **titan beetle** can measure more than 16.5 cm (6.5 in), making it the world's longest hornless beetle. And at a length of 33 cm (13 in), the **giant African millipede** is the world's longest millipede.

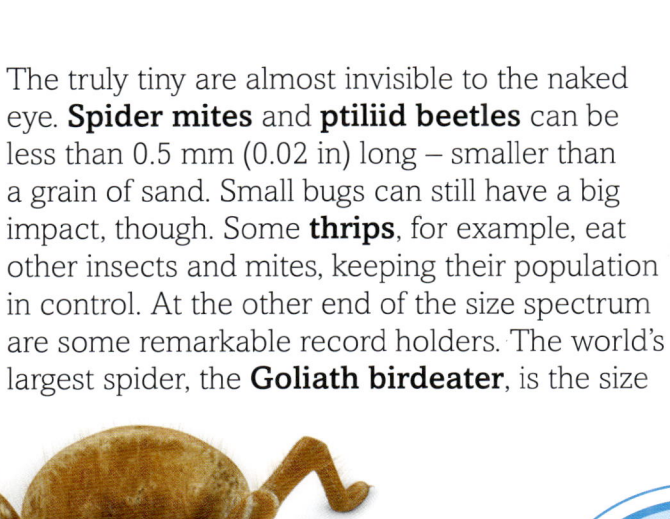

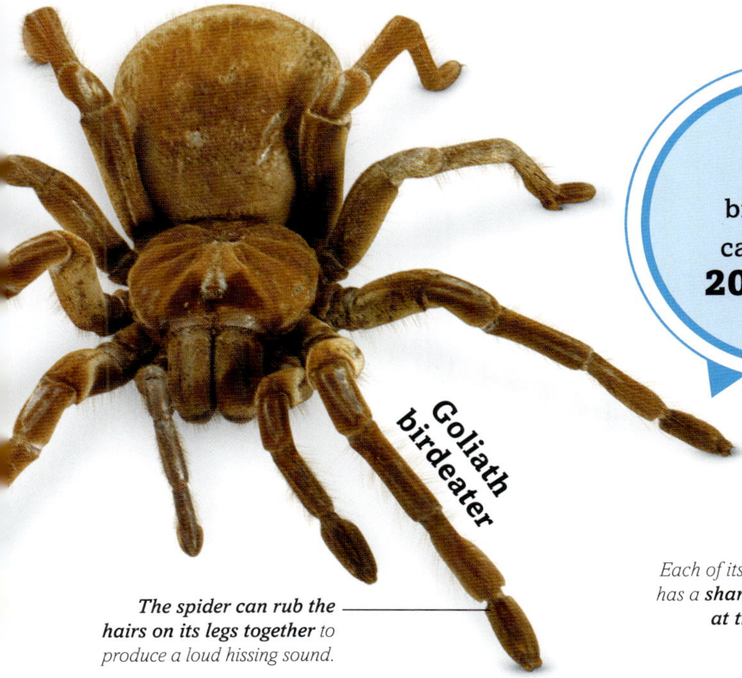

Antennae can be up to half as long as the bug's body.

Female Goliath birdeaters can live for **20 years**.

Each of its six legs has a sharp claw at the end.

Goliath birdeater

The spider can rub the hairs on its legs together to produce a loud hissing sound.

Australian giant burrowing cockroach

Tough outer shell

Goliath beetle

EXTREME SIZES

The difference in size between the smallest and largest bugs is massive. Male fairyfly wasps are around 0.14 mm (0.005 in) long, while the largest insect ever found is an as yet unnamed species of stick insect measuring 64 cm (25.2 in) with outstretched legs.

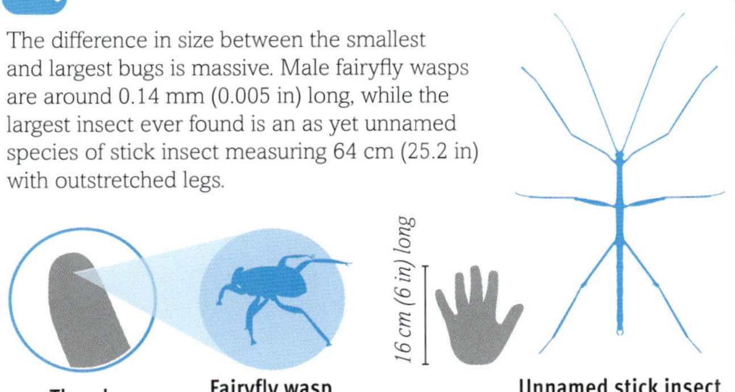

Thumb

Fairyfly wasp
0.14 mm (0.005 in) long

16 cm (6 in) long

Unnamed stick insect
64 cm (25.2 in) long

Titan beetle

Giant African millipede

Super senses

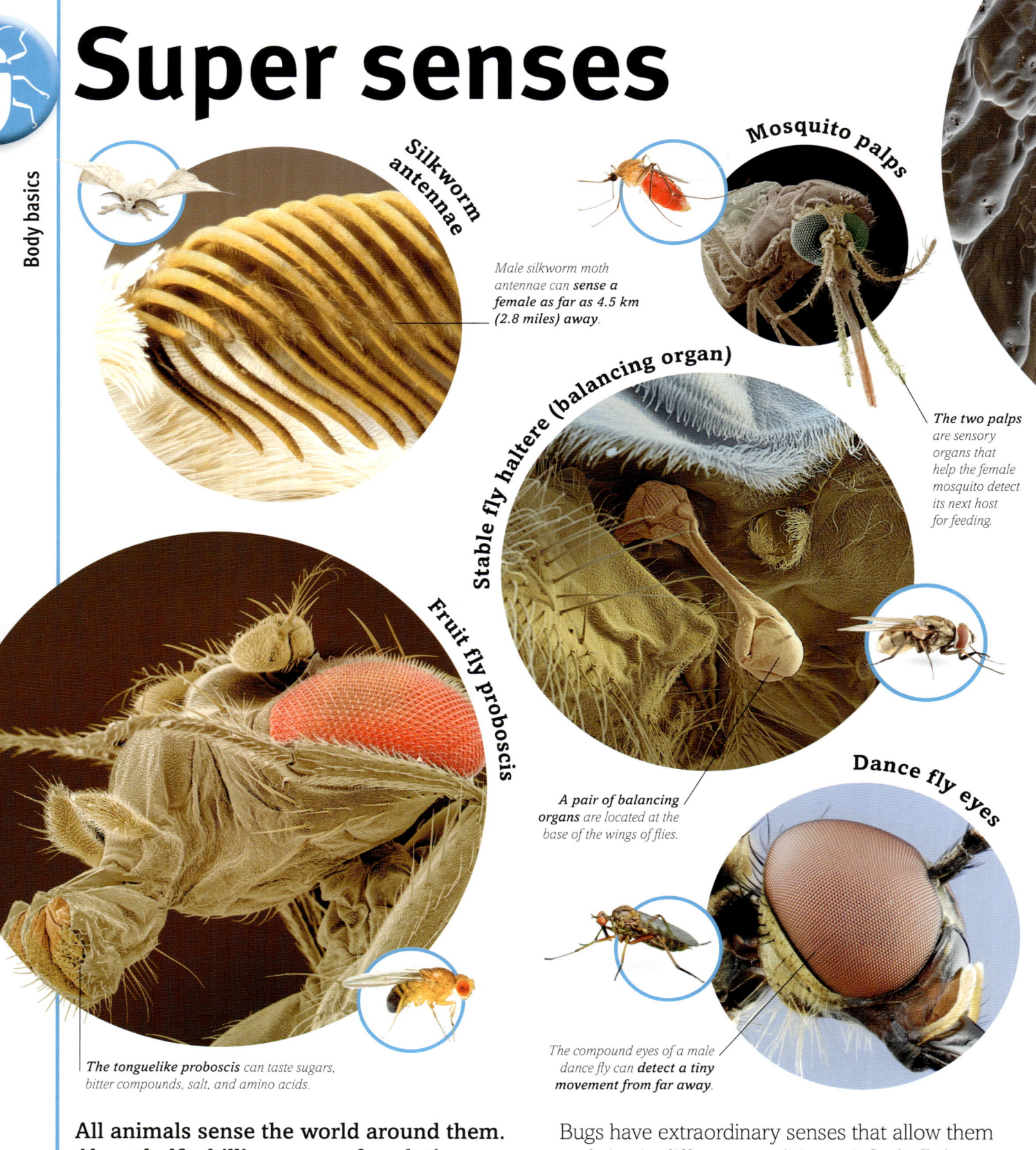

Silkworm antennae
Male silkworm moth antennae can *sense a female as far as 4.5 km (2.8 miles) away*.

Mosquito palps
The two palps are sensory organs that help the female mosquito detect its next host for feeding.

Stable fly haltere (balancing organ)
A pair of balancing organs are located at the base of the wings of flies.

Fruit fly proboscis
The tonguelike proboscis can taste sugars, bitter compounds, salt, and amino acids.

Dance fly eyes
The compound eyes of a male dance fly can *detect a tiny movement from far away*.

All animals sense the world around them. About half a billion years of evolution have helped bugs to fine-tune the way they interact with their surroundings. They have developed many weird, wonderful, and, at times, truly remarkable adaptations that they use to survive.

Bugs have extraordinary senses that allow them to thrive in different conditions. A **fruit fly's proboscis** picks up complex tastes, while enlarged **dance fly eyes** allow males to spot a single female in the middle of a swarm for mating. Other bugs can pick up on microscopic chemical changes around them. **Mosquito palps** are so

Super senses

Fire beetle sensors — Each infrared sensor, located on the rear end of the thorax, has a tiny pocket of water that expands when exposed to heat, *allowing this beetle to locate nearby fires*.

Water strider setae — *Hairlike structures* help water striders walk on water and sense movements of nearby prey.

Jumping spider foot — The longer hairs on the feet are used to *sense vibrations in their surroundings*.

Cockroach cerci (sensors) — Tiny hairs on the cercus are sensitive to *changes in air movements*.

Bumblebee hairs — These hairs help the bee identify different flowers and even sense if another bee has recently visited a flower.

Honeybee vision — Honeybees can detect *ultraviolet light*, helping them find the nectar guides on certain flowers.

sensitive to carbon dioxide, they can detect human breath from 50 m (165 ft) away. Male **silkworm antennae** can sense a single molecule of bombykol – a chemical released by the female to attract a mate. Some bugs are sensitive to physical stimuli. **Cockroach cerci** (structures sticking out of the abdomen) can feel the slightest air currents to sense predators, while **water strider setae** (bristles) can sense the tiniest vibration on a pond's surface to locate prey. The **fire beetle's infrared sensors** help it detect forest fires. The beetle lays eggs in burnt wood, a perfect place for its larvae to grow, with few predators.

Extraordinary eyes

Large eyes can change colour depending on the amount of light.

Only males have these enormous, bulging eyes that cover almost the entire head.

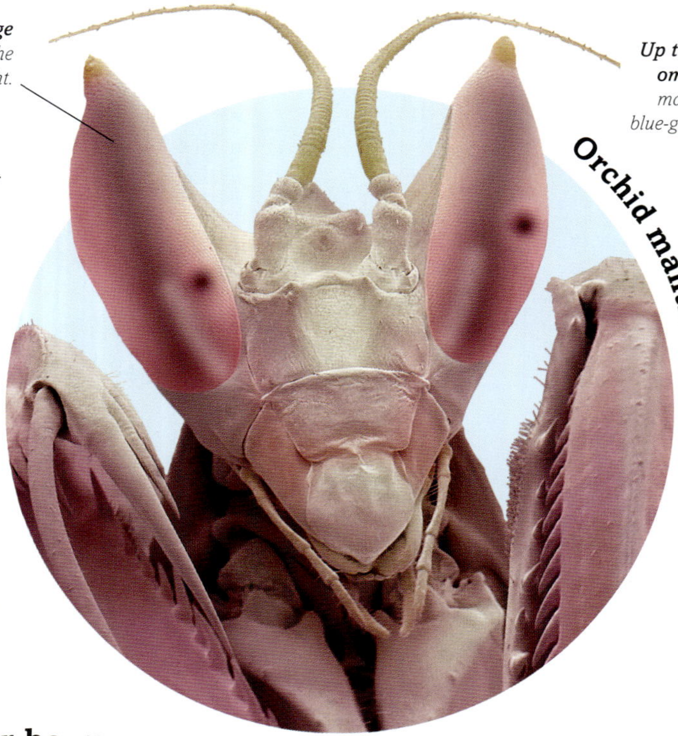

Orchid mantis

Up to 30,000 ommatidia make up the blue-green eyes.

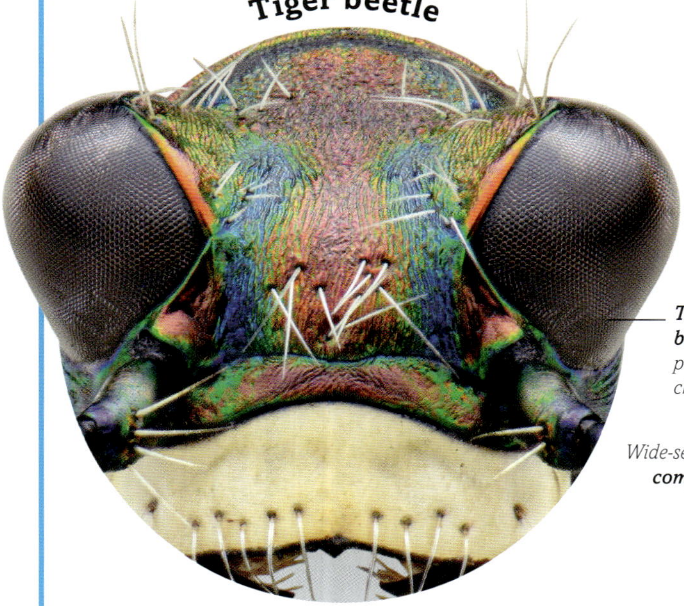

St Mark's fly

Emperor dragonfly

Eyes can be 5.5 cm (2.2 in) apart.

Tiger beetle

Male stalk-eyed flies sometimes use their eye stalks to **fight each other**.

This beetle uses its bulging eyes to spot prey easily when chasing after it.

Wide-set, blood-red compound eyes

Yellow Monday cicada

Three simple eyes

Insects have evolved unique eyes to adapt to their needs and surroundings. Most adult insects have compound eyes, which are made up of thousands of light-sensitive hexagons called ommatidia. Spiders, however, have simple eyes called ocelli. Each ocellus works like a single camera.

Compound eyes can't usually see sharp detail, but they are sensitive to movement, allowing flying insects such as the **emperor dragonfly** to easily pursue prey in midair. Some bug eyes bulge out to give a wider range of vision, like in the **tiger beetle** and the **horsefly**. Similarly, the **stalk-eyed**

Extraordinary eyes

Turban-shaped eyes help males to attract a mate.

Small spurwing mayfly

Six small eyes can see red, green, and ultraviolet wavelengths.

Regal jumping spider

C-shaped compound eyes

European hornet

Coloured patterns form when light reflects off the lenses.

Horsefly

Hairs stick out from the eyes.

Painted lady butterfly

Stalk-eyed fly

fly's amazing eyes are mounted on long poles that stick right out of its head. Multiple types of eye are seen in many insects, such as the **Yellow Monday cicada**. It has three simple eyes above its two compound eyes, which help it move around by detecting changes in light and dark. Spiders usually have poor eyesight as their eyes aren't very complex. But two of the **regal jumping spider's** eight eyes are huge, giving it excellent vision compared to other spiders.

SUPREME SIGHT
A pair of damselflies peer out through a leaf. A damselfly's enormous eyes, which occupy most of its head, allow it to detect movement quickly and see in all directions. This skill lets it navigate successfully and even take down flying prey easily in mid-air. With only weak hearing and short antennae, the bug's excellent vision is its strongest sense.

Like most insects, a damselfly has compound eyes. Each of its eyes is made up of thousands of tiny lenses that together create a sharp and detailed image of the insect's surroundings. The eyes are spaced far apart, providing all-round vision, including above and below the flying bug. Their sharp eyesight makes them formidable hunters.

Damselflies live by fresh water, which they use as a hunting ground for tiny mosquitoes and midges. When seeking prey, they may hover behind foliage to sneak up on unsuspecting victims or speed over open water to seize them mid-flight. Their bristly legs work like a trap – the hairs snag the prey, leaving no chance of escape.

Body basics

Little but loud

Grote's bertholdia moth — 🔊 85 dB

This moth produces super-fast, high-pitched clicks using organs in its thorax.

17-year periodical cicada — 🔊 100 dB

The periodical cicada chirps by vibrating rubbery organs called tymbals.

Tymbals, located in the abdomen, are made of a rubbery substance called resilin.

European mole cricket — 🔊 72 dB

The cricket lives and calls from an underground burrow, which amplifies the sound.

Death's head hawkmoth — 🔊 64 dB

This bug forces air through its proboscis to squeak.

Greater wax moth — 🔊 81 dB

As well as creating loud sounds, this moth can also detect high-frequency sounds with the specialized membranes on its thorax.

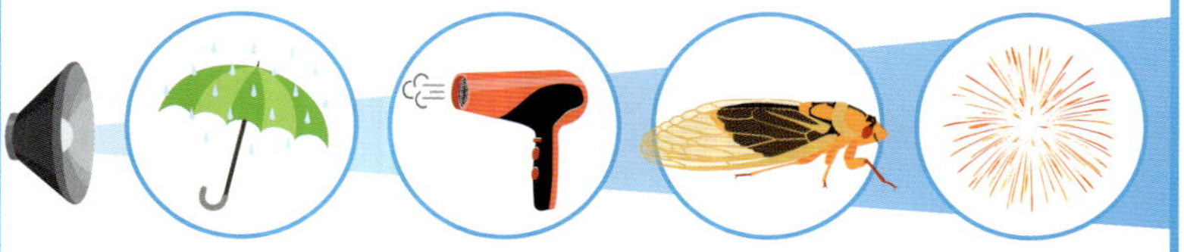

🔊 93 dB

The warning clicking sounds made by the caterpillar's mouthparts are accompanied by biting and thrashing.

🔍 HOW SOUND IS MEASURED

We measure sound in decibels (dB). A buzzing bee, at around 65 dB, is a little louder than the patter of rain on an umbrella at 50 dB. Much noisier sounds include the whine of a group of masked devil cicadas, which, at around 110 dB, is almost as loud as the bursting sound of a fireworks display.

| RAINFALL (50 dB) | HAIR DRYER (90 dB) | MASKED DEVIL CICADA (110 dB) | FIREWORKS (130 dB) |

Most insects are too tiny to make much of a racket. However, some defy their small size to hiss, chirp, or squeak to create a symphony. Many insects have developed diverse, and sometimes deafening, ways to make noise, usually to attract mates and to warn of danger.

Some bugs use sound to drive away predators. The **peacock butterfly** rubs its wings together rapidly to hiss at attackers, while the **Madagascar hissing cockroach** makes a similar sound by forcing air through its body. The **tobacco hornworm caterpillar** warns others off by clicking its mandibles (tiny jaws).

Little but loud

Peacock butterfly — 72 dB
As the flashing eyespots are not visible in the dark, the butterfly **makes hissing sounds to deter prey**.

Madagascar hissing cockroach — 90 dB
The cockroach communicates by producing **different types of hisses** with its breathing holes.

Field cricket — 100 dB
The frequency of the chirping sound, made by rubbing its wings together, decreases as the cricket gets older.

Resh cicada — 106 dB
The hollow body makes the chirps of a male even louder.

Rhinoceros katydid — 100 dB
The ridged wing is rubbed against the other to make a distinctive call.

Masked devil cicada — 110 dB
This species can use the ridges on its collarlike structure and wings to **create a unique sound**.

Tobacco hornworm caterpillar

The snapping noise of a lesser water boatman can be as **loud as a car horn**.

Lesser water boatman — 105 dB
This bug makes an extremely loud snapping sound by rubbing its ridged front legs **to attract a mate**.

Many bugs fall prey to bats that produce high-pitched calls and detect their echo as the sounds bounce off a prey. The **Grote's bertholdia moth** jams the bat's signals by producing high-pitched clicks of its own. Bugs don't only pipe up in self-defence. **Field crickets** rub their wings together to make loud chirping sounds to attract mates. Males of cicadas, such as the **17-year periodical cicada** and **resh cicada**, chirp like crickets, but a lot louder. The chorus of **masked devil cicadas** is even louder. These bugs can band together to chirp and whine louder than a lawnmower.

Fabulous antennae

Feathery, fan-shaped antennae

*Outstretched antennae have **bristles on both sides**.*

Small elephant hawk-moth

Clublike antennae on an elongated head

Feather-horned beetle

Giraffe weevil

*Extremely long antennae marked by **tufts of hair***

Striking long antennae indicate that this is a male.

Fabulous longhorn beetle

European longhorn bee

Every insect has a pair of antennae. These special organs help bugs to touch, taste, smell their surroundings, and locate mates. They are often unremarkable and in proportion with the bug's body. But, some insects have truly eye-catching antennae.

Insects use their sensor-packed antennae for many practical purposes. The **small elephant hawk-moth** controls its flight thanks to the bristles at the base of its antennae. During flight, the antennae rub against these bristles, which allows the insect to sense its surroundings and change its wing position or direction, if required.

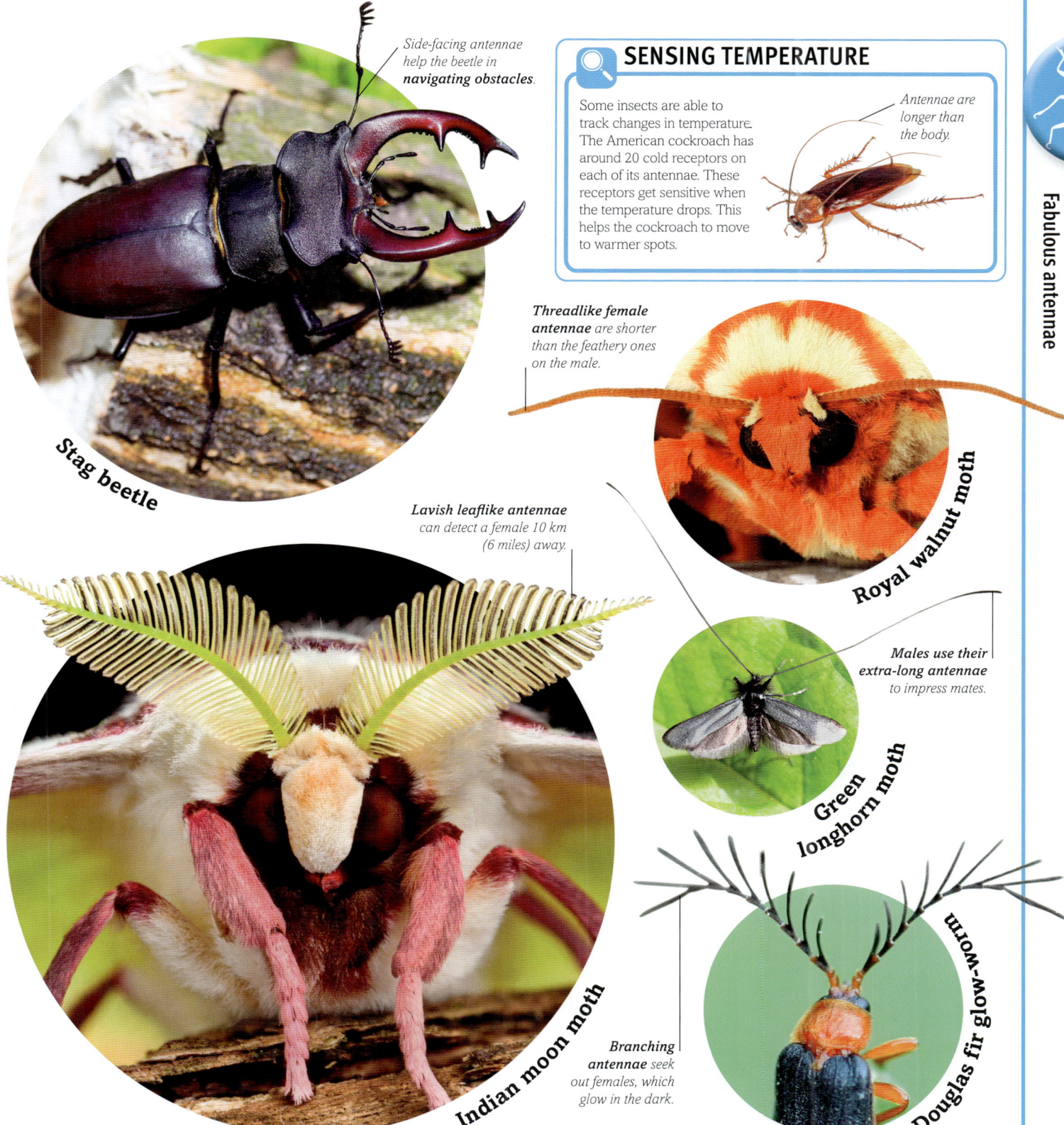

Fabulous antennae

Stag beetle — Side-facing antennae help the beetle in *navigating obstacles*.

SENSING TEMPERATURE

Some insects are able to track changes in temperature. The American cockroach has around 20 cold receptors on each of its antennae. These receptors get sensitive when the temperature drops. This helps the cockroach to move to warmer spots.

Antennae are longer than the body.

Royal walnut moth — *Threadlike female antennae* are shorter than the feathery ones on the male.

Indian moon moth — *Lavish leaflike antennae* can detect a female 10 km (6 miles) away.

Green longhorn moth — Males use their *extra-long antennae* to impress mates.

Douglas fir glow-worm — *Branching antennae* seek out females, which glow in the dark.

The **giraffe weevil** and **stag beetle** use their antennae to forage for food. In some insects, the antennae are impressive looking and attract the attention of potential mates. The males of the **green longhorn moth** and **fabulous longhorn beetle** have incredible antennae that can be several times longer than their entire bodies and are able to detect the subtle scents – called pheromones – produced by the females. Similarly, the males of the **feather-horned beetle** and **Douglas fir glow-worm** use their elaborate antennae to pick up on female pheromones.

Prehistoric bugs

Triassic cockroach

Wings seem fully developed, suggesting the cockroach could probably fly.

Fine mud has preserved even the veins of the wings.

Carboniferous cockroach

Tough forewings of this cockroach protected the more delicate hindwings beneath.

Permian dragonfly

Around 30 segments are each covered by three plates.

Carboniferous millipede

Segmented body and pincers closely resemble those of modern scorpions.

AGE OF GIANTS

An abundance of oxygen in the atmosphere in prehistoric times, among other factors, allowed some bugs to grow to super sizes. *Meganeura*, a dragonfly-like insect, was one of the largest.

At up to 75 cm (2.5 ft), the wingspan was almost as big as that of a crow.

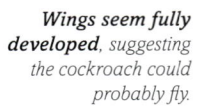

Meganeura

Carboniferous scorpion

Bugs first evolved around 480 million years ago (mya), long before even the dinosaurs were around. These creatures were some of the first to roam Earth – and the first ones to evolve wings and fly. Soon, bugs were swarming the skies, almost 250 million years before any bird.

Most ancient ancestors of modern bugs first appeared during the Carboniferous Period (359–299 mya). Some, such as the **Carboniferous scorpion**, are strikingly similar to today's scorpions. Others resemble some of their modern descendants, but with at least one giant difference – their size. The

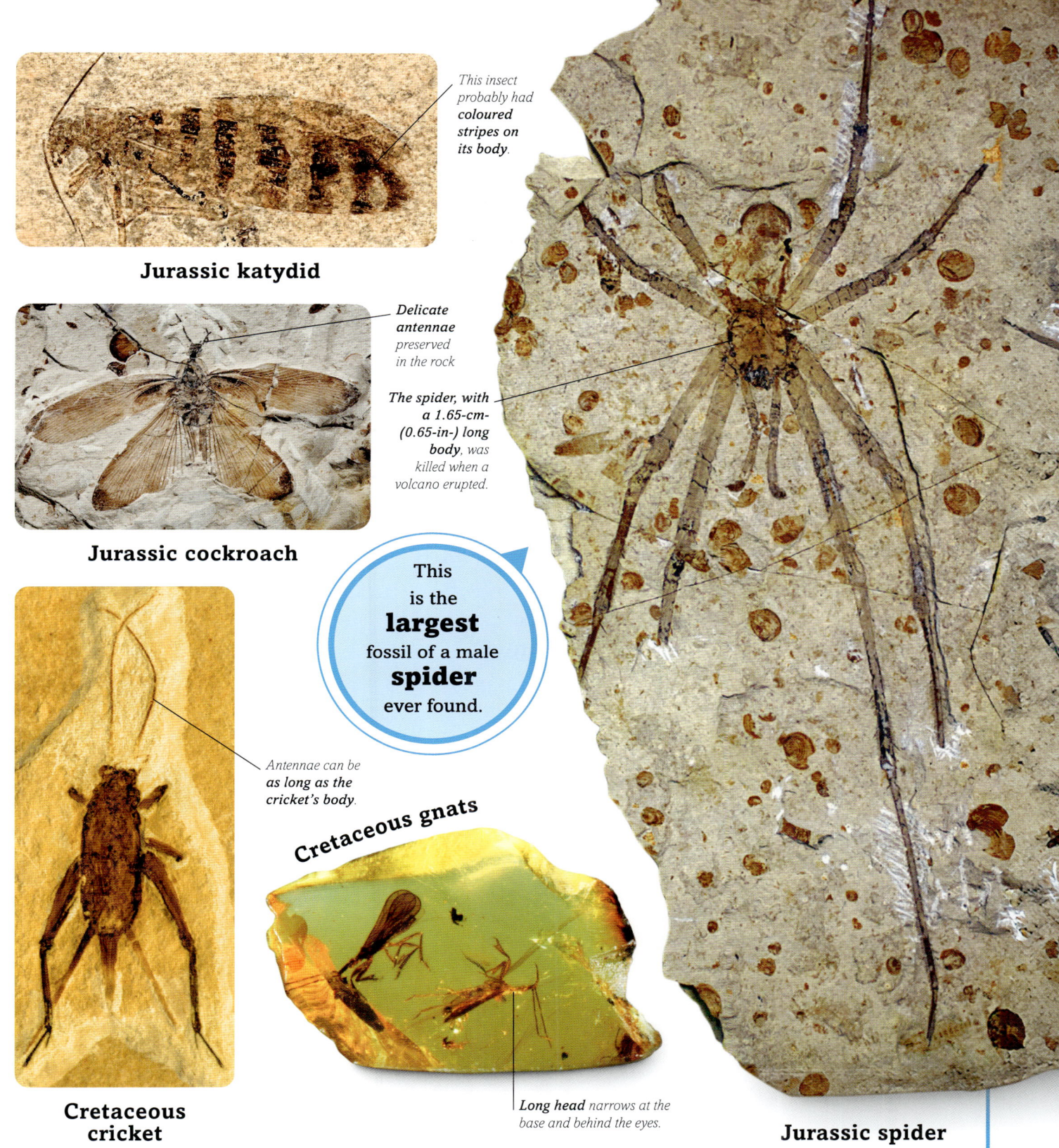

Jurassic katydid
This insect probably had coloured stripes on its body.

Jurassic cockroach
Delicate antennae preserved in the rock.

The spider, with a 1.65-cm- (0.65-in-) long body, was killed when a volcano erupted.

This is the **largest** fossil of a male **spider** ever found.

Cretaceous cricket
Antennae can be as long as the cricket's body.

Cretaceous gnats
Long head narrows at the base and behind the eyes.

Jurassic spider

Carboniferous millipede could grow as long as a modern-day alligator. The **Carboniferous cockroach** had an external ovipositor (organ that lays eggs). This ovipositor began to shrink during the Triassic (251–201 MYA) and Jurassic Periods (201–145 MYA) – an evolutionary process that has led to the internal ovipositor of today's cockroaches. Most of what we understand about the first bugs comes from fossils (delicate remains of ancient life). Some of them preserve the whole bodies in amber, such as **gnats** from the Cretaceous Period (145–66 MYA). Amber is a yellow substance formed from fossilized tree resin.

Leggy crawlers

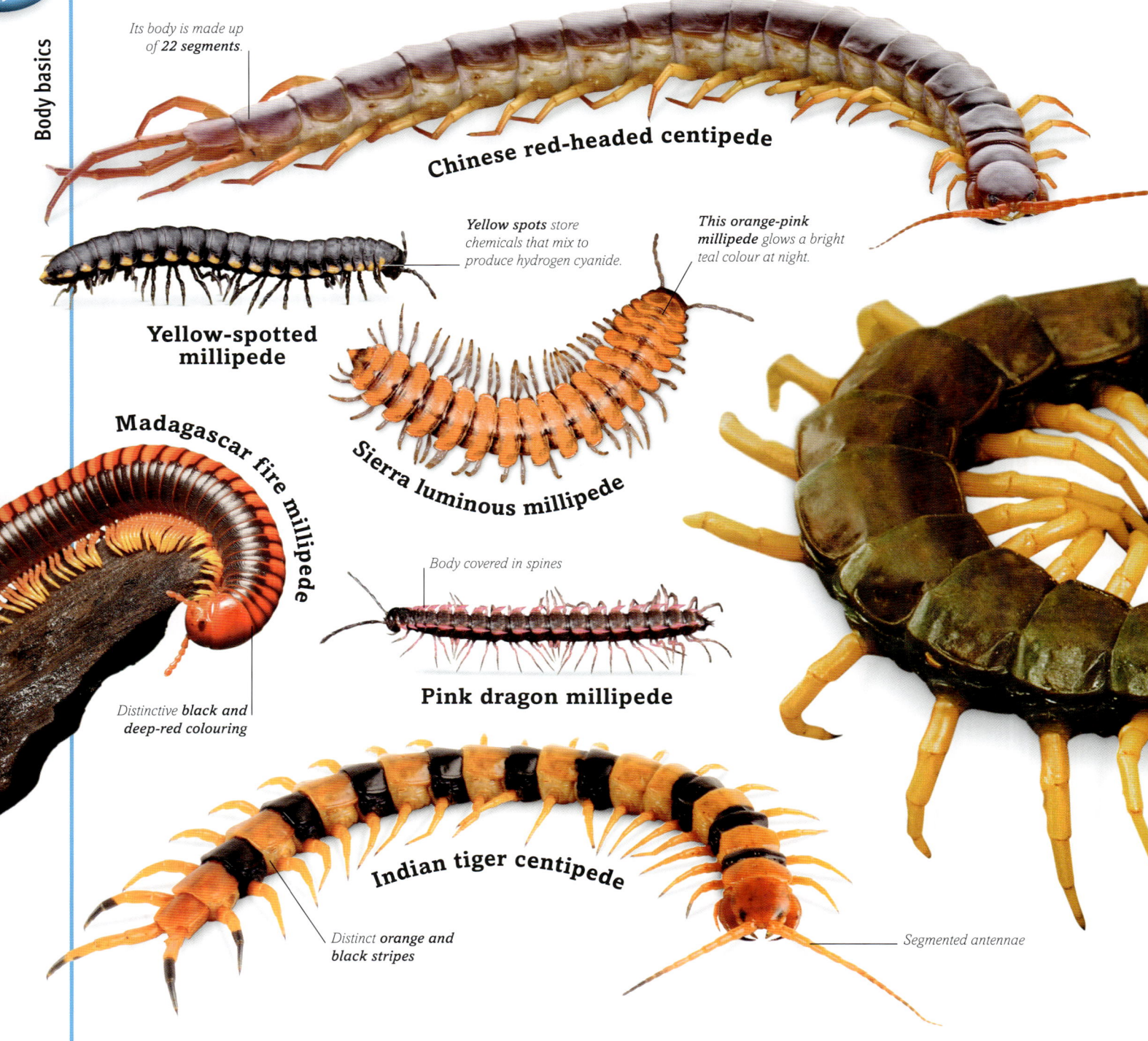

Its body is made up of 22 segments.

Chinese red-headed centipede

Yellow spots store chemicals that mix to produce hydrogen cyanide.

This orange-pink millipede glows a bright teal colour at night.

Yellow-spotted millipede

Madagascar fire millipede

Sierra luminous millipede

Body covered in spines

Distinctive black and deep-red colouring

Pink dragon millipede

Indian tiger centipede

Distinct orange and black stripes

Segmented antennae

Centipedes and millipedes can be found all over the world. They love dark and moist habitats, so many are often hidden in soil. Try lifting up a rock or rustling some fallen leaves and you might just see some scurrying around on their many, many legs.

Centipedes and millipedes belong to a group of invertebrates called myriapods, meaning "many feet". They all have a hard, protective exoskeleton, legs with flexible joints, and segmented bodies. Some are tiny, such as the **bristly millipede**, which can be as small as 2 mm (0.08 in) in length. Others are much bigger, such as the **giant desert**

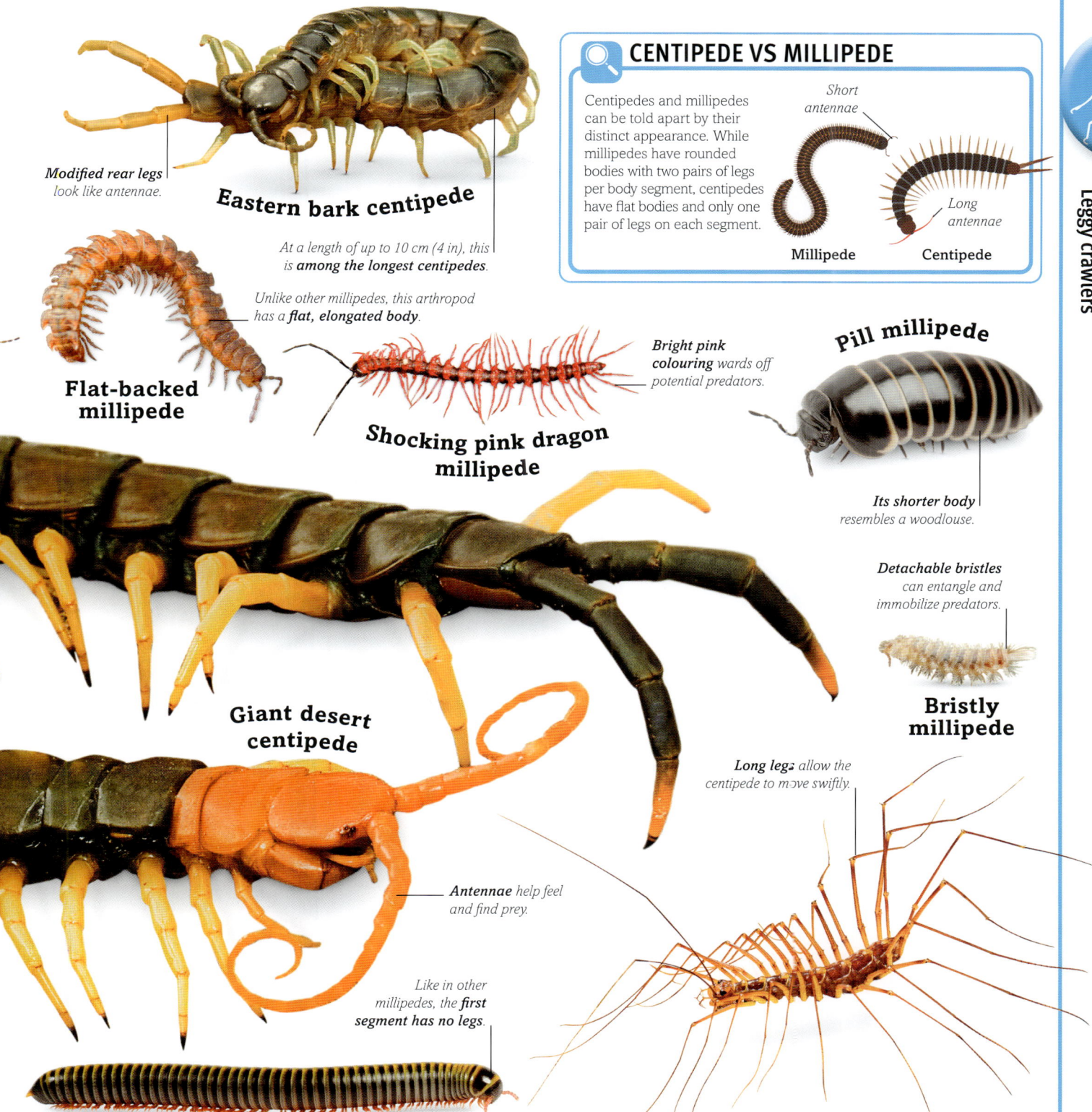

CENTIPEDE VS MILLIPEDE

Centipedes and millipedes can be told apart by their distinct appearance. While millipedes have rounded bodies with two pairs of legs per body segment, centipedes have flat bodies and only one pair of legs on each segment.

Modified rear legs look like antennae.

Eastern bark centipede

At a length of up to 10 cm (4 in), this is **among the longest centipedes**.

*Unlike other millipedes, this arthropod has a **flat, elongated body**.*

Flat-backed millipede

Bright pink colouring wards off potential predators.

Shocking pink dragon millipede

Pill millipede

Its shorter body resembles a woodlouse.

Detachable bristles can entangle and immobilize predators.

Bristly millipede

Giant desert centipede

Long legs allow the centipede to move swiftly.

Antennae help feel and find prey.

*Like in other millipedes, the **first segment has no legs**.*

Bumblebee millipede

Long-legged centipede

centipede, which can grow up to 20 cm (8 in). All centipedes are venomous. They have two modified front legs, called forcipules, which they use to inject venom into prey or predators. The **Chinese red-headed centipede** can immobilize creatures much bigger than itself. In contrast to these hunters, most millipedes, including the **flat-backed millipede**, feed on dead plants and help enrich the soil. When threatened, they often curl into a tight coil. But some species, such as the **yellow-spotted millipede** and the **Sierra luminous millipede**, can also secrete a toxic substance called hydrogen cyanide to ward off attackers.

Little speedsters

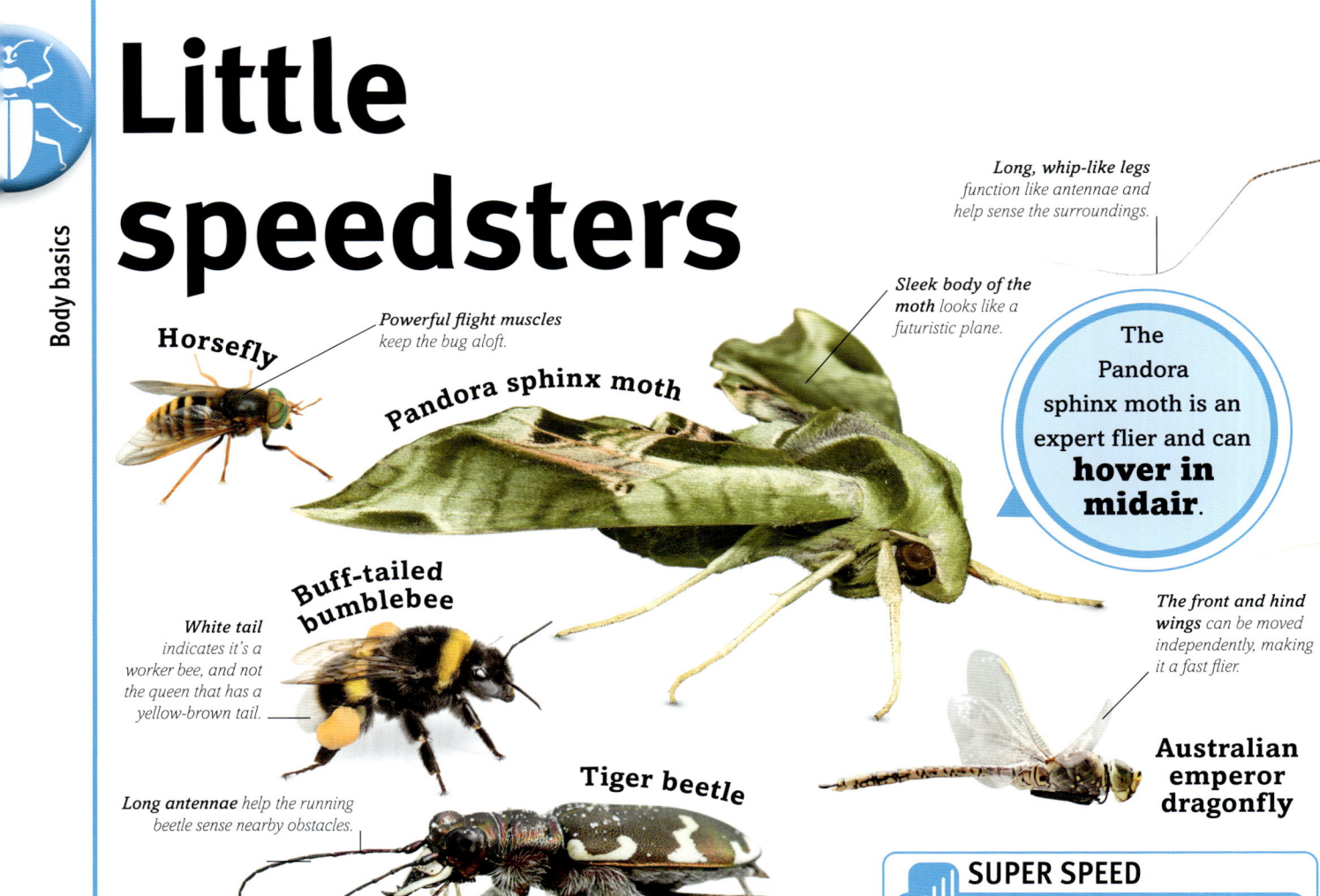

Horsefly — Powerful flight muscles keep the bug aloft.

Pandora sphinx moth — Sleek body of the moth looks like a futuristic plane. Long, whip-like legs function like antennae and help sense the surroundings.

The Pandora sphinx moth is an expert flier and can **hover in midair**.

Buff-tailed bumblebee — White tail indicates it's a worker bee, and not the queen that has a yellow-brown tail.

Tiger beetle — Long antennae help the running beetle sense nearby obstacles.

Australian emperor dragonfly — The front and hind wings can be moved independently, making it a fast flier.

Wolf spider — This long-legged spider is often found in dry grass.

SUPER SPEED

Despite their numerous legs, most millipedes don't move much faster than a snail. Butterflies are surprisingly speedy. However, horseflies take the gold – they can sometimes reach speeds of up to 145 kph (90 mph).

- Millipede — 0.05 kph (0.03 mph)
- Butterfly — 60 kph (37 mph)
- Male horsefly — 145 kph (90 mph)

Whether scurrying across the ground, darting through the air, or even racing across the water's surface, some bugs can move like lightning. Their speed and agility help them to snatch their next meal or avoid the danger of becoming a predator's next target.

Few bugs pursue their prey more ferociously than the **wolf spider** and the **Brazilian wandering spider**, which sprint at breakneck speeds after their victims before pouncing on top of them. But even these speedy spiders would struggle to chase down the **tiger beetle** – the fastest insect on land. Some species of this

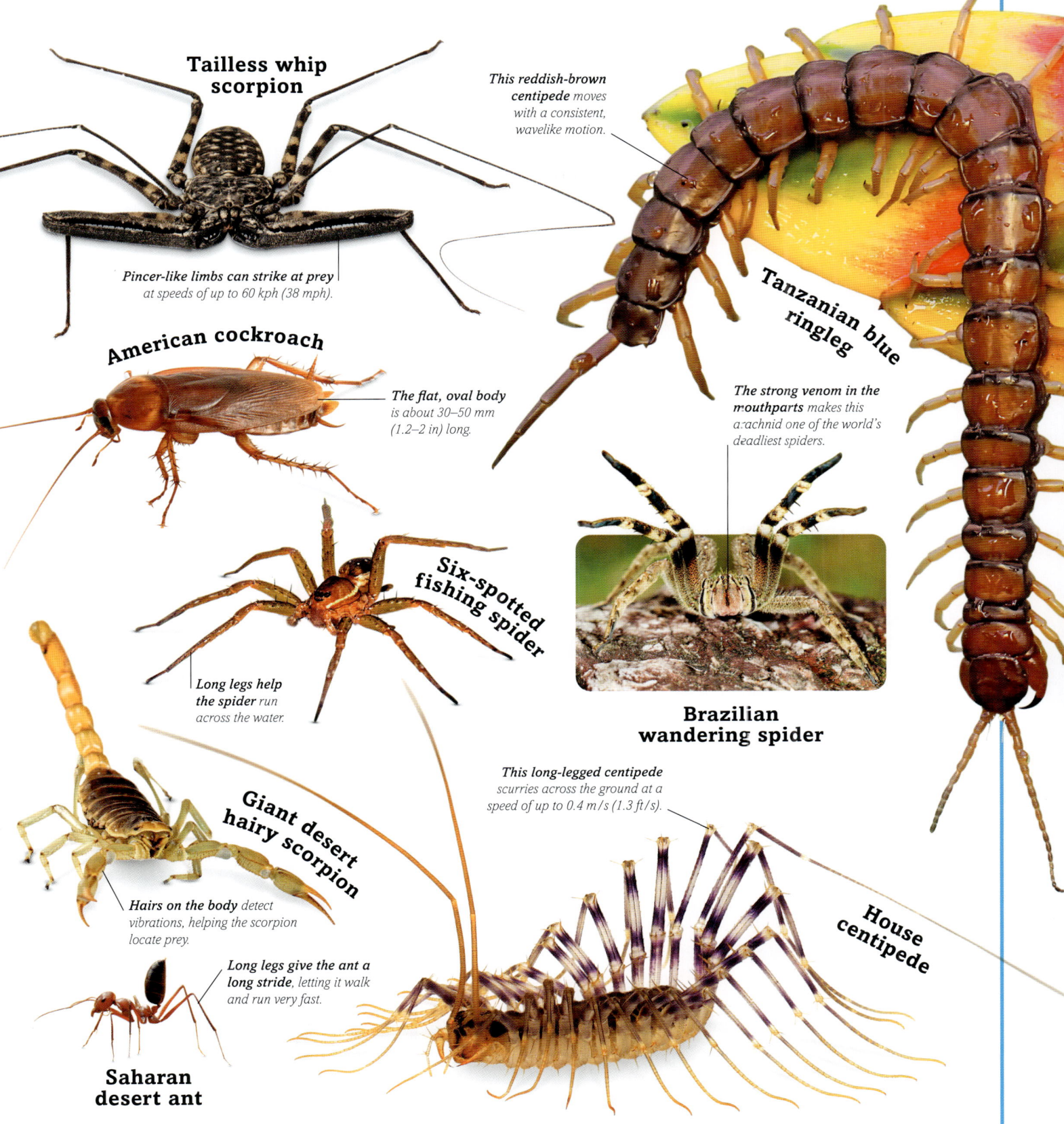

beetle can run the length of their body 125 times per second whereas a cheetah – the fastest land animal – can only run about 15 times its body length per second. Each of these bugs, along with the **American cockroach**, which can run as fast as 5.5 kph (3.4 mph), reach their top speeds in quick, short bursts of movement.

Although clumsy on the ground, the **buff-tailed bumblebee** is speedy in the air, beating its wings 200 times a second to zip between flowers. Other fast fliers include the **Pandora sphinx moth**, which can dart up to around 15 m/s (49 ft/s).

Colours and patterns

Wings and thorax of this moth are cream coloured with **small black and large red spots**.

Crimson speckled footman

Picasso bug

Small, oval body is covered in **stunning geometric patterns**.

The **lines and dots pattern** on the back look like calligraphy.

Dogwood leaf beetle

Happy-face spider

Red smile shape on the abdomen

Tasmanian peacock spider

Net-winged beetle

Vivid orange colour gives a warning that this beetle tastes unpleasant.

Bright yellow body with distinct spots **on top of the flat body**

The male Tasmanian peacock spider puts on a **dance display** to win over females.

Purple emperor butterfly

Eight-spotted crab spider

Many bugs light up the natural world with their vibrant colours and extraordinary patterns. Their unique visual displays are for all kinds of reasons – from attracting mates and producing offspring to deterring predators.

Insects and arachnids occasionally display their beauty by flashing their colourful bodies or wings to catch the eyes of potential mates. Often the males of a species, such as the **purple emperor butterfly** and the **Tasmanian peacock spider**, are brightly coloured, while the females have muted and mottled tones. Some bugs use startling

colours and unusual patterns to show that they are unpleasant to eat or even toxic to hungry predators. The warning colours can be seen in the spotty patterns of both the **crimson speckled footman** and **spotted lanternfly**. The **sunburst diving beetle** searches for food underwater, armed with a secret weapon. Its yellow spots send a clear warning to predators that it can produce a nasty chemical. Although bright colours may make some species an easy target for predators, they can help in certain habitats. The colourful **eight-spotted crab spider** hides among similarly bright flowers, waiting to pounce on pollinating insects.

DON'T EAT ME! Bright red, newly hatched giant shield bug nymphs scuttle along a green leaf. Their striking colours, clearly visible even before they emerge from their see-through eggs, act as a warning to predators to keep their distance. These young bugs believe in safety in numbers, often sticking together in groups to make their eye-catching warning even more obvious to any prying predators.

The use of colour as a means of protection is seen in lots of bugs, who use it to warn predators, particularly birds, not to eat them. A bird sees a bright colour on an insect meal as a warning that it might be toxic or taste terrible. This alert can be more useful than the insect's defences themselves, since being poisonous or unpalatable doesn't help a bug that's already been caught. Some other bugs have even evolved to copy the warning colours of another species that packs more of a punch. Harmless hoverflies can escape predators by looking like aggressive wasps. Most predators have learned to associate bold colours such as red, yellow, and orange in prey with an unpleasant taste. They steer clear of it.

Brilliant butterflies

Orange-barred sulphur — Named for the **dark orange marks on wings**

Regal purple tip — Bright white wings with **striking purple tips**

Painted Jezebel — Bright yellow and red colours with big black veins are typical of a female.

Common brimstone — **Leaf-shaped wings** provide excellent camouflage when closed.

Lemon emigrant — **Lemon yellow** is one of the many colours of this butterfly.

Great orange tip — Wings secrete a **foul-tasting toxin** that protects against predators.

Queen Alexandra's birdwing — **Black tips** on the fringes of vivid yellow wings

Ulysses — **Bright blue colour** is easy to spot, so the butterfly flies quickly to avoid predators. Wingspan of up to 30 cm (12 in) in females

Common grass yellow

The very first butterflies evolved around 100 million years ago. Thousands of species now populate skies, meadows, forests, mountains, and countless other habitats all around the globe, turning the diverse natural world into a kaleidoscope of colour.

It's easy to know when you've seen a butterfly – just look out for six legs, two long antennae, and, most importantly, four colourful and fragile-looking wings, covered in tiny colourful scales. But for all these similarities, there's a huge variation between different species, such as their wings. Some butterflies, such as the **green peacock**, **giant**, and

Menelaus blue morpho — *Microscopic scales on the wing reflect sunlight, giving a shiny blue colour.*

Monarch butterflies — *Bright colour and striking patterns warn predators that this insect is poisonous.*

Red cracker — *The upperside of the wings have a black and blue marbled pattern.*

Great eggfly — *Males of the species have black wings with three pairs of white spots.*

Leopard lacewing — *Named for the lacelike wing pattern*

Wallace's golden birdwing — *Males are typically bright orange in colour.*

Wallace's golden birdwing is **found** only on the **Maluku Islands** of Indonesia.

White-barred emperor — *A distinctive white bar runs through the length of the underside of each wing.*

Old World swallowtail — *Orange spots on the inner edge of the hindwings*

Giant swallowtail — *Long lobes are used to confuse predators.*

Green peacock swallowtail — *Green-dusted wings are striped with blue and black.*

Old World swallowtails, have long lobes at the back of their hindwings. Others, such as the **regal purple tip** and the **great orange tip**, have wings tipped with colourful decoration. Butterfly wings can also feature vibrant patterns. The wings of the **red cracker** and **white-barred emperor** flaunt a multicolour patchwork. On the other hand, the **monarch butterfly** has mainly orange wings, but its black veins and wing margins, highlighted with small white patches, create a striking pattern that warns of its toxicity. Butterflies come in all sizes, too. The world's largest butterfly is the **Queen Alexandra's birdwing**, which is almost the size of a small bird.

Long-tailed skipper
Each hindwing has a *tail 1.25 cm (0.5 in) long.*

Indian sunbeam
Males have a thin, *black margin.*

Common tit
Unique orange and black spot on the underside of the wing

Common branded skipper
White spots on the underside of each hindwing

Brazilian skipper
Extra long proboscis is used to sip nectar from larger flowers.

Pea blue

Brown hairstreak
Bright orange patch on each forewing

Two-barred flasher
Iridescent (shiny) blue body with white bands on forewings

Sergius firetip
Red tuft at the end of the abdomen

Silver-spotted skipper
Silver band on each underwing

At the other end of the size spectrum are much smaller species such as the **white-M hairstreak**, **imperial hairstreak**, and **periander metalmark**, all with an average wingspan about the length of a grape. The **silver-spotted skipper** is smaller still – some only slightly bigger than a peanut. These vast variations in size are matched by the incredible range of colours that makes up the world of butterflies – the male **Indian sunbeam's** bright orange wings are a marked contrast to the muted grey of the **common tit**. The vibrant colour schemes aren't

Three distinct white bands run across each hindwing of a female.

Four-spotted sailor

Imperial hairstreak

Cupid metalmark

Delicate tails resemble antennae — a clever trick to confuse predators.

Large blue

Dusty blue wings with black spots and edges

Periander metalmark

Named for the **metallic spots** on the hindwings

The proboscis of the blue-winged eurybia can be **twice its length**.

Metallic blue colour of wing is framed by black edges.

Shiny blue patch

Blue-winged eurybia

Reddish patches on hindwings stand out against the darker colours.

White-M hairstreak

just for show — they have evolved to serve a practical purpose. Some butterflies use their colouring for camouflage, as seen in the **long-tailed skipper**, which uses its light-brown body and wings to blend in among fallen leaves. For others, bright colours and misleading patterns might protect them from attack. The spots on the **blue-winged eurybia's** wings look like the eyes of a threatening animal, potentially deterring a predator. Colour can sometimes play a part in mating, too. Females might be more likely to mate with males that have the brightest colours.

39

Body basics

Life of a butterfly

The life cycle of a butterfly is like many other insects, such as moths, beetles, mosquitoes, and ants. Its body changes completely between the larval form and the adult form. When fully grown, this insect is unrecognizable from where it started out. This slow and dramatic process – called complete metamorphosis – occurs in separate stages.

2 Growing larva › The newly hatched larva is called a caterpillar. The caterpillar grows by eating constantly. It soon becomes too big for its outer skin, which needs to be shed – in a process called moulting. The caterpillar gets bigger each time it moults.

*The caterpillar uses an armlike structure called a cremaster to attach its rear end to a **silk pad it has woven on a branch**.*

Thickened skin

*Turning yellowish green as it grows keeps the tailed jay caterpillar safely **camouflaged against the leaf**.*

The developing butterfly can spend between five and 21 days in the chrysalis before it is ready to come out.

***The larva hatches from the egg** and begins feeding on the leaf.*

1 Laying eggs › A female butterfly lays a cluster of eggs on a leaf. The eggs usually take a few days to hatch. However, in extreme conditions such as cold winters, the eggs may take months to hatch.

3 Forming pupa › In the next stage, the caterpillar makes a protective covering for its body, known as a chrysalis, which is a type of pupa. Inside the chrysalis, the caterpillar transforms into a butterfly.

Tailed jay

Two sensitive antennae *help the butterfly explore its surroundings and find food.*

*With the butterfly gone, the **empty chrysalis** is discarded.*

5 Adult life ❯ By the final stage, the butterfly is a mature adult ready to reproduce. After mating with a male, the female lays her eggs, and the cycle of life starts again.

4 Fully transformed ❯ The young butterfly pushes against the chrysalis to break free. Metamorphosis is completed as the butterfly emerges for the first time. The wet wings must dry in the sunlight before the butterfly can take off.

The mottled wing pattern features leafy colours to help the tailed jay butterfly avoid predators.

Hungry caterpillars

Caterpillars are ravenously hungry in preparation for metamorphosis. They eat leaves, bark, twigs, moss, poo, the larvae of other insects, and even other caterpillars. Butterflies feed on nectar from flowers, so they are not in competition with caterpillars for precious food.

Magnificent moths

Body basics

"Eye" spots make the hooded snake shape look more real to a predator.

Lace-like pattern on the wings gives this moth its name.

Lace border moth

Furry covering provides a layer of warmth in cold weather.

Oak eggar moth

Distinctive marking on the thorax looks like a human skull.

Death's-head hawk-moth

Atlas moth

Long proboscis to suck nectar from tubular flowers

Hummingbird hawk-moth

Flappy wings look like an elephant's ears.

Elephant hawk-moth

The **forewing tip** of an Atlas moth looks like the **head of a snake**.

Moths are eye-catching, fast-flying insects, very similar to butterflies. Although some nocturnal moths are dark to camouflage at night, daytime moths often dazzle with spectacular colours and patterns.

Like butterflies, moths have two pairs of wings, six legs, and two antennae. Their bodies are covered in tiny scales that provide warmth and boost flight. There are nearly 160,000 types of moth, with differences in colour and size. The **Atlas moth** is bigger than a human hand, while the **four-spotted palpita moth's** wingspan is narrower than a

Slim antennae help the moth **maintain balance during flight**.

Scarlet tiger moth

Notched antennae are seen on an adult male.

Grape leaffolder moth

Six red spots on each front wing warn that the moth is poisonous.

Six-spot burnet moth

Delicate wings are *semi-transparent*.

Four-spotted palpita moth

Shimmering blue-green wings camouflage the moth in leafy vegetation.

Green forester moth

Madagascan moon moth

Long tail on the hindwings help evade bat predators.

Io moth

Eye spots mimic the eyes of a larger animal to scare away predators.

The wings have four eye spots, two of which are visible even when the wings are closed.

Slate grey body has bright **red bands and spots**.

Cinnabar moth

Spanish moon moth

Furry, pink and yellow wings help the moth to hide among vibrant maple tree leaves.

Rosy maple moth

Speckled wing pattern helps the moth blend into surrounding woodland.

Light brown apple moth

human thumb. The most vibrant moths fly by day, and may use their bright hues to warn hungry birds that they taste horrible. The striking patterns of the **scarlet tiger moth** and **six-spot burnet moth** signal to predators that they are best avoided. The **cinnabar moth** is poisonous to predators because its larva feeds on the toxic ragwort plant. Most moths have a straw-like proboscis to feed on flower nectar or tree sap. But some moths, such as the **Spanish moon moth** and **Madagascan moon moth**, have no mouthparts and never feed. They survive on energy stored during their caterpillar stage, living as an adult only for a week or two.

Bright beetles

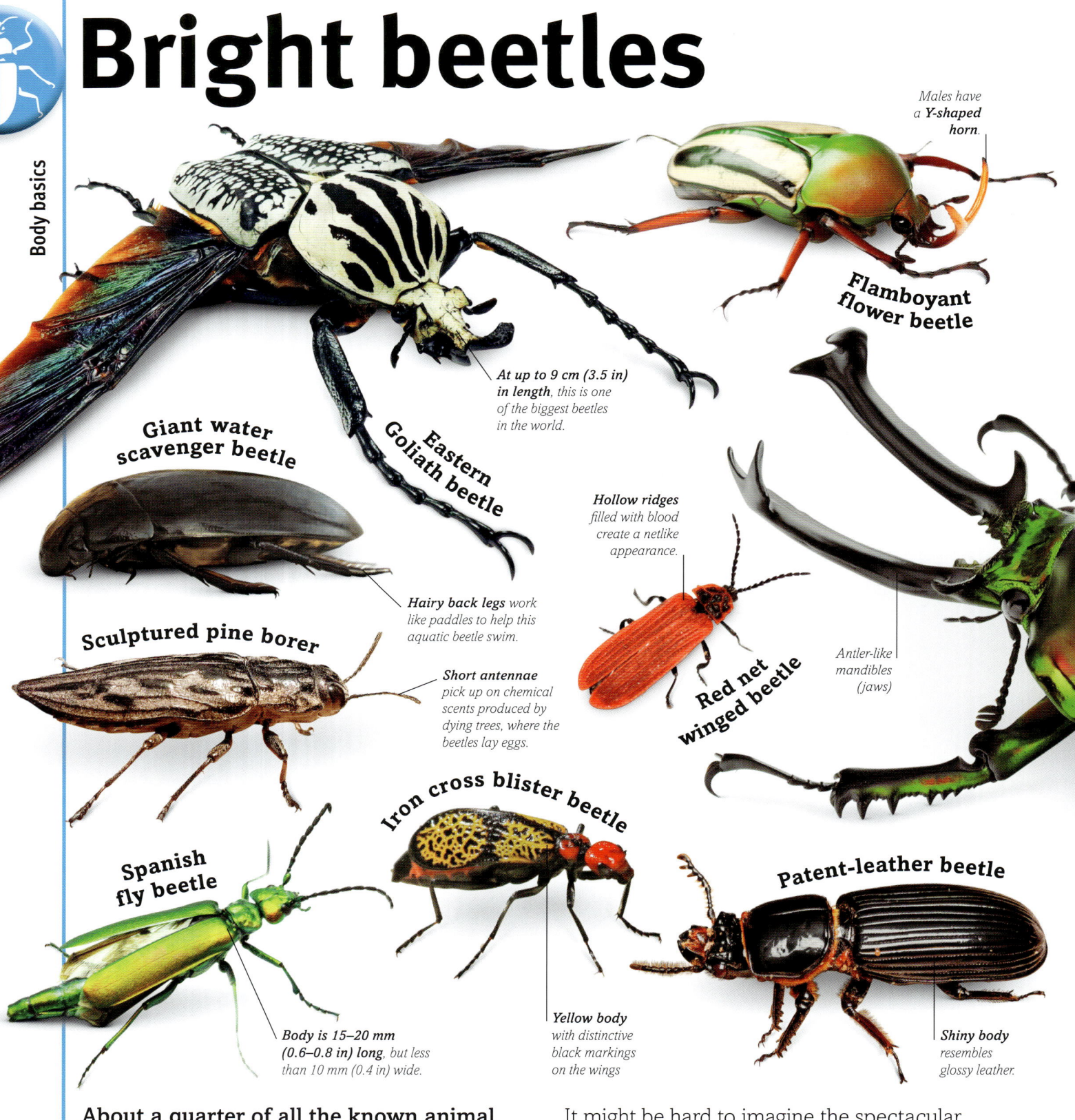

Males have a **Y-shaped horn**.

Flamboyant flower beetle

Eastern Goliath beetle

At up to 9 cm (3.5 in) in length, this is one of the biggest beetles in the world.

Giant water scavenger beetle

Hollow ridges filled with blood create a netlike appearance.

Hairy back legs work like paddles to help this aquatic beetle swim.

Sculptured pine borer

Short antennae pick up on chemical scents produced by dying trees, where the beetles lay eggs.

Red net winged beetle

Antler-like mandibles (jaws)

Iron cross blister beetle

Spanish fly beetle

Patent-leather beetle

Body is 15–20 mm (0.6–0.8 in) long, but less than 10 mm (0.4 in) wide.

Yellow body with distinctive black markings on the wings

Shiny body resembles glossy leather.

About a quarter of all the known animal species on Earth are beetles. Among the roughly 350,000 varieties, many beetles are bright and beautiful, with a spectrum of iridescent (shiny) colours. Their natural brilliance can serve as warnings, provide camouflage, or attract mates.

It might be hard to imagine the spectacular **rainbow stag beetle** or **spring dumbledor** being able to camouflage. But their eye-catching colours can produce a hazy silhouette in bright sunlight and on rain-soaked plants, which helps them to go unnoticed by predators, such as birds and rodents. The effect is caused by tiny creases

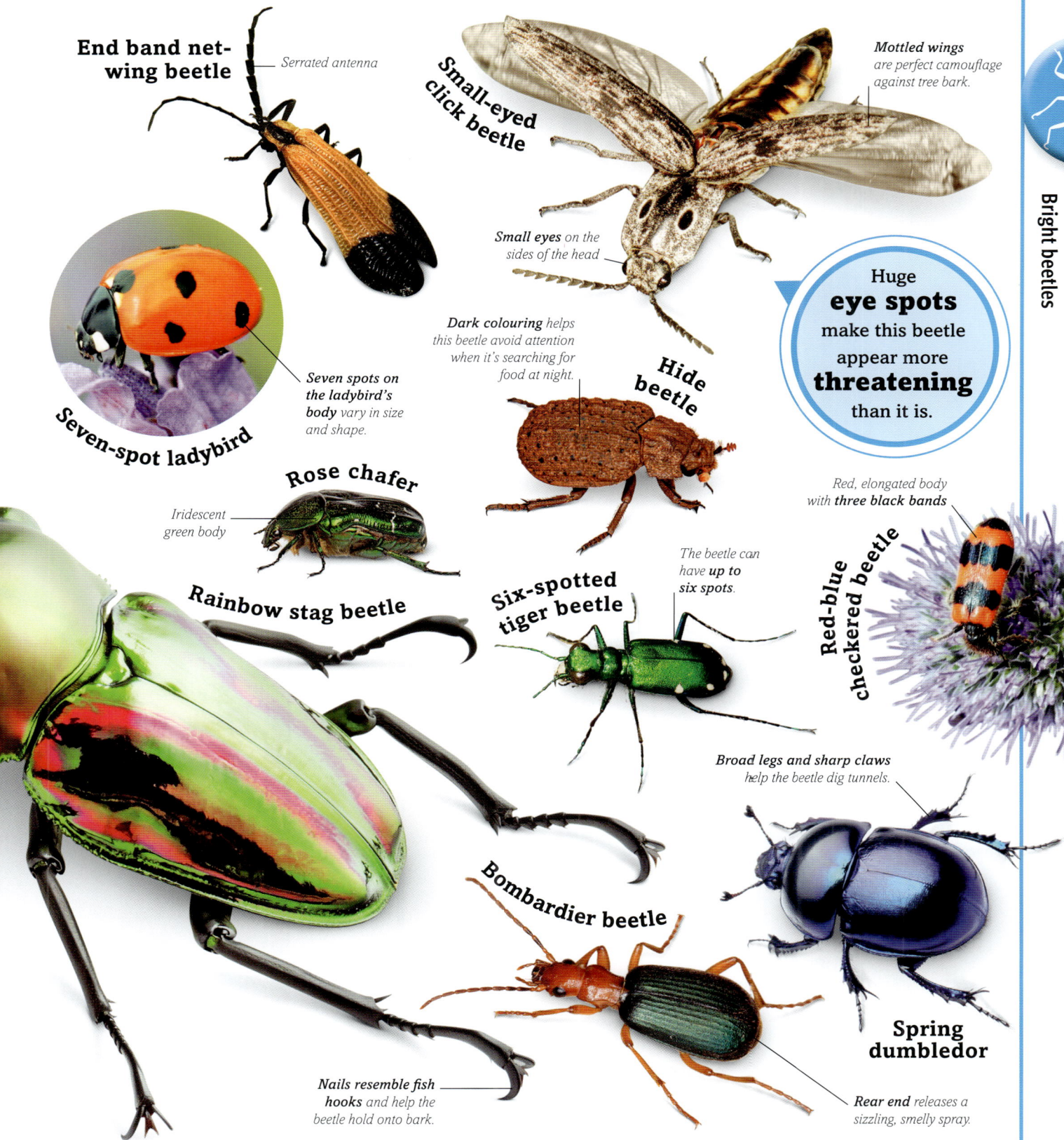

Bright beetles

and crinkles on the exoskeleton (outer skeleton) that channel light in different directions, creating a blurry effect. In contrast, some beetles don't need to hide from predators at all. The **Spanish fly beetle** and the **iron cross blister beetle** display dangerous colours and release a toxic substance when touched. When in danger, the **red net winged beetle** can release blood that contains a foul-smelling poison to deter attacks. And despite being less than 2.5 cm (1 in) long, the **bombardier beetle** blasts enemies with burning chemicals that can travel up to 30 cm (12 in) away.

45

Body basics

Hooded beetle 
Protective hoodlike covering

Red-shouldered bostrichid 
Red markings give this beetle its name.

Common tuft bearing longhorn beetle 
Black fluffy tufts on each antenna

Banded sexton beetle

Red milkweed beetle 
Antennae are almost as long as the entire body.

Spotted tortoise beetle 
Dome-shaped body is similar to a tortoise's shell.

Golden buprestid 
Colourful body helps this beetle camouflage in bright sunlight.

Clubbed antennae help detect the scent of dead animals on which it feeds.

Emerald ash borer 
Flat head with black kidney-shaped eyes

Dogbane beetle 
Blue-green body with a copper shine helps the bug blend with the dogbane leaves it mostly feeds on.

Acorn weevil 
Long, curved snout is used to break and drill into the hard acorn nut.

HOW BEETLES BREATHE

Like many insects, a beetle's body is dotted with tiny holes in the sides. These openings, known as spiracles, let air into a network of tubes called trachea inside the bug's body, through which the air reaches every part of the beetle.

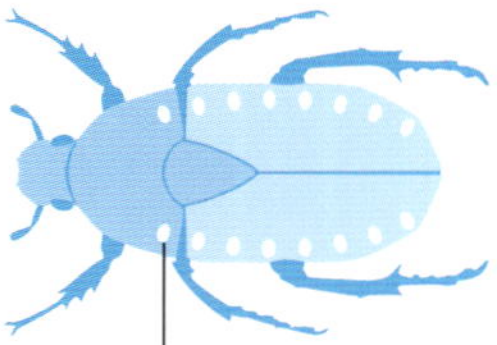

Up to 16 openings along the abdomen

Many beetles feature spot-based patterns to show predators that they taste bad or are truly toxic. This warning colouration can be seen in the **spotted tortoise beetle**, **red milkweed beetle**, and **22-spot ladybird**. Another way to avoid attackers is to blend in with the surroundings with camouflage colours.

The **varied carpet beetle**, often found in homes, has a mottled pattern that can make it hard to see against shaggy carpets and rugs, while the **emerald ash borer** looks much like its leafy surroundings. Other beetles have protective body armour, such as the **ironclad beetle** that can withstand being squashed. It also plays dead

by lying completely still, folding away its legs and antennae. As most animals prefer a fresh meal, they ignore this clever beetle. But predators aren't the only risk for beetles – harsh climate can kill just as easily. The **red flat bark beetle's** blood contains a natural antifreeze that helps it survive subzero temperatures of −150°C (−238°F). When it comes to finding a mate, beetles pull out all the stops. The dramatic visual display of the male **red speckled jewel beetle** attracts passing females, while the male **rainbow scarab** both draws in females and battles with competing males with its single tough horn.

47

Dragonflies and damselflies

Dark wings and a shiny green body camouflage this damselfly near streams in leafy woodlands.

Ebony jewelwing

Blue emperor

This big dragonfly has a **bright green thorax**.

Blue jewel damselfly

Blue markings on abdomen and thorax

The dazzling iridescent body of this insect confuses predators when it flits over streams and rivers.

Azure damselfly

Dark patches on the wings are common in the males of this damselfly species.

Banded demoiselle

Yellow wings with brown bands

Halloween pennant

Perched atop bare twigs, this dragonfly swings back and forth like a flag in the wind.

This small-bodied, female dragonfly has **brown eyes**.

Black darter

Among the most agile and acrobatic insects are dragonflies and damselflies. They have four long, lightweight wings that help with fast and flexible flight. Their breathtaking aerial displays aren't complete without them zipping through the air and hovering still.

Dragonflies and damselflies live on every continent except Antarctica. Dragonflies, such as the **blue emperor**, typically have bigger, stronger bodies with outstretched wings at rest. Damselflies, such as the **blue jewel damselfly**, are usually smaller and perch with their wings neatly closed. What most dragonflies and damselflies have in common

are thin, transparent or translucent wings strengthened by a network of veins. They are capable of fast flight, as seen in the **swift river cruiser**, a long, dark brown dragonfly that zips around at up to 64 kph (40 mph). Transparent wings also camouflage some of these flying insects, such as the **azure damselfly**, whose pale blue body allows it to blend into freshwater habitats. Some have spots on the edges of their wings, such as the **four-spotted chaser**, because this pattern acts as tiny weights, stabilizing the dragonfly when it's gliding. Others, such as the male **banded demoiselle**, stay bold and bright to appeal to females. The **ebony jewelwing** and the **Sudanese gossamerwing** have darker wings, which absorb sunlight to keep them warm.

Body basics

Life of a dragonfly

Like cicadas, dragonflies change gradually as they transform from an egg to an adult. They grow bigger at every stage until they reach adult size. This life cycle is known as incomplete metamorphosis because – unlike a caterpillar turning into a moth – the dragonfly does not totally change its appearance.

1 A new start › The life cycle begins when an adult female dragonfly lays hundreds of eggs, often on plants in a pond or lake. The eggs hatch within a few weeks. The newly hatched dragonfly larvae are known as nymphs.

Nymph looks like a mini adult.

The brittle, moulted skin may remain attached to vegetation for weeks.

2 Growing nymphs › With every stage of growth, the aquatic nymph becomes too big for its outer skin. This is when the skin splits open – a process called moulting. Each shedding of the skin is called a moult. For the final moult, the nymph leaves the water and crawls onto land, securing a spot on a plant stem or other vegetation.

3 Breaking out › The nymph holds on to the stem firmly and starts pumping a bloodlike fluid faster through its body. Its body puffs up and the outer shell splits, as the adult dragonfly begins to climb out of it. Its head, thorax, and legs are quite wrinkled at first.

4 Ready to perch › The adult dragonfly completely pulls its abdomen out of the skin. This newly emerged adult uses its front legs to perch on its moulted skin as it waits.

5 New wings ›
The dragonfly dries out its new wings, stretching and straightening them in a process that can take several hours. The body of the dragonfly is not yet at its full size either – its thorax and abdomen will continue to grow.

6 Preparing to fly ›
Despite its large wings, the dragonfly is not yet a strong flier. It spends its early days feeding on insects away from water to grow strong enough to fly expertly. It then returns to water to find mates and renews the life cycle.

The **delicate wings** of the dragonfly can take **3 hours** to dry.

Dragonfly wings are very thin, strengthened by a network of tiny veins.

A mature dragonfly has a hard body that displays brilliant colours.

Dragonfly larvae

Dragonfly larvae have big appetites. They live under water and feast on a wide variety of prey – from aquatic insects to small tadpoles and fish. These tiny hunters are among the top insect predators underwater, thanks to their deadly, hooked lower lip, which can be extended to grab prey easily.

Distinct pairs

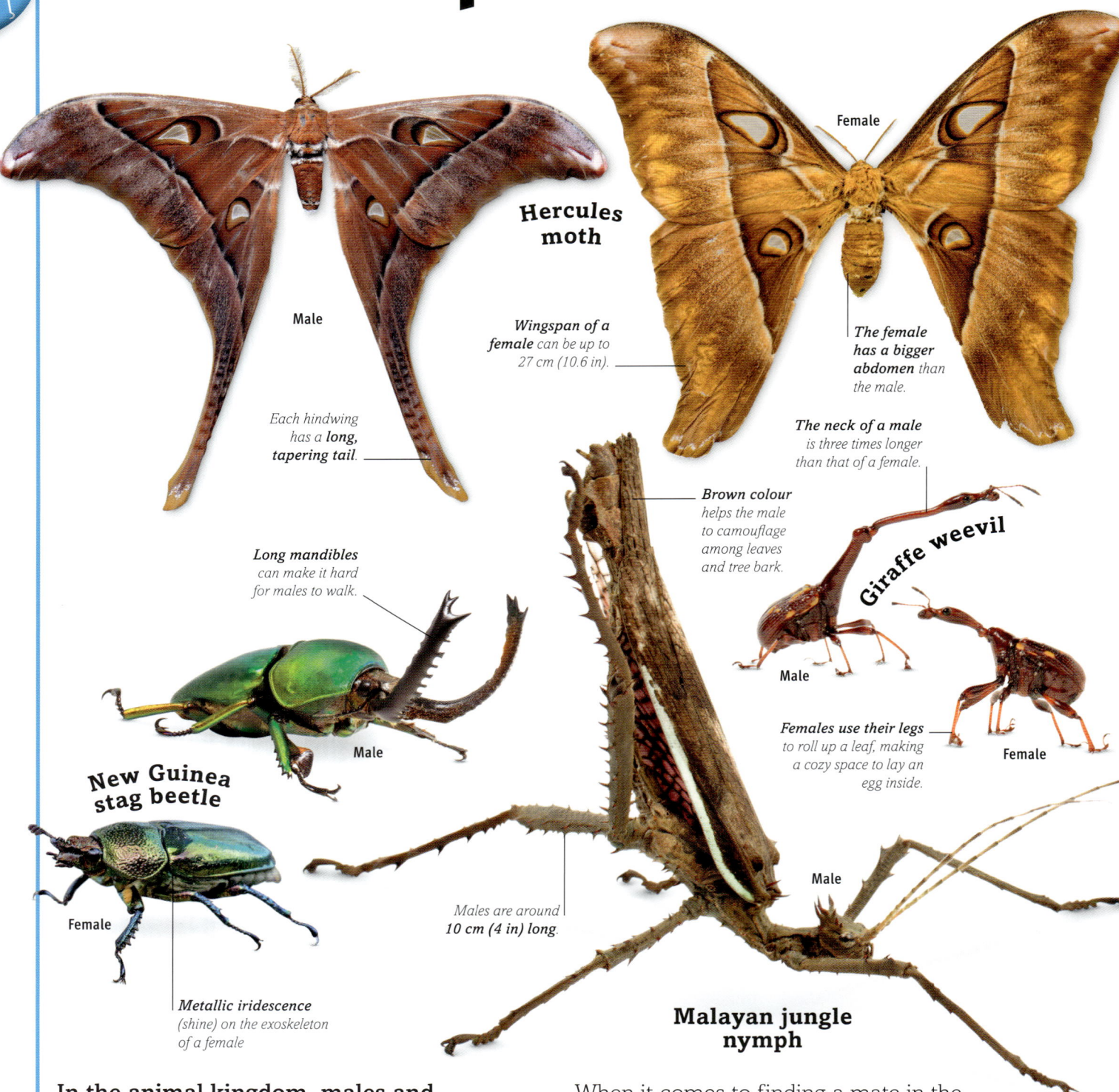

In the animal kingdom, males and females of the same species may look strikingly different. There are many examples of it in bugs. These unique differences between couples – called sexual dimorphism – are related to mating and reproduction.

When it comes to finding a mate in the world of bugs, competition between males can be fierce. Many male bugs have evolved features to either attract females or defeat other mating rivals. Male **giraffe weevils** grow long necks to battle each other, and **New Guinea stag beetles** use their massive

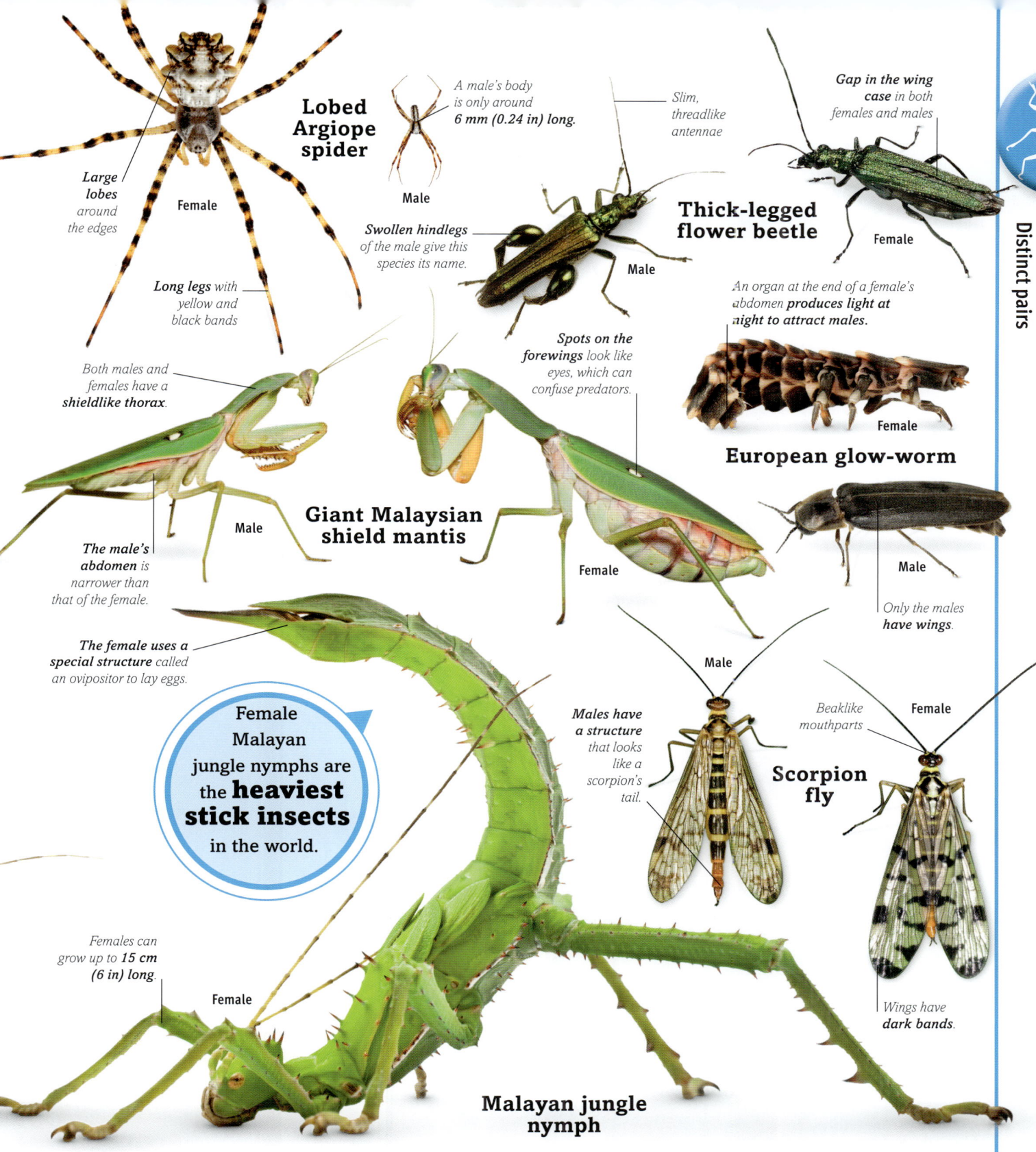

hornlike mandibles (jaws) to fight. Other insects have more subtle ways of finding a mate. Male **Hercules moths**, for example, have feathery antennae, which they use to detect pheromones released by females up to 2 km (1 mile) away. Sometimes the size differences are stark. The females of a species may be larger than the males – as in the **lobed Argiope spiders**. The females can be up to five times larger than the males. Some pairs can be told apart by their colour differences – the darker male **Malayan jungle nymphs** mate with larger, green females.

WHERE BUGS LIVE

Where bugs live

Habitats

A habitat is the place where animals and plants live. Like most living things, bugs need a habitat with food, water, and shelter. Even a rock, pool, or plant can provide a home. Bugs are part of an ecosystem, a wider community of animals and plants that depend on each other to survive.

LIFE IN LAYERS
This spectacular tropical rainforest in Borneo offers countless bugs a diverse range of places to live. Bugs have set up home in every layer of this rainforest, taking advantage of the plentiful rainfall, abundant food, and leafy shelter.

Bee nest in canopy ❯
A swarm of honeybees is hanging from a lofty branch in the rainforest roof, called the canopy. These nectar-feeding bees stay here temporarily while some of them scout around looking for a permanent home in a cavity or crevice.

Ants in understorey ❯ Weaver ants build leafy nests in the understorey layer of the forest that is full of bushes and small trees. This space is hidden from predators and safe from heavy rainfall. The understorey also provides the ants with insect prey and sweet honeydew.

Termites on forest floor ❯
Busy termites move in groups along the forest floor, feeding on rotting wood and fallen leaves. Damp ground prevents termites from drying out. They roll fungi balls from here to the colony to strengthen their nests.

Types of habitat

Bugs are amazingly adaptable, and this is why they exist in just about every habitat on Earth, from the grassy savannah and the dry desert to the Arctic tundra and tropical rainforest. Huge numbers of bugs also thrive alongside people in towns and cities.

Savannah

Desert

Boreal forest and Arctic tundra

Butterfly in canopy
Butterflies frequent every level of the rainforest. However, the canopy is a favourite for butterflies that are migrating in search of food or mates. This birdwing butterfly drinks nectar from the rainforest flowers and pollinates plants in the process.

Lantern bug in understorey
The spotted lantern bug prefers the trees growing in the understorey. This layer keeps predators at bay and helps its residents avoid flooding on the forest floor. This bug's piercing mouthparts suck out tree sap and produce honeydew for other bugs to eat.

Millipede on forest floor
The darkness, dampness, and decay of the forest floor attract millipedes. They live under rocks, and keep their body moist on the rain-soaked ground. By eating the rotting leaves, they put nutrients back into the soil.

Underground creatures

*Animals that **live in caves** are known as **troglofauna**.*

Broad pincers can be used to block the entrance of a burrow to protect it from intruders.

Boehm's burrowing scorpion

Antennae are thick to avoid getting damaged while burrowing.

European mole cricket

Cave millipede

This insect is almost transparent as it lives in dark caves with no need to camouflage or warn off predators.

The second pair of legs is used to sense surroundings in the dark.

Cave harvestman

Giant burrowing cockroach

Platelike structure at the front of the body helps while digging.

Long, threadlike body makes burrowing through soil easy.

Soil centipede

There are numerous bugs that spend their whole lives in dark places, with little to no light. They bury themselves in the ground, dig tunnels, or make their home in caves so dark that some of them don't have eyes. Instead, they use other senses and organs to survive.

Fascinating bugs can be found under the ground's surface. The **antlion larva** digs a funnel-shaped pit in the sand and buries itself in the bottom, ready to seize any prey that slips into the pit. The **soil centipede** travels lower, slithering down through the layers of soil to find prey. The **European mole cricket** and the **burrowing**

Mucus-covered silk threads are used to catch prey.

New Zealand glowworm larva

Burrowing wolf spider

Front legs, used for digging, are heavier than the rest.

The larva moves underground to weave a cocoon and pupate.

Antlion larva

Termite nests have intricate tunnels to **control temperature and airflow**.

The pincers are used to detect **prey in the dark**.

Sensitive, long legs help the beetle detect danger in the dark.

Cave beetle

False scorpion

African termite

wolf spider have legs adapted to help them dig tunnels. The **African termite** builds large underground nests, with towering chimneys for ventilation. **Boehm's burrowing scorpion** digs complex systems of tunnels, and hides in them for days at a time to escape heat and predators. Some bugs have developed unique adaptations to live inside extremely dark and wet caves. The **New Zealand glowworm larvae** live on the ceilings of caves and create a spectacular lightshow to attract prey. Cave-dwelling bugs have little need to see, and many of them, including the **cave beetle** and **cave harvestman**, are completely blind.

Insect architects

*Potter wasps use soil and water to build **pot-shaped nests**.*

Mud pot

Fresh, flexible leaves are used to make the Asian weaver ant nest.

Leaf nest

These tunnels made by the European spruce bark beetles widen as the larvae grow inside.

*Nest contains tiny **wax pots**, brooding cells, and wax covering.*

Oak marble galls

*Wasp larvae grow inside these **brown, marble-shaped growths**.*

Bumblebee nest

As many as 100,000 worker bees form a wall of protection around the outer layer of the nest.

Bark beetle tunnels

Giant honeybee nest

When it comes to building homes, insects are capable of incredible architectural feats. Some work alone to build small, cozy hideouts, whereas others band together to construct monumental nests. Insects try to make their homes safe spaces – camouflaged or hidden from sight, or built strong enough to withstand harsh weather conditions and predator attacks.

Insects use a variety of materials to build their spectacular homes. Some use substances found in nature, while others create their own. A female potter wasp builds a **mud pot** for each of its eggs. Asian weaver ants construct **leaf nests** by gluing leaves together with silk produced by the ant larvae. **Bald-faced hornet nests** are made from chewed up wood fibres, and **cathedral termite mounds** are made from mud, saliva, and even the

*Abbot's bagworm moth caterpillar protects its cocoon using **plant remains**.*

Cathedral termite mounds can be up to **8 m (26 ft)** tall.

*The calleta silkmoth caterpillar **weaves a silk cocoon** to protect itself from predators and changing weather.*

Cocoon

*Leafcutter ants build **underground** nests and grow fungi using leaves to feed their larvae.*

Log-cabin

Fungus garden

Cathedral termite mound

Made of paperlike material, the nests are about the size of a basketball.

*These hollow mounds have **strong walls** and ventilate the underground termite nests.*

Bald-faced hornet's nest

poo of the termites. Some insects take over existing structures to make their homes. **Bark beetle tunnels** are carved out by the bugs burrowing under the bark of spruce trees. **Oak marble galls** are made by wasps that cause the growth of hard, woody balls on the twigs of oak trees. The female wasps lay their eggs inside the galls.

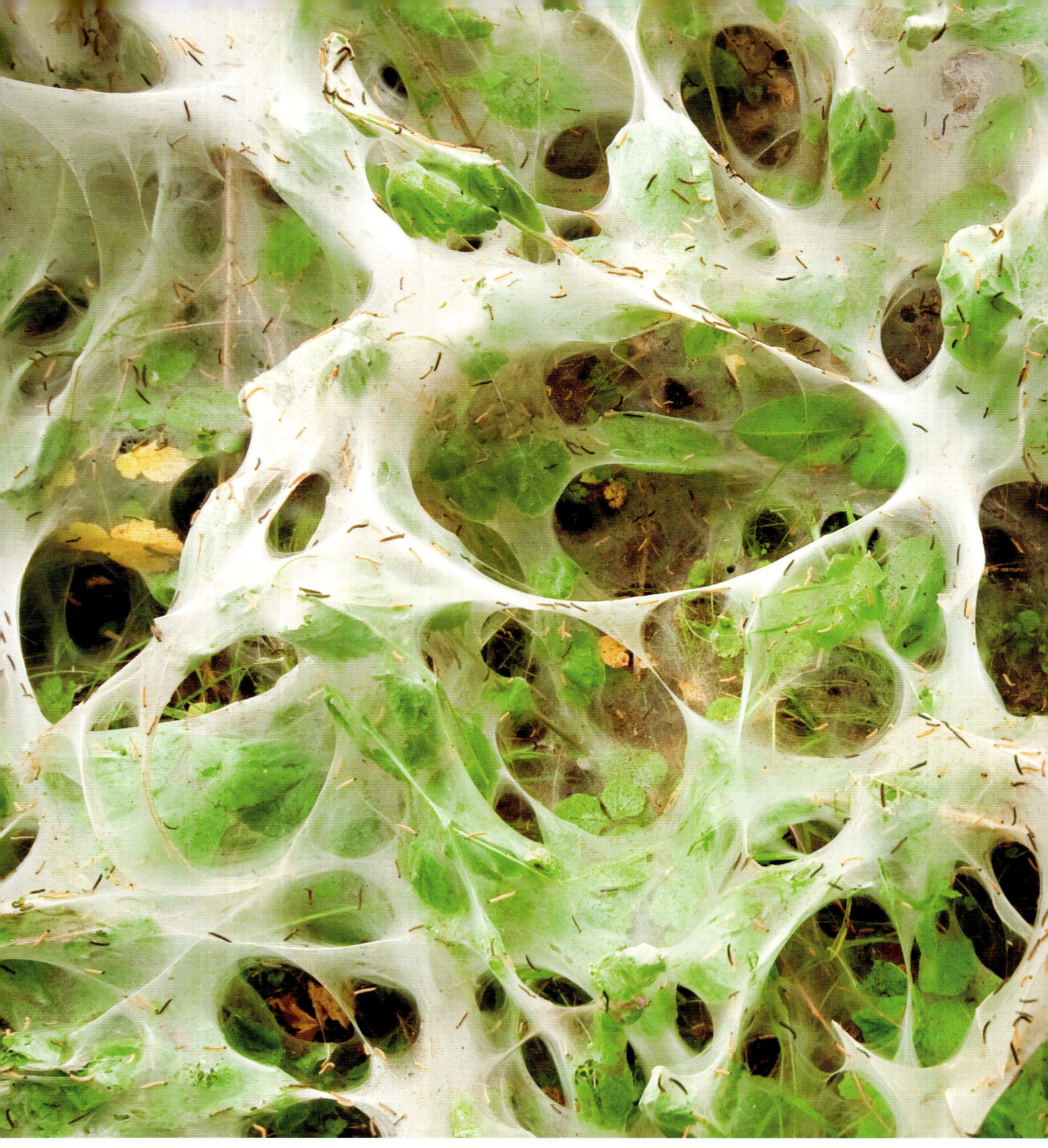

SAFE HAVEN
From spring until early summer, the bird cherry tree becomes unrecognizable in parts of Europe and Asia. It stands shrouded in a strange, spooky silk that resembles colossal cobwebs. This eye-catching design is the handiwork of the caterpillars of the bird cherry ermine moth. They spin supersize, silken webs in the trees to create a barrier that stops predators from coming close.

By living in large communities of hundreds or even thousands, these small caterpillars stick together and find safety in numbers. The white web serves as a safety net for the growing caterpillars – keeping predators and bad weather at bay. The immense, cloudlike web serves as a warning, threatening invaders with the risk of becoming entangled in its dense silk.

Protected by the surrounding silk, these hungry bugs are free to feast on the leaves, growing to a sufficient size to transform into adult moths. Although the webs do not harm the trees, the caterpillars leave the branches bare. When they have completed their metamorphosis, the web wears off and the trees begin to recover their leaves.

Desert dwellers

American sand wasp — *The wasp drinks sweet nectar from desert flowers.*

Fog-basking darkling beetle — *Rear end is raised so water from the desert fog flows easily into its mouth.*

Sacred scarab dung beetle — *Toothed front legs are used for digging.*

Desert blister beetle — *This beetle can squirt toxic fluid from its leg joints, when threatened.*

Blue death-feigning beetle — *Blue bumps on forewings ooze out wax.*

Arabian fat-tailed scorpion — *Potent tail sting is used to paralyse prey, making this scorpion one of the deadliest bugs.*

EXTREME LIVING

Bugs seek out all kinds of shelter to survive in deserts. While the scorpions hide under rocks or debris, the beetles live among cacti spines. Others, like spiders, burrow into the sand, while the termites reside in rotten wood.

- Under the rocks
- Inside burrows
- Inside rotten wood
- Near cacti plants

Deserts are among the most challenging habitats on Earth. With blazing sunshine, extreme temperatures, scarce food, and limited water, desert bugs must be both strong and smart to survive. To live in their harsh surroundings, they've developed cunning ways of adapting.

The simplest way to cope with the intense heat is to avoid it altogether. The **Arabian fat-tailed scorpion** is nocturnal, hiding in crevices by day and emerging at night when the temperature goes down. Similarly, the **desert millipede** creates its own burrow underground to keep cool. Deserts face a continual shortage of water,

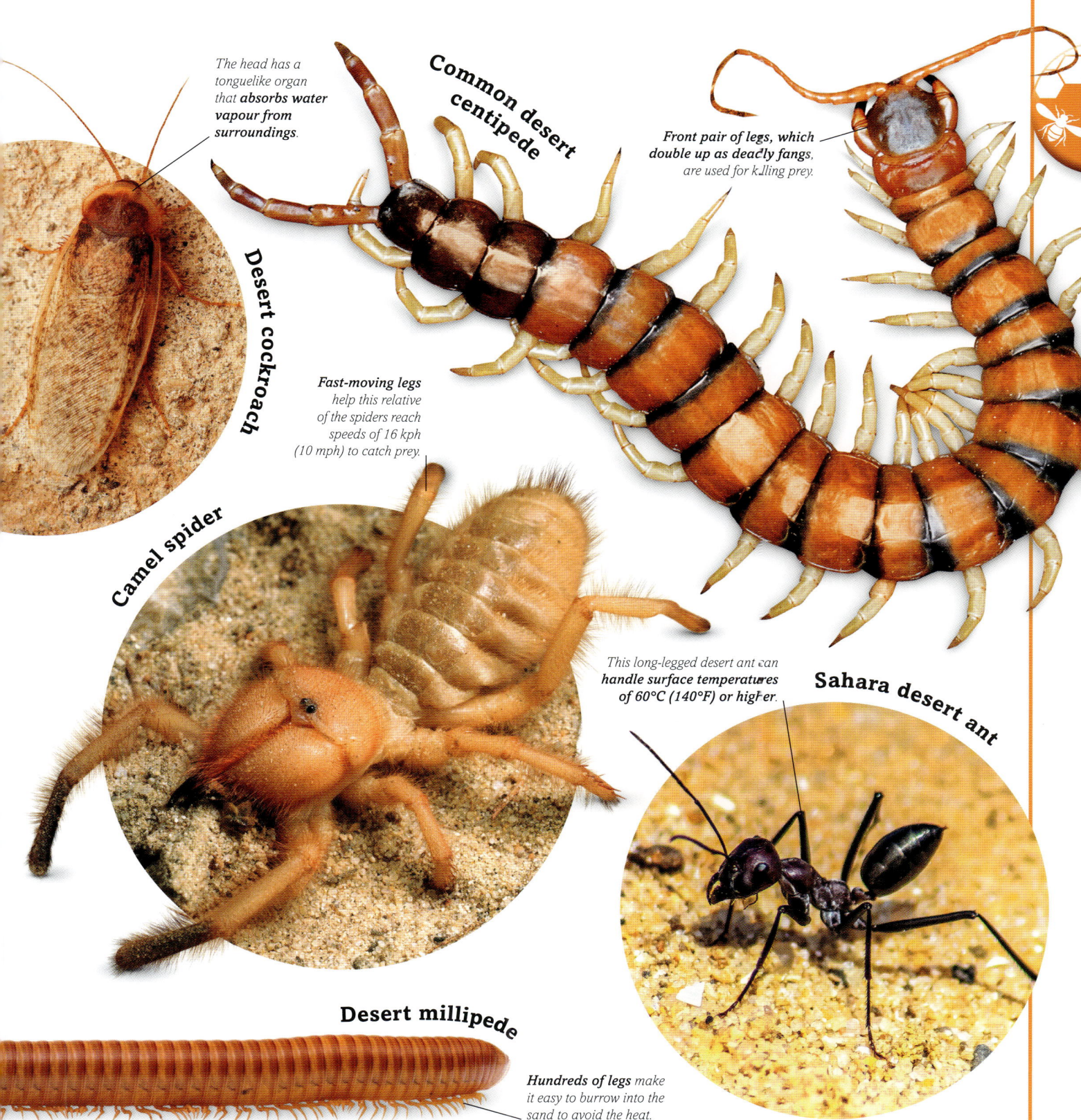

Desert cockroach — The head has a tonguelike organ that *absorbs water vapour from surroundings*.

Common desert centipede — Front pair of legs, which *double up as deadly fangs*, are used for killing prey.

Camel spider — *Fast-moving legs* help this relative of the spiders reach speeds of 16 kph (10 mph) to catch prey.

Sahara desert ant — This long-legged desert ant can *handle surface temperatures of 60°C (140°F) or higher*.

Desert millipede — *Hundreds of legs* make it easy to burrow into the sand to avoid the heat.

so bugs must get creative to find this valuable resource. The **fog-basking darkling beetle** takes advantage of the morning fog in the desert dunes by letting water droplets trickle into its mouth. The **blue death-feigning beetle's** waxy coating helps the bug to retain precious water, while the **camel spider** gets all the water it needs from the variety of bugs it hunts and eats. Plenty of desert dwellers, including the **desert cockroach**, scavenge for decaying animal and plant matter. The **sacred scarab dung beetle** takes it one step further – it eats dung (poo) to make sure absolutely nothing goes to waste.

Up in the mountains

Black body with a **copper-brown** abdomen

White wings help the butterfly to blend in snow-covered ground.

Mountain Apollo butterfly

Alpine bumblebee

This black and orange coloured cicada looks for sunny spots to escape the cold.

Mountain cicada

Highland ant

The highland ant works **hard** *in the summer and becomes inactive during cold months.*

An elongated body **covered with tiny hairs**

Males have **feathery antennae**.

Sierra Nevada ice crawler

Glacier midge

Named after the **Greek god** of the Sun, **Apollo**, this butterfly loves sunny slopes.

The shiny, stripy coloured **beetle** *hibernates to survive the cold weather.*

Rainbow leaf beetle

It's a tough life for bugs found in mountain ranges around the world. Despite the challenges of low temperatures, unpredictable weather, snowy slopes, and limited resources, these resilient creatures have successfully adapted in high altitudes to survive.

One way to brave the harsh mountain habitat is to grow thick hair for insulation, which helps retain heat. The **Alpine bumblebee** and the **mountain ringlet** keep warm with a dense covering of body hair. The tiny **glacier midge** and **splay-footed carpenter bee** have black bodies to absorb as much sunlight as possible.

TOP OF THE WORLD

These three record-breaking insects and arachnids live at the highest altitudes in the world. The Himalayan jumping spider lives on mountains, including Zhumulangma Feng (Mount Everest), making it the highest-living spider on Earth.

QUEEN OF SPAIN FRITILLARY BUTTERFLY AT 6,000 M (19,685 FT)

HIMALAYAN JUMPING SPIDER AT 6,700 M (21,982 FT)

TERMITE AT 5,800 M (19,029 FT)

Himalayan jumping spider
The spider is just 5 mm (0.19 in) in size.

Splay-footed carpenter bee
Vibrant wing colour can surprise attackers.

Mountain ringlet
The dark brown and black wings act like solar panels that help the butterfly survive harsh winters.

Snow flea
This small bug is around 0.25 cm (0.09 in) in length.

Queen of Spain fritillary butterfly
Dark orange wings with black spots

Club-legged grasshopper
Darker forms of this grasshopper warm up faster in the cold mountain air.

In extremely cold regions, some insects, such as the **snow flea**, produce anti-freeze proteins that prevent their blood from freezing. On the other hand, the **Queen of Spain fritillary butterfly** makes a mountain migration – moving down the slopes during the cooler months to benefit from the warmer temperatures found at lower altitude. Many bugs are faced with slim pickings for food. The **Himalayan jumping spider** watches out for tiny bugs blown up the slopes on the wind. However, the **Sierra Nevada ice crawler** has a diverse diet, from fungi and algae to small bugs.

Up in the mountains

Where bugs live

Rainforest bugs

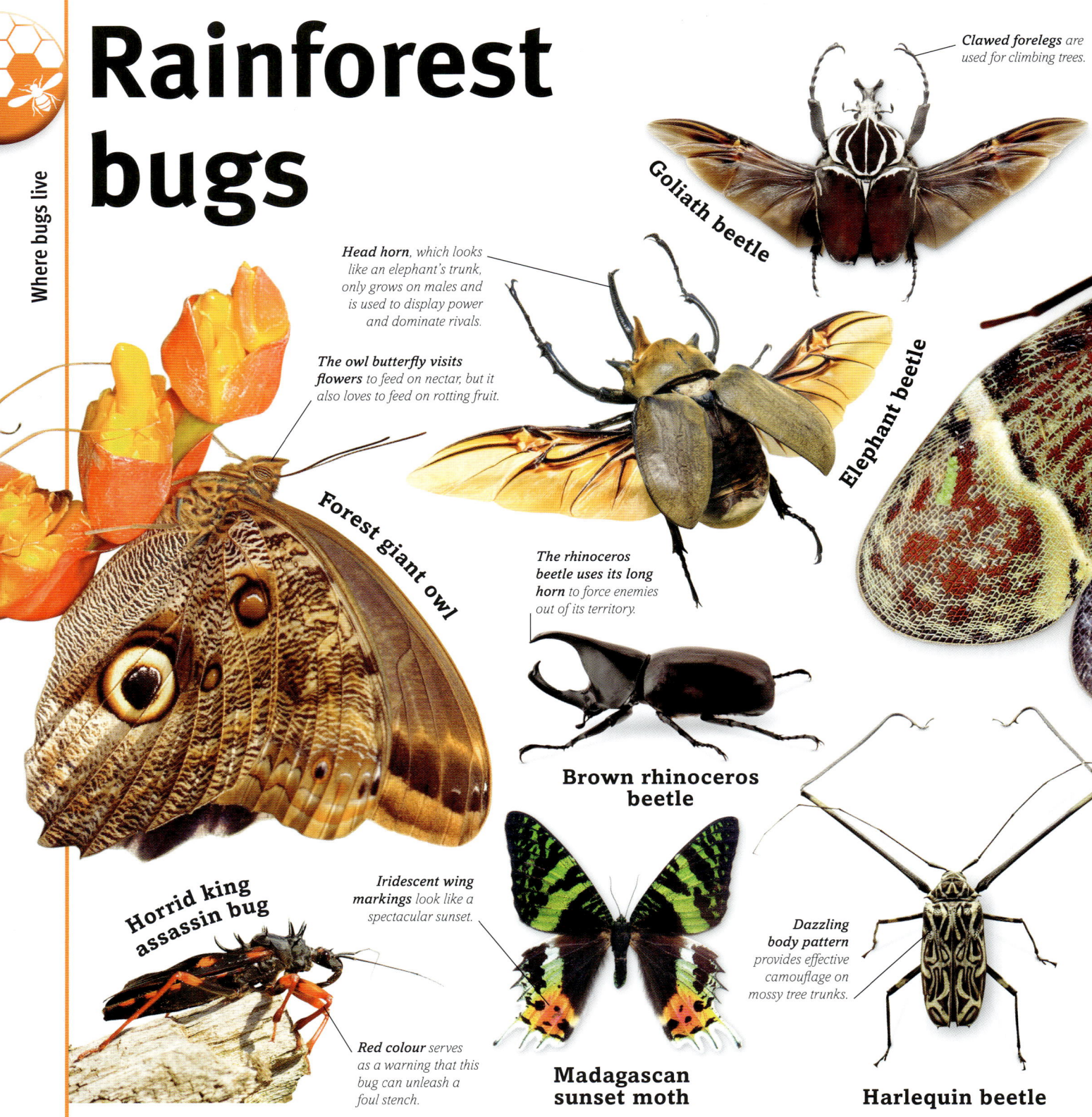

Clawed forelegs are used for climbing trees.

Goliath beetle

Head horn, which looks like an elephant's trunk, only grows on males and is used to display power and dominate rivals.

The owl butterfly visits flowers to feed on nectar, but it also loves to feed on rotting fruit.

Forest giant owl

Elephant beetle

The rhinoceros beetle uses its long horn to force enemies out of its territory.

Brown rhinoceros beetle

Horrid king assassin bug

Iridescent wing markings look like a spectacular sunset.

Red colour serves as a warning that this bug can unleash a foul stench.

Madagascan sunset moth

Dazzling body pattern provides effective camouflage on mossy tree trunks.

Harlequin beetle

Tropical rainforests are home to more than half of all the species on Earth and around 90 per cent of these could be bugs. From the tallest treetops to the forest floor, bugs thrive in this lush habitat with its leafy shelter, warm temperatures, plentiful rainfall, and abundant food supply.

Rainforest bugs use the dense trees and leafy plants as a safe sanctuary hidden from prying predators. The **pink toe tarantula** spends most of its time in trees, tucked away safely in its web. The **Goliath beetle** – one of the biggest and heaviest insects around – climbs high up in trees to avoid predators. Food is also on offer at every

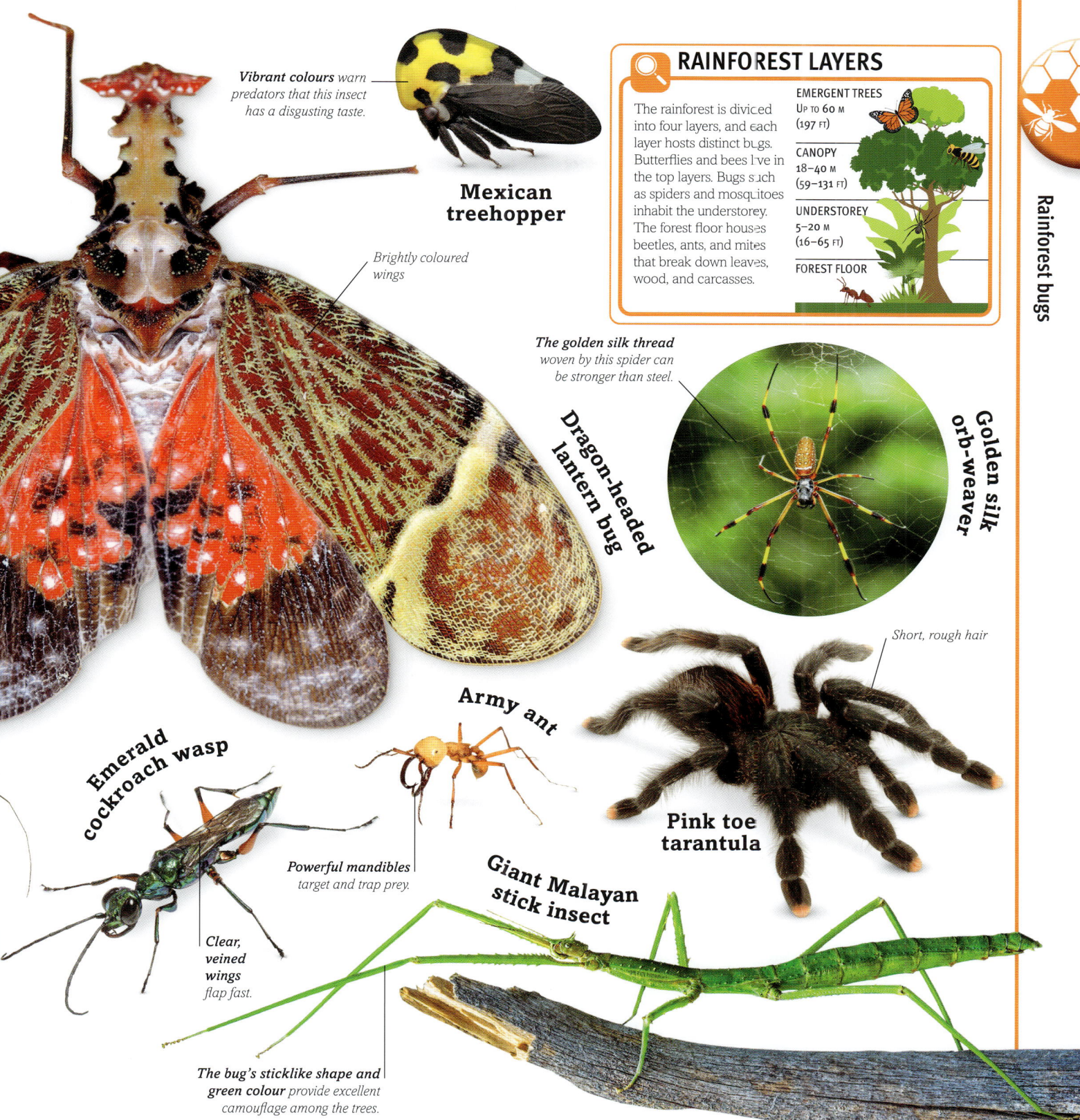

Vibrant colours warn predators that this insect has a disgusting taste.

Mexican treehopper

Brightly coloured wings

RAINFOREST LAYERS

The rainforest is divided into four layers, and each layer hosts distinct bugs. Butterflies and bees live in the top layers. Bugs such as spiders and mosquitoes inhabit the understorey. The forest floor houses beetles, ants, and mites that break down leaves, wood, and carcasses.

EMERGENT TREES Up to 60 M (197 FT)
CANOPY 18–40 M (59–131 FT)
UNDERSTOREY 5–20 M (16–65 FT)
FOREST FLOOR

The golden silk thread woven by this spider can be stronger than steel.

Dragon-headed lantern bug

Golden silk orb-weaver

Short, rough hair

Emerald cockroach wasp

Army ant

Powerful mandibles target and trap prey.

Pink toe tarantula

Giant Malayan stick insect

Clear, veined wings flap fast.

The bug's sticklike shape and green colour provide excellent camouflage among the trees.

Rainforest bugs

level. The **Mexican treehopper** uses its strawlike mouth to suck plant sap, the **Madagascan sunset moth** feasts on the sweet nectar of flowers, and the **elephant beetle** feeds on fruit fallen onto the ground. Other bugs see this habitat as a hunting ground, with the **emerald cockroach wasp** and the **horrid king assassin bug** injecting deadly venom to stun their victims. Similarly, the **golden silk orb-weaver** sets up large, sticky webs between trees to prey on insects. Water is always available as regular rainfall collects in the leaves, ready for bugs such as the **giant Malayan stick insect** to pass by and quench their thirst.

Where bugs live

Super spiders

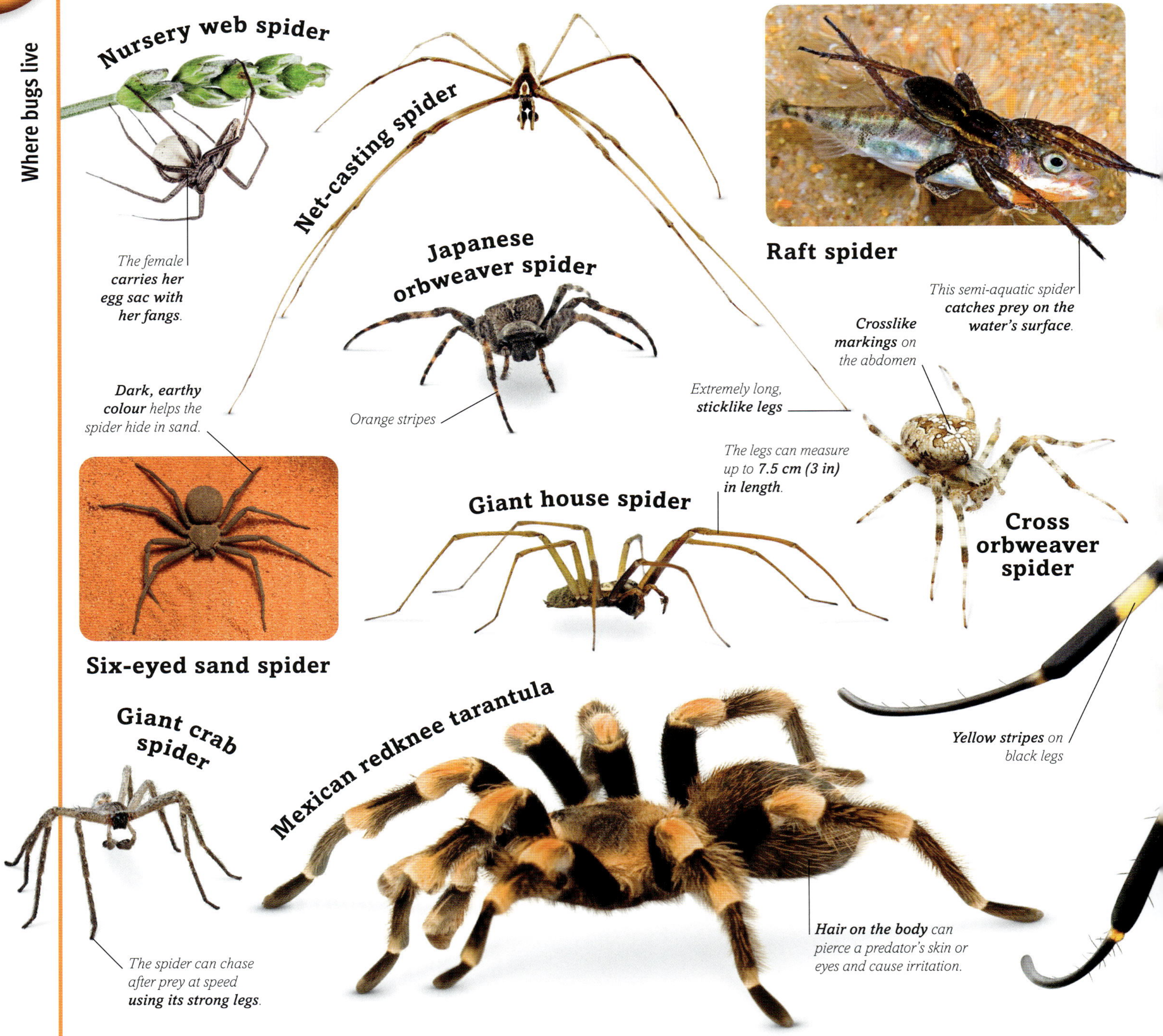

Nursery web spider
The female carries her egg sac with her fangs.

Net-casting spider

Japanese orbweaver spider
Orange stripes

Raft spider
This semi-aquatic spider catches prey on the water's surface.

Six-eyed sand spider
Dark, earthy colour helps the spider hide in sand.

Giant house spider
Extremely long, sticklike legs
The legs can measure up to 7.5 cm (3 in) in length.

Cross orbweaver spider
Crosslike markings on the abdomen

Giant crab spider
The spider can chase after prey at speed using its strong legs.

Mexican redknee tarantula
Hair on the body can pierce a predator's skin or eyes and cause irritation.

Yellow stripes on black legs

What's so special about spiders? Unlike insects, which have three body parts, arachnids such as spiders have two parts – the head and the abdomen. Spiders are great hunters that move around on eight legs. They can all produce silk. Most of them have eight eyes, but some of them have fewer, and others don't have any at all.

Spiders come in all sizes. On the lower end of the scale is the tiny **spinybacked orbweaver**, which isn't much bigger than a ball-pen tip. Much larger than this are the titan tarantulas such as the **Mexican redknee** and the **barking spider**, which is the size of a tennis ball. Female spiders are usually bigger than males, especially those of the **giant wood spider**, which can be ten times

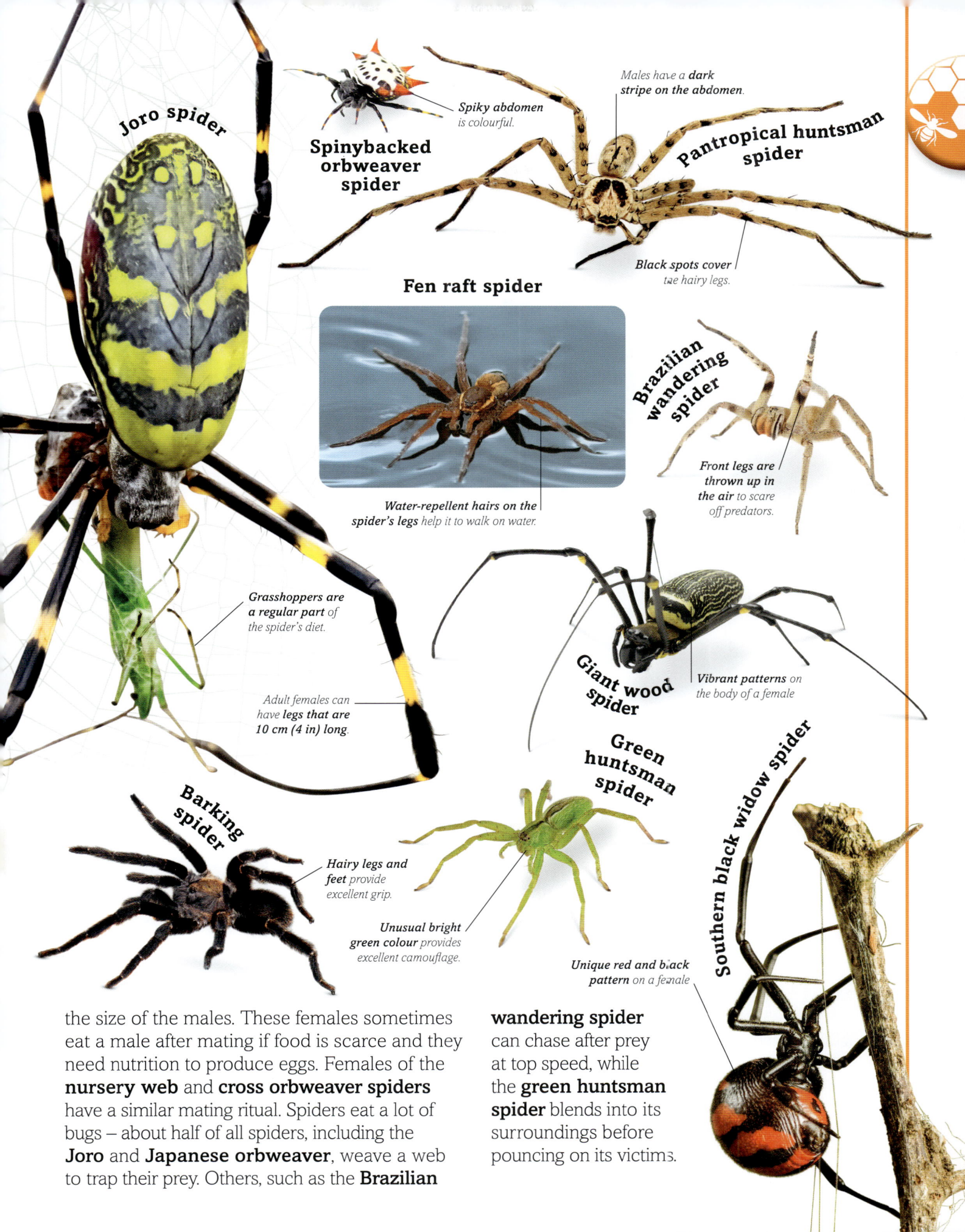

the size of the males. These females sometimes eat a male after mating if food is scarce and they need nutrition to produce eggs. Females of the **nursery web** and **cross orbweaver spiders** have a similar mating ritual. Spiders eat a lot of bugs – about half of all spiders, including the **Joro** and **Japanese orbweaver**, weave a web to trap their prey. Others, such as the **Brazilian wandering spider** can chase after prey at top speed, while the **green huntsman spider** blends into its surroundings before pouncing on its victims.

FOAMY HIDEAWAY Young spittlebugs live up to their name by producing a frothy foam to form a cosy sanctuary. This build-up of bubbles on the stem of a plant completely conceals the baby insects, keeping the nymphs warm and safely tucked away from predators, such as assassin bugs and spiders. The foam also adds a vital layer of moisture to prevent the nymphs from drying out.

Even though it is known as "cuckoo spit", this white foam doesn't come from a bird or even the spittlebug's mouthparts. Instead, the nymphs release a mixture of air, undigested plant sap, and a sticky fluid from their rear end in the form of bubbles. The young ones live inside the bubbles, feeding freely on plant sap, while growing bigger. These sociable insects sometimes live together, sharing bubbles on the same plant to stay safe. They are not picky about which type of plant they inhabit, and create their bubble bases on all kinds of flowers, including lavender and rose. Despite its dramatic appearance, this bubble home doesn't harm plants and disappears once the nymphs grow into adults.

Urban insects

Where bugs live

The reddish-brown beetle infests stored foods, such as grain and flour.

Confused flour beetle

These busy ants are known to nest in pavements.

Central European bicoloured ant

This beetle feeds on fur, carpets, woollens, and feathers, often found in museum exhibits.

Museum beetle

Unique parallel grooves on wing covers

Biscuit beetle

This insect can feed on the starch found in papers and glue.

Long-tailed silverfish

Flat body of the firebrat slips easily inside boiler rooms and bakeries.

Firebrat

Insects inhabiting towns and cities have adapted well to live in urban spaces. They share spaces with people in their homes and workplaces, in parks, and roadsides. Their small sizes help them to go unnoticed, while their appetites are satisfied by food stores and leftover waste.

Bugs can set up home in all kinds of urban spaces. Cloth stores and bedroom wardrobes play host to the **case-bearing clothes moth caterpillar**, which feeds on clothing fibres and thrives in the warm spaces of shops and homes. Restaurants and bakeries are quite popular with hungry bugs. The **biscuit beetle**

Spindle ermine moth

This polka-dotted moth thrives on spindle trees in urban areas, where its caterpillars spin dense webs and feed on the leaves.

Dark colour merges with the wood of door panels and window frames.

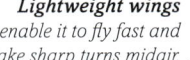

European powderpost beetle

Lightweight wings enable it to fly fast and take sharp turns midair.

Fruit fly

A silken-spun case protects the caterpillar's body.

Case-bearing clothes moth caterpillar

HIDING HOLES

Being small comes in handy when bugs, such as these red firebug nymphs, want to hide or escape danger. They can squeeze into the tiniest cracks and crevices in urban areas, from pavements and tiles to bricks and bins.

Deathwatch beetle

This oval-shaped burrowing beetle lives in rotten wood and old beams.

The red mason bee likes to nest in existing structures such as brick holes and hollow stems.

Red mason bee

Clawed legs

Vine weevil

enjoys sugary treats as well as stored pasta and cereal. The **fruit fly** hangs around rubbish bins to take advantage of any juicy fruit thrown out. While the **vine weevil** is attracted to the city lights, it prefers the parks and nurseries for their tempting range of leafy plants and flowers. The **Central European bicoloured ant** has earned the nickname "ManhattAnt", thanks to its increasing numbers in New York, US. It scavenges for leftovers on streets and climbs trees on the pavements in search of honeydew – the sugary excretion of aphids and scale insects.

Where bugs live

Aquatic bugs

Many bugs live near water sources, but some actually live on, or even in, the water itself. Inhabiting most aquatic habitats – from the stagnant waters of marshes and swamps, to ponds and the flowing currents of rivers and streams – these water-loving insects and spiders have unique adaptations that help them survive underwater.

Middle and back legs spread the insect's weight over the water's surface.

Pond skater

Sensitive legs help this bug find prey by detecting vibrations on the water's surface.

Water measurer

Great diving beetle

Air trapped under the wings provides oxygen to breathe underwater.

Water stick insect

Extremely long legs propel this bug through the water.

Silk glands inside the mouth are used to build a protective case around the body.

Caddisfly larva

Protective case made from natural materials

The diving bell is the **only** spider species that **lives underwater**.

Phantom midge larva

See-through body makes it nearly invisible to both predators and prey.

Each foot has a pair of small claws.

Stonefly nymph

Diving bell spider

Air bubble is trapped by small hairs on the spider's abdomen.

Aquatic bugs, such as the **pond skater**, **water measurer**, and **pond wolf spider**, just skim across the water's surface. Others spend their time underwater by carrying their air supply. The **saucer bug**, **lesser water boatman**, and **great diving beetle** trap an air bubble inside the water and use it like an oxygen tank. The **diving bell spider** spins a pouch to store air underwater. Oxygen in the surrounding water seeps into this pouch while carbon dioxide seeps out, keeping the air inside the pouch oxygenated. While these bugs scuba dive, others go snorkelling. The **water scorpion** and **water stick insect** breathe through long tail-like siphons that stick out of the water. But, some insects don't need air at all. The **stonefly nymph** and **caddisfly larva** both have gills to breathe underwater.

Aquatic bugs

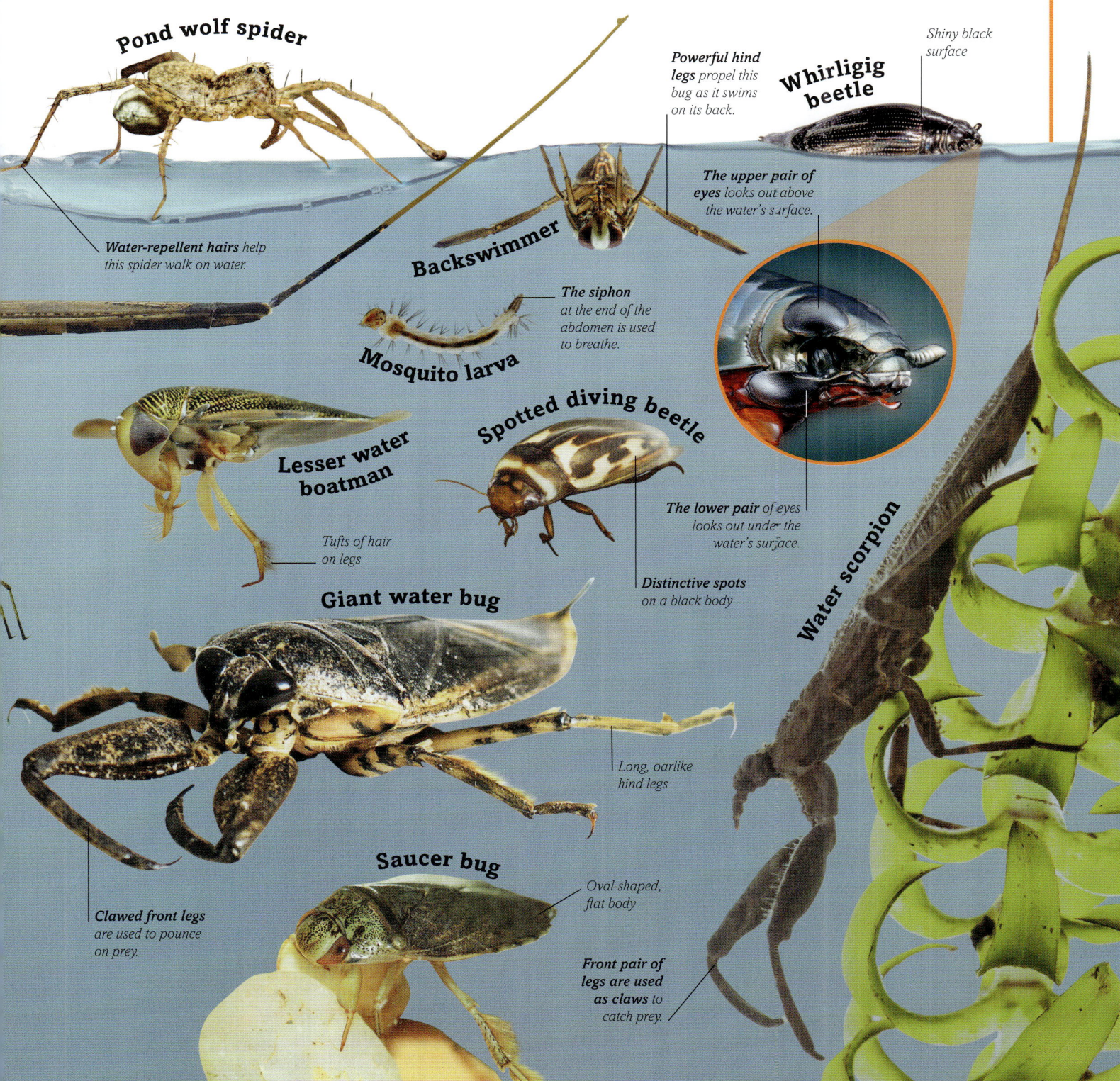

A BUG'S LIFE

Bug behaviour

Bugs can communicate, move, find food, care for their young, and survive in a world full of predators and dangers. Some bugs form complex communities with defined roles so everyone works together and stays safe.

Caring parents

Although many bugs adopt a lay-and-leave approach to their eggs, some care for their offspring until they are grown. In most cases, it is the mother that takes care of the young. The giant water bug is unusual because in this species the father carries the eggs on its back for safety until they hatch.

Male giant water bug with its eggs

Mimicking others

Many bugs imitate more powerful or dangerous creatures to protect themselves, avoid predators, or approach prey. Visual mimicry involves looking like another creature, while behavioural mimicry is acting like another creature. This harmless hoverfly uses visual mimicry to mask as a wasp or a bee, so that predators assume it has a deadly stinger and steer clear.

Hoverfly feeding on nectar

LIVING TOGETHER

Ants, bees, termites, and wasps are among the insects that live in highly organized colonies. By working as a team, they ensure there is enough shelter, food, and care for the young. Living alongside hundreds or thousands of colony mates brings safety in numbers, making it harder for predators to attack. Ants often live in large nests, where each ant has a job to do.

Larvae ❯ After ant eggs are laid, it takes about two weeks before larvae hatch out of them. Without eyes or legs, these larvae are entirely dependent on worker ants feeding them. They spend their days eating, and keep shedding their skin as they grow bigger and bigger.

Pollinating flowers

Plenty of insects, including bees and butterflies, help plants reproduce by transferring pollen from one flower to another, without even realizing it. This process is called pollination. It is essential to keep ecosystems healthy and produce an abundance of fruit and vegetables.

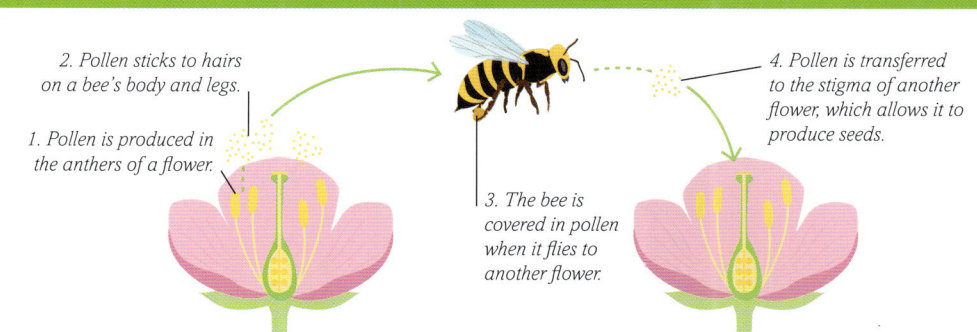

1. Pollen is produced in the anthers of a flower.
2. Pollen sticks to hairs on a bee's body and legs.
3. The bee is covered in pollen when it flies to another flower.
4. Pollen is transferred to the stigma of another flower, which allows it to produce seeds.

Worker ant ❯ All the worker ants are females, tasked with finding food for the colony. They search for anything edible, from nectar to insects, and carry it back for everyone to share. They also keep the colony clean, take care of the queen, and look after the eggs and larvae.

Queen ant ❯ Every ant colony has a queen who resides inside the nest as the only female to lay the eggs. In her lifetime, the queen may lay thousands or even millions of eggs in total. The many worker ants feed the queen and her larvae.

Soldier ant ❯ Not all ant colonies have soldier ants, but the ones that do benefit from their protection. Soldier ants are the biggest ants in the colony, responsible for defending everyone. If the colony comes under attack, they use their strong jaws, powerful sting, or toxic spray to drive off predators.

Ant larvae turn into pupae before transforming into adults. The pupa is small and pale, with its legs and antennae folded close to its body.

Pollinators

Tawny mining bee
White hair at the front sets apart males from females.

White-tailed bumblebee
White furry rear end

Hairy-eyed flower fly
Smooth rear lacks a stinger.
The marks on the thorax look a little like a bat.

Batman hoverfly

Pellucid hoverfly
See-through abdomen gives this insect the name "pellucid", which means "translucent".

Blue tiger butterfly
Blue stripes on the wings look like a tiger's markings.

Narcissus bulb fly
This fly looks like a bumblebee, which may deter predators.

Small tortoiseshell butterfly
Clubbed antennae help the butterfly detect the scent of flowers.

European wool carder bee
Females have sharp teeth to snip off plant hairs, which they use to build their nests.

Bugs called pollinators collect pollen for food, and as they travel from flower to flower, they help plants reproduce. This is a vital process in nature. While bees may be the most famous pollinators, butterflies, wasps, and beetles are busy helping out too!

Many bugs have evolved to be the perfect pollinators. Some, such as bees, are covered in tiny hairs called setae, which pick up pollen when the insect visits a flower to forage for food. This is most noticeable on fuzzy bees, such as the **tawny mining bee** and the **white-tailed bumblebee**. But even insects that have a

smoother appearance, such as the **Batman hoverfly** and **European wool carder bee**, are covered in pollen-catching setae if you look closely. Some insects, such as the **blue tiger butterfly** and **bee beetle**, aren't too picky about which plants they pollinate as long as they get a good amount of nectar. Others have more specific taste – the **imperial orchid bee** prefers to feed on nectar from orchids, and ends up pollinating a wide variety of orchid species. Similarly, the female **fig wasp** has evolved to pollinate just one kind of plant – figs. It pollinates the flowers inside an unripe fig and also lays its eggs there.

EATING POLLEN

Beetles eat just about anything. They have an incredibly diverse diet, and feed on everything from plants to dung and other insects. The spotted maize beetles are particularly partial to pollen, and there's plenty of that to go around on this sunflower. While this may seem like a large gathering of hungry beetles, hundreds can sometimes be seen feeding on the same flower.

By moving from one flower to the next to feed, these beetles will transfer pollen and help the plants reproduce in the process. Although bees are the best-known pollinators, beetles have been doing it for a lot longer. Some flowers, such as magnolias, are so old that bees didn't even exist when they first appeared. They relied instead on beetles to pollinate them, and they are still the main pollinators today. Other plants have evolved specific traits to attract beetles. While most flowers use sweet scents to entice pollinators, the aptly named skunk cabbage, corpse flower, and dead horse arum lily stink of rotting flesh, which draws in beetles with an appetite for decaying animal carcasses.

Buzzing bees

Leafcutter bee

Busy, buzzy bees zip from flower to flower for sweet nectar and pollen. Even though there are more than 20,000 kinds of bee, only a few make honey. All bees play a vital role in pollination – many crops, including vegetables and fruits, depend on bees to spread their pollen so they can reproduce.

The bee holds the leaf with its legs and uses its tough jaws to cut it into pieces to build a nest.

At more than 6 cm (2.5 in) long, this is the world's biggest bee.

Virginia carpenter bee

Shiny black, mostly hairless abdomen

Wallace's giant bee

Alkali bee

Blue stripes turn iridescent (shiny) under light.

Blue-banded bee

Veins reinforce wings during flight.

> One honeybee queen can lay up to **250,000 eggs in a year**.

Indian carpenter bee

Bee seals off the honeycomb cell with a layer of wax.

Blue carpenter bee

Bright blue hairs cover most of the female bee's body.

Western honeybee

Wings held above its back help the bee balance while feeding.

Indian honeybee

Some bees, such as the **alkali bee** and wild **American bumblebee**, have yellow and black stripes to warn that they are dangerous. But the **blue carpenter bee** and the male **green metallic sweat bee** have different warning colours. Honeybees, such as the **Indian honeybee**, are sociable creatures, with thousands sharing nests where they make honey and take care of their young. However, most bees, such as the **leafcutter bee**, prefer to live alone. Female bees are known for their painful tail sting, which can kill predators. The **orchid bee** and **Wallace's giant bee** are among the bees that sting repeatedly when under threat. Unfortunately for honeybees, they die after a single sting as the stinger gets ripped from their body, killing them.

HEXAGONAL CELLS

Honeybees make their honeycomb in a neat structure of multiple hexagons (six-sided shapes). When honeybees eat honey, they produce wax. They then shape this wax into hexagons one by one to make the honeycomb. These shapes require the least wax to build while providing the maximum storage space.

Each hexagon aligns perfectly with the next without any gaps in between.

Honeycomb structure

A bug's life

Social insects

The world's biggest wasp measures 5 cm (2 in).

Asian giant hornet

A trap-jaw ant uses its antennae to recognize colony mates.

Trap-jaw ant

The soldier termites rushing out to defend their nest

A cone-shaped head suggests this termite is a soldier.

Cathedral termites

Conehead termites

These tree-dwelling ants have formed a bridge to help each other move across leaves.

Weaver ants

Worker ants don't have wings.

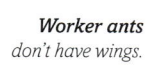

Red wood ants

Worker ants collect dead bugs to feed the colony.

Ghost ants

The leafcutter ant carries the leaf over its head like an umbrella.

Leafcutter ants

The team players of the insect world are ants, bees, termites, and wasps. They live together in organized colonies. These bugs find strength in numbers, coming together in thousands or even millions to build nests, forage for food, care for their young, and defend themselves.

Many insects organize themselves in a social order with different rankings and responsibilities. Like other social bees, **red dwarf honeybees** are led by an egg-laying queen bee. Hundreds of male drones mate with the queen bee, and thousands of female worker bees build and maintain the colony. **Cathedral termites** follow a similar system – the

Lesser banded hornets — Hanging nest made from chewed wood mixed with saliva

German wasps — Thousands of German wasps inhabit a single wood-pulp nest.

Red dwarf honeybees — A colony of red dwarf honeybees swarms around an open-air honeycomb.

Giant honeybees — A bee nest is used for storing honey and rearing the brood.

Asian honeybee — Long hairs near the eyes sweep up pollen grains from flowers.

French paper wasps — White eggs are laid within exposed honeycomb cells.

queen and the king produce all the eggs. Worker termites build giant cathedral-like mounds for the colony to live in, while soldier termites protect against predators. Insects also cooperate to find food. Hungry **Asian giant hornets** launch coordinated attacks on honeybee hives, with large numbers swarming in to devour their prey.

The **giant honeybee** performs a waggle dance to share the location of nectar-laden flowers with other bees. Some bugs band together against enemies. **Asian honeybees** take revenge on any predatory giant hornet by collectively forming a ball around it. Their bodies produce such intense heat that the hornet boils alive.

Active ants

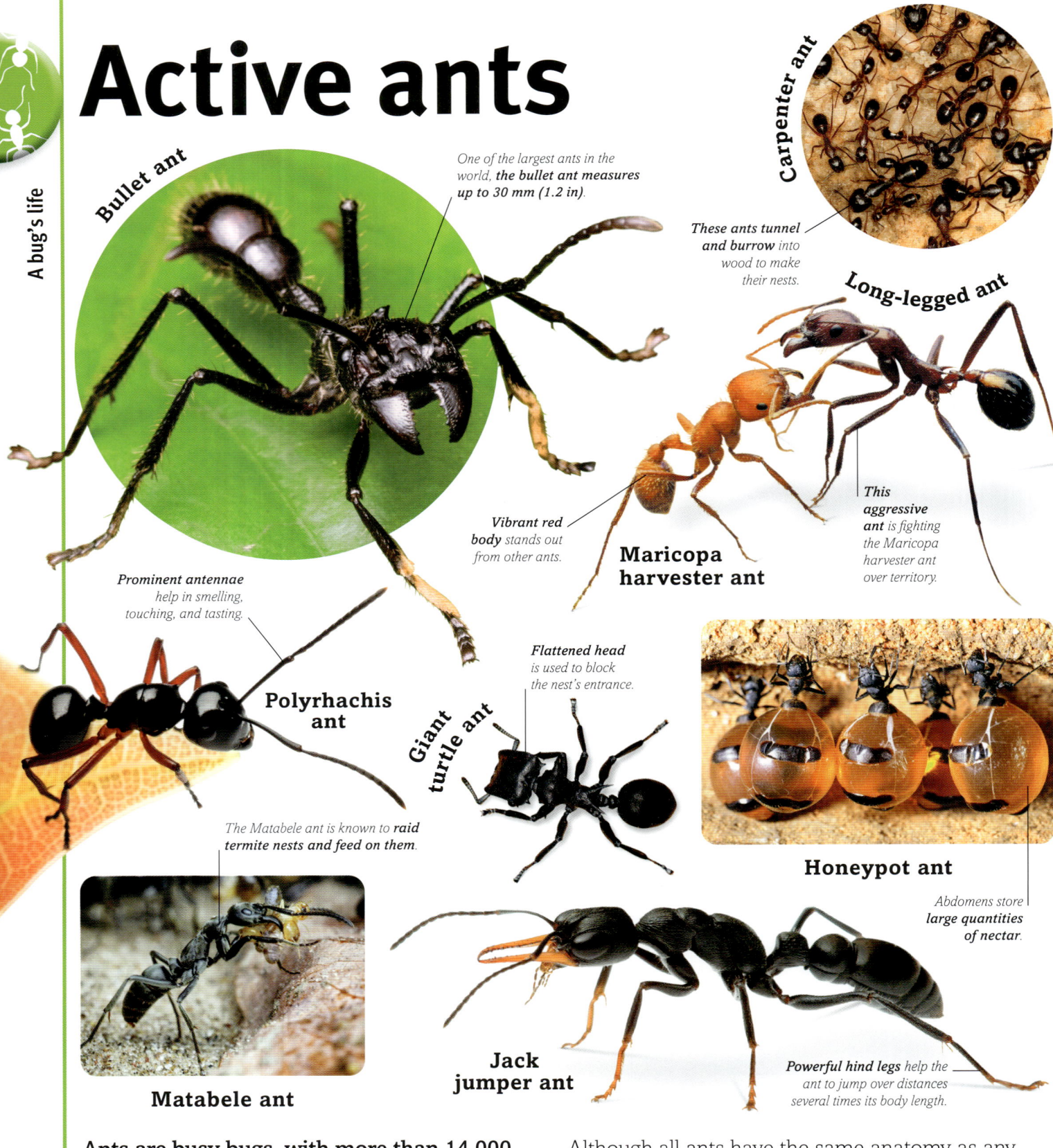

Bullet ant — One of the largest ants in the world, **the bullet ant measures up to 30 mm (1.2 in)**.

Carpenter ant — These ants tunnel and burrow into wood to make their nests.

Long-legged ant — This aggressive ant is fighting the Maricopa harvester ant over territory.

Maricopa harvester ant — Vibrant red body stands out from other ants.

Polyrhachis ant — Prominent antennae help in smelling, touching, and tasting.

Giant turtle ant — Flattened head is used to block the nest's entrance.

Honeypot ant — Abdomens store large quantities of nectar.

Matabele ant — The Matabele ant is known to raid termite nests and feed on them.

Jack jumper ant — Powerful hind legs help the ant to jump over distances several times its body length.

Ants are busy bugs, with more than 14,000 species living almost everywhere in the world. Although tiny, ants are strong insects. Thousands or even millions live together in colonies, where they work as a team to build nests, store food, and raise their young.

Although all ants have the same anatomy as any other insect, ant species vary in how they look and behave. They are usually black, brown, red, or yellow in appearance. The **long-legged ant** lives up to its name with lengthy limbs allowing for easy movement. The long legs are also useful when battling other ants over territory. Similarly, the **jack**

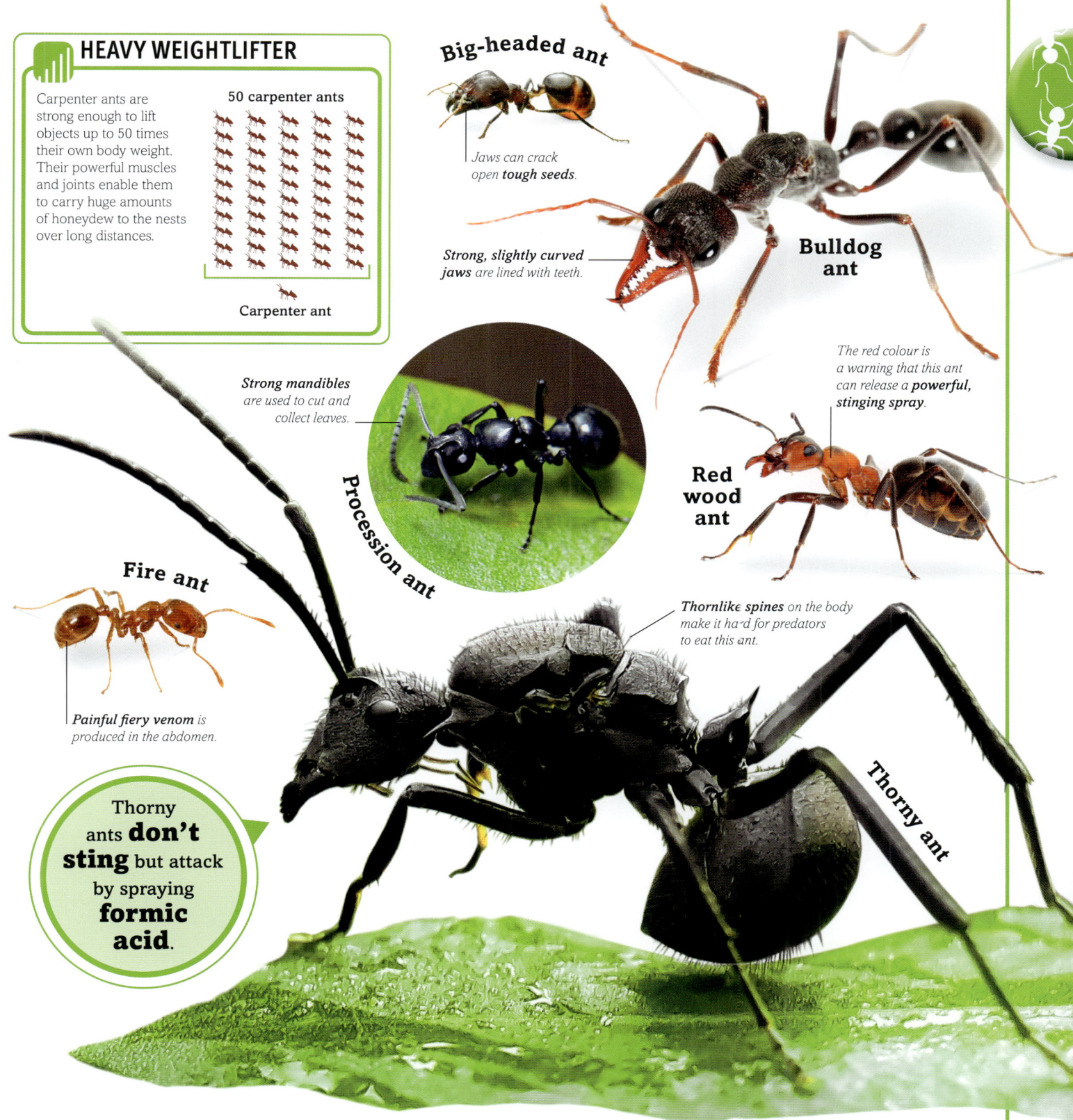

HEAVY WEIGHTLIFTER

Carpenter ants are strong enough to lift objects up to 50 times their own body weight. Their powerful muscles and joints enable them to carry huge amounts of honeydew to the nests over long distances.

50 carpenter ants

Carpenter ant

Big-headed ant
Jaws can crack open **tough seeds**.

Bulldog ant
Strong, slightly curved *jaws* are lined with teeth.

Procession ant
Strong mandibles are used to cut and collect leaves.

Red wood ant
The red colour is a warning that this ant can release a **powerful, stinging spray**.

Fire ant
Painful fiery venom is produced in the abdomen.

Thorny ant
Thornlike spines on the body make it hard for predators to eat this ant.

Thorny ants **don't sting** but attack by spraying **formic acid**.

jumper ant relies on its oversized legs to leap away from danger. Strong muscular jaws ensure the **bulldog ant** and the **bullet ant** can put up a fight and hold intruders in place as they deliver painful stings. The **Maricopa harvester ant** comes armed with the most potent venom of any insect. In contrast, the **giant turtle ant** is entirely harmless. Under threat, this ant crouches down and hides its legs and antennae, making its body harder to attack. Foraging for food is an important activity for all ants, and they use different strategies for it. To cover large areas more efficiently, **procession ants** form long trails that they use in search for food.

PROTECTIVE PATROLLERS
Tree-dwelling acrobat ants in West Africa leave nothing to chance and smash all the eggs of butterflies to prevent their newly hatched caterpillars from devouring the leaves. These fearless ants patrol the branches day and night, keeping an eye out for any predators to protect their nesting trees.

Some species of ants and trees share a relationship that is beneficial to both. The ants fiercely guard the tree against harmful caterpillars, and receive plentiful sweet nectar from the tree's flowers and the opportunity to nest inside its hollow structures. But sometimes ants build a rapport with aphids, caterpillars, and leafhoppers so that they can feed on the sugary secretions produced by the bugs. In return, the ants protect these vulnerable insects against bigger or stronger predators. Some crafty caterpillars, though, trick ants by smelling, sounding, or acting like ant larvae. The ants take care of them but get nothing in return.

A bug's life

Wasps and sawflies

The yellow and black colour is similar to that of a common wasp.

European wheat stem sawfly
The club-shaped segmented antennae are nearly half the length of the body.

Scabious sawfly
Transparent wings with darker blotches

Broad-leaved willow sawfly
Copper and yellow striped body

Giant woodwasp

Birch sawfly
Pale stripe on a black abdomen makes this sawfly easily recognizable.

Sand wasp
Beaklike, triangular upper lip is unique to the species.

Steel blue cricket hunter
Shiny blue body and wings

Black and yellow mud dauber
The wasp uses a stinger to deliver potent venom that can paralyse spiders.

Rust-coloured body gives the wasp its name.

Rusty spider wasp

> The **dauber fills** its **nest** with **spiders** on which its **larvae feed**.

Mud is collected by females for building a nest.

Wasps and sawflies can look alike and share much in common. But there is one main difference between the two – wasps possess a venomous stinger for self-defence while sawflies don't. Instead, some sawflies look like wasps to fool birds and other predators.

Although wasps and sawflies can both take flight, wasps are stronger and faster in the air. Wasps can be recognized by their slender waists, as seen in the **giant scoliid wasp**. Sawflies, however, have chunky bodies – the **broad-leaved willow sawfly** is a typical example. Wasps use their sharp tail stinger to prey on other animals.

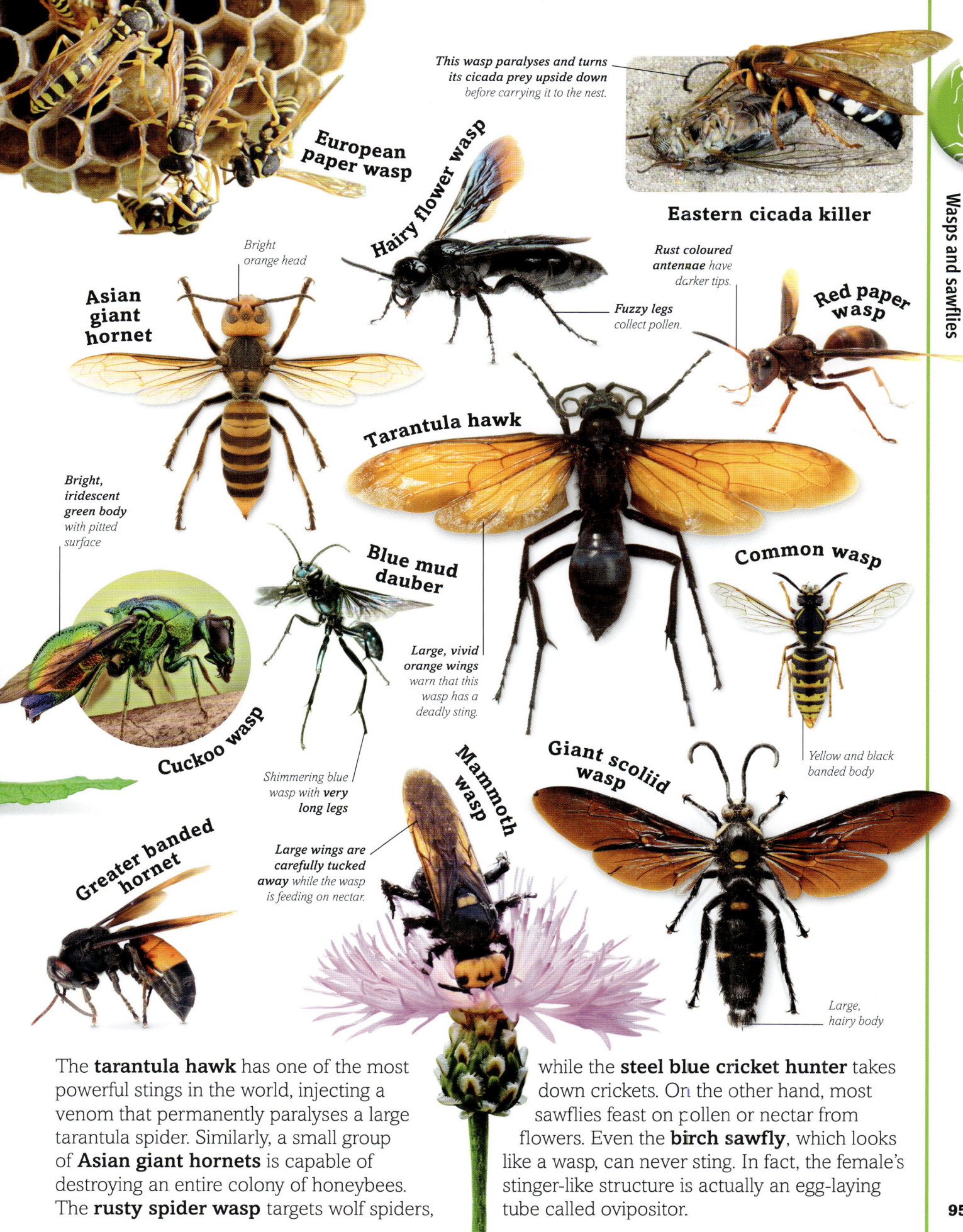

Wasps and sawflies

The **tarantula hawk** has one of the most powerful stings in the world, injecting a venom that permanently paralyses a large tarantula spider. Similarly, a small group of **Asian giant hornets** is capable of destroying an entire colony of honeybees. The **rusty spider wasp** targets wolf spiders, while the **steel blue cricket hunter** takes down crickets. On the other hand, most sawflies feast on pollen or nectar from flowers. Even the **birch sawfly**, which looks like a wasp, can never sting. In fact, the female's stinger-like structure is actually an egg-laying tube called ovipositor.

A bug's life

Parental care

The female harvestman lays eggs in a safe space, and sometimes stays with its young for several days.

The young beetle larvae feed on a dead animal.

Common sexton beetle

Harvestman

The female lays an egg inside each dung ball, and when it hatches, the larva feeds on the dung.

Dung beetle

The baby spiders link their legs to avoid falling off their mother's back.

The young nymphs stay with their devoted mother for around 8 weeks.

Wolf spider

The female wolf spider carries its eggs in an **egg sac** made of **silk**.

The female wolf spider can carry more than 100 spiderlings on its back.

Parent bug

All bugs spend time and energy to mate and produce offspring. Many of them lay eggs and leave them to survive on their own. But, some bugs choose to stay with their eggs and guard them until they hatch. Others care for their newly hatched babies and feed them, too.

Only a handful of bug species care for their eggs or young. The female **organ pipe mud dauber wasp** makes sure that its young larvae are well fed once they hatch, so it lays the eggs in a nursery full of food. The **Pacific giant centipede** and **earwig** mothers stay with their eggs to guard them from potential predators. The female **bark**

Bark scorpion

The scorpion babies climb up their mother's legs to get on the back, where they stay for a week or two.

Tsetse fly

The tsetse fly larva grows inside its mother's body for 9 days.

A larva hatches from eggs carried by a male giant water bug.

Giant water bug

Termite

Young termites are cared for by an army of workers inside their colony.

Pacific giant centipede

The eggs are nestled inside the centipede's protective coil.

Earwig

The earwig's eggs are regularly licked clean by the mother.

The mother wasp carries a crab spider to feed its young.

Organ pipe mud dauber wasp

Parental care

scorpion and **wolf spider** even carry their young around with them until they are stronger and able to defend themselves. For **giant water bugs**, the male performs a similar role, carrying the eggs on its back until they hatch. But no one can beat the care that the **common sexton beetles** give. Both parents stay with their eggs and later, tend to their young. One of the best single parents of the bug world is the female **tsetse fly**. The mother fly grows a single offspring in its body, feeding it with a milklike liquid until it is as big as the parent. The female then gives birth to the larva that quickly burrows into the ground.

Faking it

Thorn bugs / **Ant-mimicking treehopper**
- *A helmet-like structure at the back provides the disguise of an ant.*
- *The bug's head looks like an ant's abdomen.*

Clearwing borer
- *Yellow and black bands help the bug to impersonate a wasp.*

Giant owl butterfly
- *The bug's prominent horns have turned a harmless branch into a thorny one.*
- *A big butterfly with a wingspan of up to 15 cm (6 in)*

Asian ant mantis
- *Front two legs betray an otherwise perfect ant impersonation.*

Malaysian leaf insect
- *Typical leaflike central vein and side veins on the body*

BEE ORCHID

Mimicry is common in the natural world – and even plants use this clever tactic. Some flowers pretend to be female bees to attract male pollinators. This bee orchid has the look and smell of a female bee to encourage male bees to come closer. In this way, pollen is transferred, and the plant reproduces.

Many bugs are experts at camouflage. Some mimic the appearance of harmful plants and animals, while others have learnt the art of blending in with their surroundings. These powerful survival techniques help them to avoid predators or ambush their prey.

Several bugs have evolved camouflage to look like inedible and uninteresting plants to deter predators. **Thorn bugs** have hornlike growths on their backs identical to plant thorns, while the **plume moth** closes its wings shut and expertly plays the role of a dry twig. Some harmless insects mimic dangerous bugs, known as Batesian

Migrant hoverfly — Males have broader yellow markings than the ones on the females.

Buffalo treehopper — Curved body of the treehopper vaguely resembles a buffalo's hump, giving this bug its name.

Peppered moth — White wings speckled in black allow the moth to merge with the background of a lichen-covered tree.

Sphinx moth caterpillar — Dark spots resemble a snake's eyes.

Plume moth — The moth rolls up its large wings in order to rest.

Citrus flatid planthopper nymph — A white, cottonlike protective layer makes the planthopper nymph look like inedible fungi.

The sphinx moth caterpillar **inflates** its **head** to look like a **snake**.

Ladybird mimic spider — Round, dome-shaped abdomen

Indian stick insect — Long, twiglike body of the stick insect looks like another branch of the tree.

Faking it

mimicry. The **ant-mimicking treehopper** and young **Asian ant mantis** have bodies similar to ants and adopt antlike movements to appear more threatening. The **ladybird mimic spider** disguises itself with the same spots as a toxic ladybird, and the **migrant hoverfly** shares the same colours as stinging bees or wasps.

The **giant owl butterfly** goes even further, using large wing spots to imitate the scary eyes of an owl. Other bugs uncannily blend into their surroundings without a trace. The **buffalo treehopper** and the **Malaysian leaf insect** appear to be lush leaves and can go unnoticed.

99

MASKED MOTH The imperial moth is a master of disguise, performing a disappearing act every time it lands on leaves. Its wing colours and patterns perfectly mimic the appearance of surrounding foliage, so the moth cannot be seen without very close inspection. Clever camouflage can mean the difference between life and death, as without it, the imperial moth would be an easy target for predators.

Adult imperial moths live for a maximum of two weeks, without eating, so their time is limited. They are nocturnal creatures, flying at night to search for mates in the darkness. These moths must reproduce quickly before they are caught by a predator or they die of natural causes. The secret to their survival during this brief lifespan is camouflage. In the day, imperial moths can rest undisturbed on the forest floor because their distinctive yellow and brown colours allow them to merge with dry and dead leaves. The mottled wings of these flying insects also feature veined lines and eye spots that imitate leaf markings, blending in perfectly. Any predators looking at the leaf litter would struggle to spot them.

Nocturnal bugs

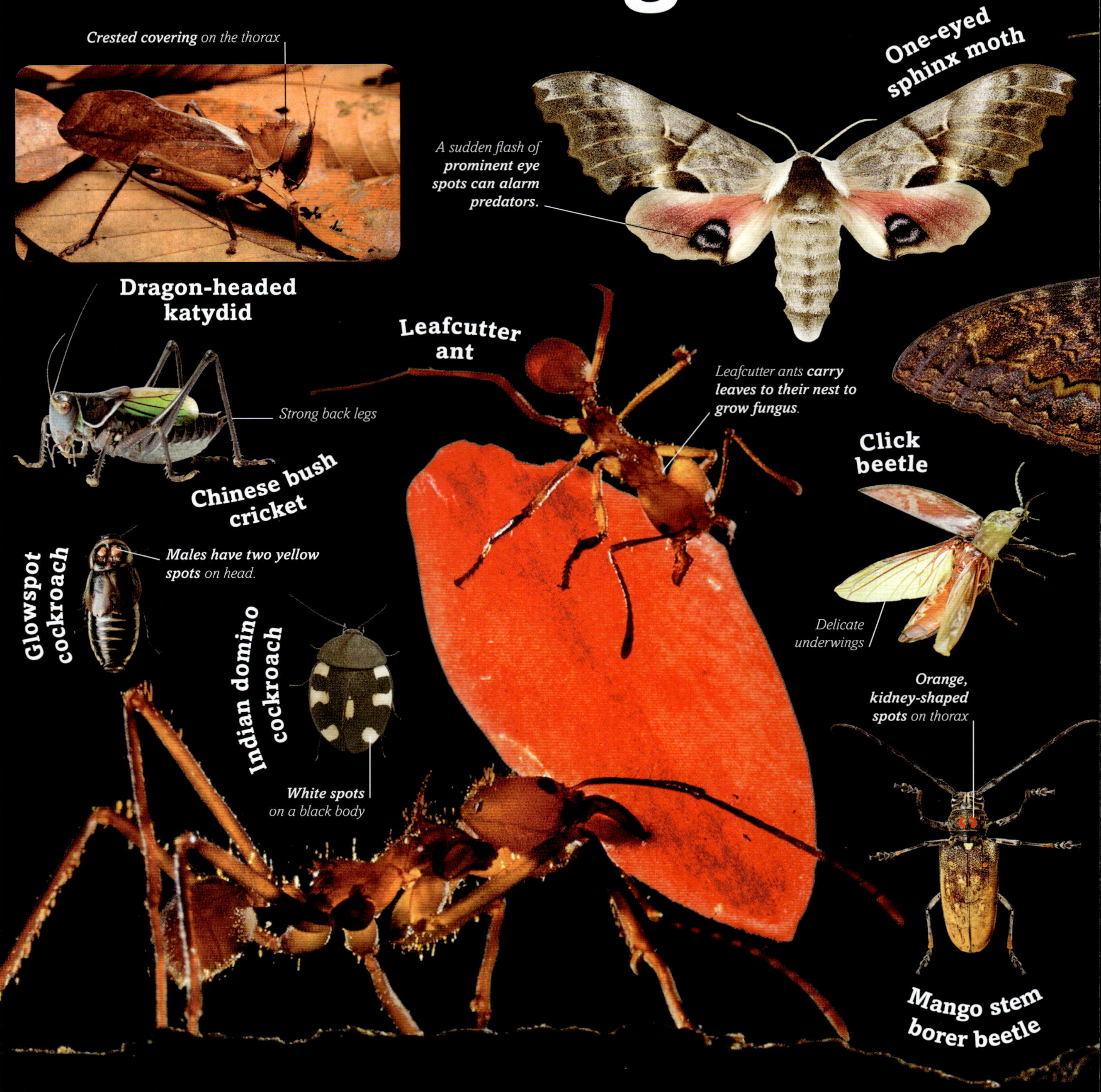

Crested covering on the thorax

Dragon-headed katydid

A sudden flash of prominent eye spots can alarm predators.

One-eyed sphinx moth

Chinese bush cricket
Strong back legs

Leafcutter ant
Leafcutter ants carry leaves to their nest to grow fungus.

Click beetle
Delicate underwings

Glowspot cockroach
Males have two yellow spots on head.

Indian domino cockroach
White spots on a black body

Orange, kidney-shaped spots on thorax

Mango stem borer beetle

A whole world of bugs wakes up and becomes active at night. Staying out of sight in the day, these nocturnal creatures only emerge after dark to find food and mates. The natural cover of darkness helps them avoid predators and enjoy their meals in relative peace.

Many bugs have adapted their bodies and behaviours to the night. Instead of sight, the **dragon-headed katydid** relies on sound to find mates. Their noisy call is easier to hear at night when the surroundings are much quieter. Some insects emit their own light in the darkness. The female **European glow-worm**

The bug raises its small, vibrant red hindwings when threatened.

Black beauty stick insect

The black beauty stick insect **sprays** a **toxic chemical** at predators.

Light-emitting female closely resembles the larval form, giving it the name "glow-worm".

European glow-worm

Multicolour, iridescent (shiny) pattern on wings

Broad, whitish-pink border on hindwings

Black witch moth

Suraka silk moth

Kissing bug

Isabella tiger moth

Pale wings blend with the flowers the moth lands on for nectar.

Flat abdomen is outlined by red stripes.

Elytra (hard outer wings) lift to reveal the fragile flight wings.

Jewel scarab beetle

DAYTIME DANGERS

Some bugs choose to be nocturnal as there are many drawbacks to being active during the day. Insects can't avoid other creatures competing for the same food or evade hungry predators. They also have to tolerate high temperatures.

- Greater competition
- More predators
- Extreme heat

produces a bright yellow light to attract males. Night-time provides room for perfect camouflage for many bugs. The **Indian domino cockroach** uses the darkness as a protective shield to scavenge for food scraps. Similarly, the **black beauty stick insect** blends easily into the shadows at night to munch on leaves. Some bugs are drawn to the night because of their unique eating habits. Unlike most assassin bugs that prey on other insects, the **kissing bug** feeds on human blood. It is drawn to the carbon dioxide gas that sleeping humans exhale and bites them around the mouth to get its meal.

Light lovers

Six long legs make this fly easy to spot.

European crane fly

An adult mayfly's mouth doesn't work so it never eats.

Mayfly

Feathery antennae help the male moth detect females.

Gypsy moth

Fluffy front and mottled white colour resemble an ermine's winter coat.

White ermine moth

Speckled wing pattern helps this moth to camouflage on tree bark.

Peppered moth

Lemon-coloured patch inside grey eyespots

Polyphemus moth

Luna moth

White-lined sphinx moth

Dark olive brown wings with a white band running through the middle

Creamy fringe

Common emerald moth

Vivid green wings look just like leaves when the moth lands to feed.

When the Sun goes down, insects can be seen swarming around artificial lights. They are attracted by the glow in the dark, perhaps mistaking it for the natural light in the night sky.

Many nocturnal insects travel in darkness using the light of the Moon and the stars. The **luna moth** and **gypsy moth** are among many moths that follow starlight to keep going forwards. The **dung beetle** relies on the Moon to keep moving its dung balls in the right direction. There are other bugs, such as the **firefly**, that create their

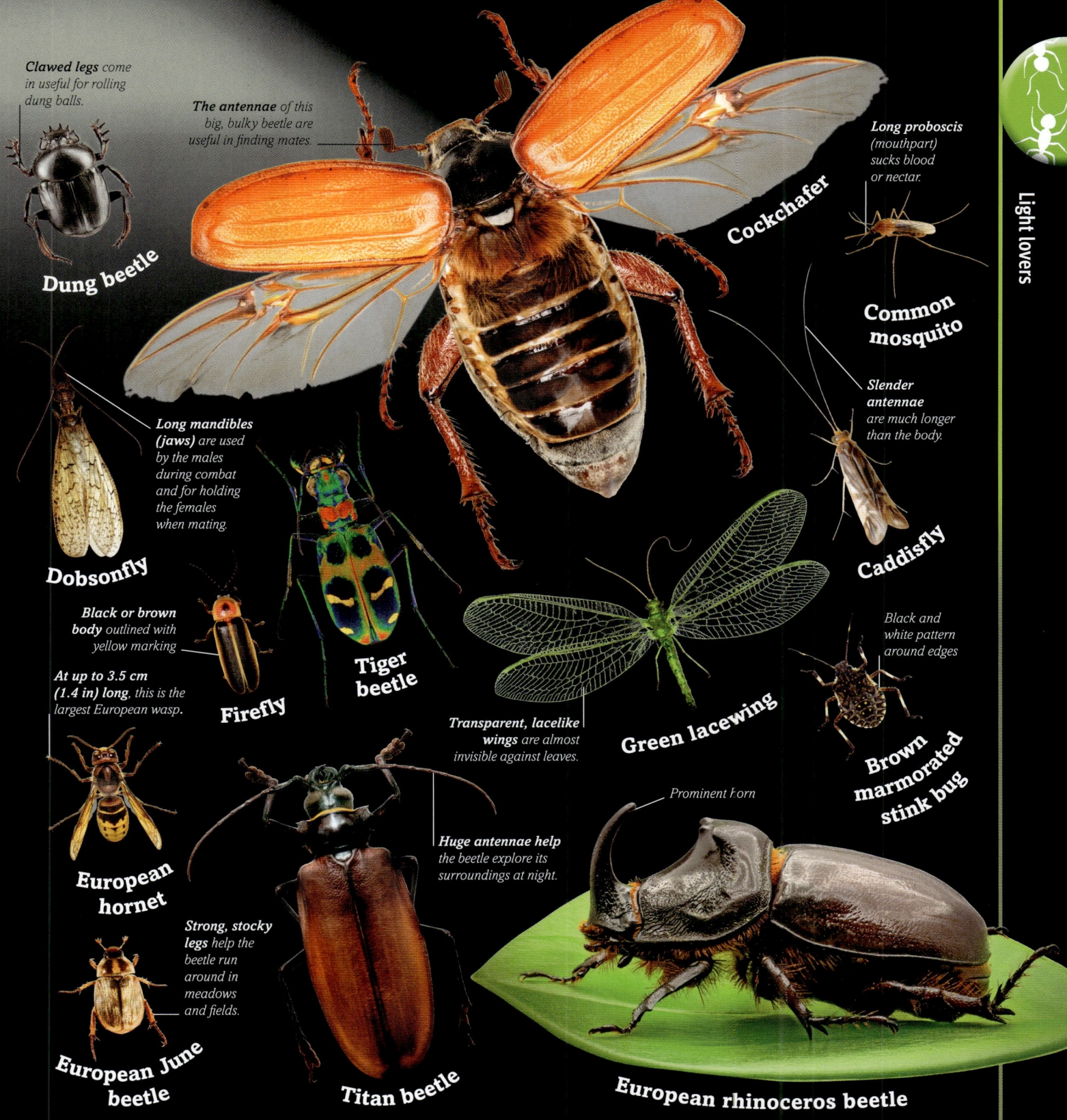

own natural light to attract each other in the dark. Streetlights and other electric lights can confuse insects by appearing too close and bright. As insects face away from the light, they may end up going in circles around artificial lights, running the risk of overheating or becoming an easy target for predators. Bugs such as the **cockchafer** and **European June beetle** may accidentally bump into illuminated windows or fall into fire-lit chimneys. Some insects, such as the **brown marmorated stink bug**, are attracted to artificial light and enter human homes through small cracks and open windows.

NIGHT LIGHTS Nature puts on the most spectacular light show at night in the form of flashing fireflies – seen here in summer in Gifu, Japan. When thousands of these brilliant bugs generate their powerful light at the same time, the result is a landscape that glitters like gold. Marine creatures, as well as certain types of algae and bacteria, also emit light in a process called bioluminescence.

Fireflies are flying beetles that produce a natural glow from light organs in the tail ends of their bodies. The light is created by an internal chemical reaction, which fireflies can turn on and off as they choose. This synchronized display of bioluminescence is an important courtship ritual that catches the eye of other fireflies. They are drawn to the flashing lights, and this is how they find mates and reproduce. Different kinds of firefly flash with distinctive patterns of light. They can emit yellow, orange, or green light. Most other types of bioluminescent creatures are found in seas and oceans – giving off light helps them to attract mates, hunt prey, and scare predators.

Great gatherings

Periodical cicada broods emerge every 13 or 17 years depending on the species.

Western honeybees gather around a tree cavity, ready to start a new colony.

Periodical cicadas

Western honeybees

A termite alate has four wings of the same size.

Termites

When insects of the same species get together to form a huge group, it is called a swarm. These large crowds can create breathtaking displays, often accompanied by the loud buzz of wings or other sounds. Bugs swarm for many reasons – from mating to finding food or a new home.

No insect waits longer than the larvae of the **periodical cicada** to become a winged adult. After more than a decade underground, a whole brood emerges at once to breed – forming swarms big enough to blanket a forest. Males sing loudly to mate with females. **Mosquitoes** also swarm to breed, with males forming

Male mosquitoes gather in swarms near water.

Mosquitoes

Desert locusts change colour when they start to swarm — young locusts turn from brown to pink, and adults from brown to yellow.

Desert locusts

massive clouds and performing impressive aerial acrobatics to pursue the small number of females that enter the swarm. When a **western honeybee** nest gets too crowded, the queen gathers a group of workers, and leaves in a swarm to start a new colony. **Termites** send out winged adults called alates, which swarm before pairing up and flying off in all directions so each couple can set up a colony of their own. Some insects swarm when there is not enough food. A swarm of **desert locusts** can contain billions of locusts and cover distances of up to 150 km (93 miles) a day, wreaking havoc wherever they go by stripping crops bare.

A bug's life

Migratory insects

Each year, trillions of insects take to the skies and leave the place they were born. From local trips to expeditions across the globe, insects set out on these voyages for many reasons, including tracking down food, finding a suitable place to breed, and escaping harsh winters.

A black stripe with two rows of white spots border the wings.

Striking eyespots on each wing

Queen butterflies

Common buckeye butterflies

*Migratory locust swarms can **travel up to 130 km (80 miles) a day**.*

Migratory locusts

Yellow wings have black edges.

Common grass yellow butterflies

The bugs feed on the nutrient-rich seed pods of the milkweed plant.

Large milkweed bugs

110

Many insects, such as the **convergent ladybug** and the **large milkweed bug**, relocate from their breeding areas to protected spots every winter as they become temporarily inactive. The **queen butterfly** and **common grass yellow butterfly** set off in search of nectar, as does the **common buckeye butterfly**, which can sometimes travel up to 800 km (500 miles) to find fresh flowers to drink from. However, these flights are short-haul compared to the long-distance journeys that some other insects undertake. The **marmalade hoverfly's** 1,000-km (600-mile) flight across Europe and the **painted lady butterfly's** 12,000-km (7,500-mile) trip from the Arctic Circle to sub-Saharan Africa each year are epic voyages. But these insects don't live long enough to complete them – instead, they breed several times along the way, with each generation continuing the journey.

Migratory insects

Huddling together helps the beetles stay warm during winter.

Convergent ladybugs

These 1-cm (0.4-in) long creatures migrate during winter in search of a warm climate.

In 2009, **26 million** painted ladies migrated from the UK.

Marmalade hoverflies

Orange wings stretch around 5–7 cm (2–2.8 in) wide from one tip to the other.

Painted lady butterflies

*Enormous numbers of this dragonfly **migrate every few years**.*

Four-spotted chaser

MIGRATING MONARCHS
Every year millions of monarch butterflies take off on an epic migration of 4,800 km (3,000 miles) from north to south that might last many generations. This spectacle fills the skies with fluttering wings, but to the butterflies, this is the difference between life and death. Their breeding grounds in Canada become so cold that they must travel to warmer Mexico for survival.

The longest-living monarch butterflies hatch out of eggs at the end of summer. Over their eight-month lifespan, they embark on a journey from Canada to Mexico. They stop along the way to rest and feed on nectar from flowers. They arrive in Mexico exhausted and sleep for months on trees. When winter ends, the monarchs head north, back to Canada. But these butterflies don't have enough time to get home before they die. Instead, they travel as far as they can and lay their eggs on the way. The newly hatched butterflies then resume their journey to Canada. They fly until they lay eggs and die, and the cycle continues. It takes about four generations of butterflies to make it back to where it all started.

A bug's life

Bug talk

Bugs communicate in many ways to find mates, share food, protect each other, or warn of danger. Although most of us won't be able to pick up on these special signals, bug experts can interpret their communication to help us understand their messages.

Sound

Bugs don't use vocal sounds to communicate as humans do. Instead, some of them use sound organs inside their bodies or rub body parts, such as wings and legs, to make noises understood by other bugs.

This wing has a hard scraper that rubs against the toothed wing.

One wing has a file of teeth that looks much like a hair comb.

Close-up of a cricket's wings

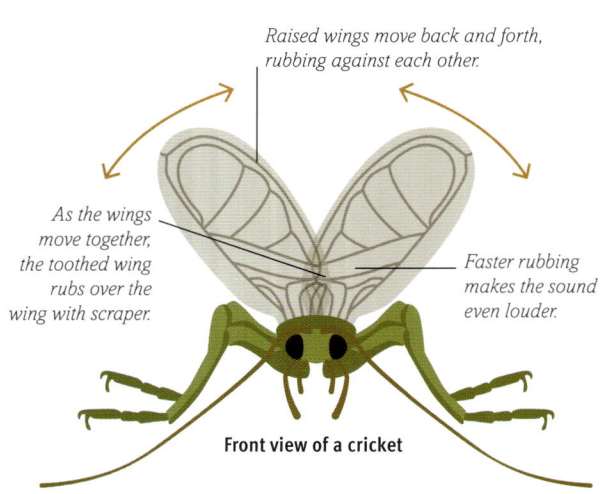

Raised wings move back and forth, rubbing against each other.

As the wings move together, the toothed wing rubs over the wing with scraper.

Faster rubbing makes the sound even louder.

Front view of a cricket

Rubbing body parts together to make sound is called stridulation. Crickets are skilled at stridulation, scraping their wings to make a clear chirping sound that attracts females.

Flash of light

A few types of insect create their own natural light, called bioluminescence. They use the light to generate specific patterns for communication, such as attracting mates and helping members of the same species identify each other.

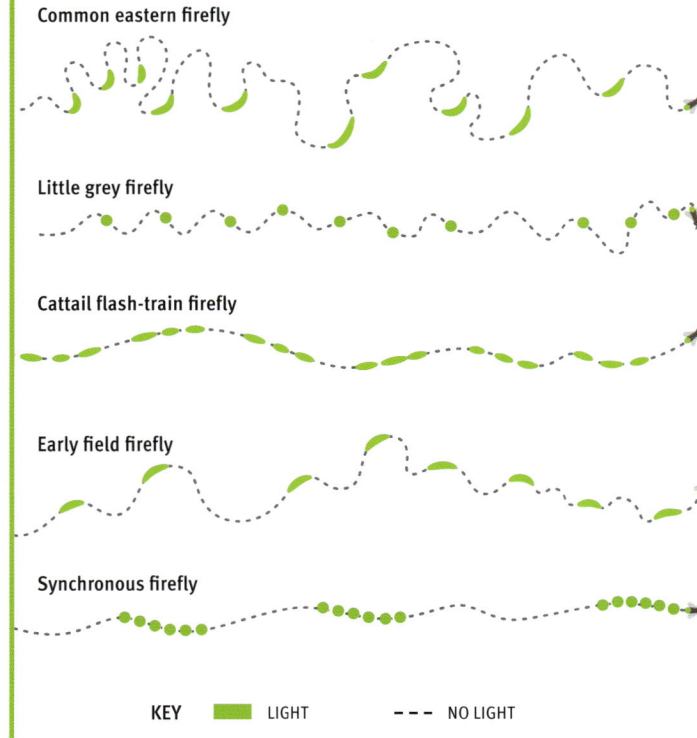

Common eastern firefly

Little grey firefly

Cattail flash-train firefly

Early field firefly

Synchronous firefly

KEY — LIGHT — — — NO LIGHT

Different species of fireflies turn their lights on and off in flashing patterns for varied lengths of time. Seen here are patterns of light given off by five kinds of firefly.

Sensing vibrations

One of the main reasons bugs communicate is to find a mate and produce offspring. Spiders have sensitive hairs on their legs that can detect the vibrations of another spider across their woven web. Males make the web move in a specific way to send a signal to females that they are potential mates and not prey.

Two garden spiders on a web

Chemical signals

Many bugs produce chemical signals, called pheromones, to communicate. These signals can be carried on the air to find mates, create scent trails, or warn others of danger.

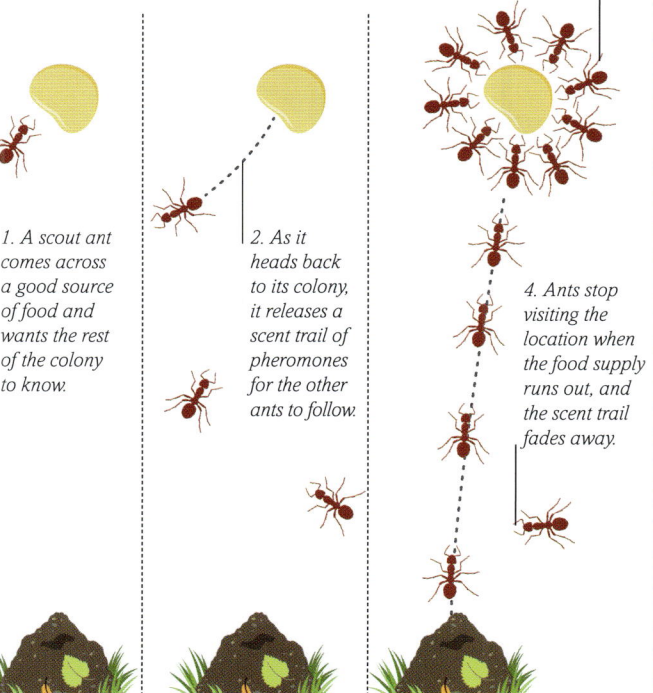

1. A scout ant comes across a good source of food and wants the rest of the colony to know.

2. As it heads back to its colony, it releases a scent trail of pheromones for the other ants to follow.

3. Other ants detect the pheromones and follow the trail, adding their own pheromones, too.

4. Ants stop visiting the location when the food supply runs out, and the scent trail fades away.

The most adventurous ants are scout ants, responsible for travelling beyond the colony to search for food. When they find a food source, they produce a chemical trail to alert their colony mates.

Body language

Bugs can position themselves or move their bodies to convey messages. Their movements can be subtle or obvious and eye-catching, depending on the species and situation.

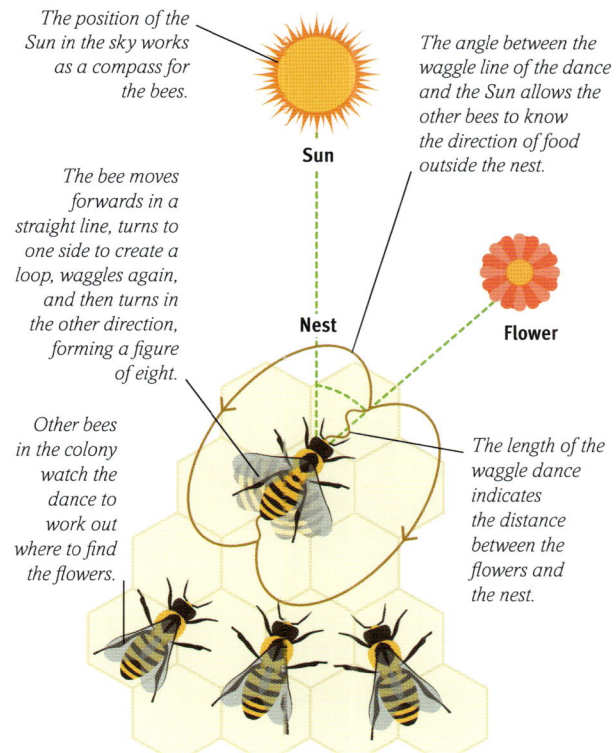

The position of the Sun in the sky works as a compass for the bees.

The angle between the waggle line of the dance and the Sun allows the other bees to know the direction of food outside the nest.

Sun

The bee moves forwards in a straight line, turns to one side to create a loop, waggles again, and then turns in the other direction, forming a figure of eight.

Nest

Flower

Other bees in the colony watch the dance to work out where to find the flowers.

The length of the waggle dance indicates the distance between the flowers and the nest.

Honeybees tell other hive members where to find the best flowers by performing an intricate waggle dance. The direction and duration of the dance moves reveal the precise location of the flowers.

Crickets and grasshoppers

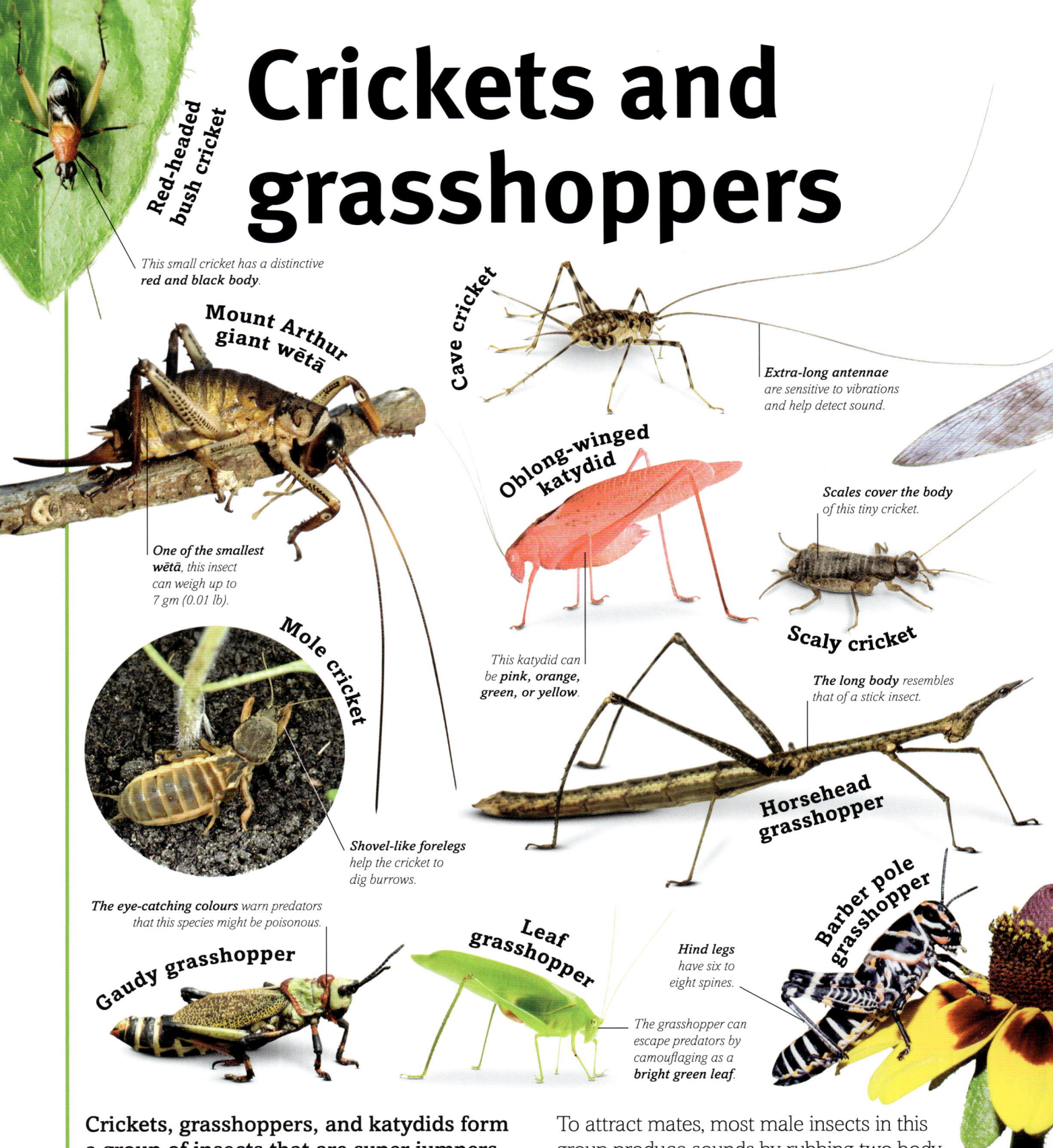

Red-headed bush cricket — This small cricket has a distinctive *red and black body*.

Mount Arthur giant wētā — *One of the smallest wētā*, this insect can weigh up to 7 gm (0.01 lb).

Cave cricket — *Extra-long antennae* are sensitive to vibrations and help detect sound.

Oblong-winged katydid — This katydid can be *pink, orange, green, or yellow*.

Scaly cricket — *Scales cover the body* of this tiny cricket.

Mole cricket — *Shovel-like forelegs* help the cricket to dig burrows.

Horsehead grasshopper — *The long body* resembles that of a stick insect.

Gaudy grasshopper — *The eye-catching colours* warn predators that this species might be poisonous.

Leaf grasshopper — The grasshopper can escape predators by camouflaging as a *bright green leaf*.

Barber pole grasshopper — *Hind legs* have six to eight spines.

Crickets, grasshoppers, and katydids form a group of insects that are super jumpers with strong legs, sensitive antennae to touch and feel, and the ability to produce remarkable sounds. Although crickets and grasshoppers have much in common, there are ways to tell them apart.

To attract mates, most male insects in this group produce sounds by rubbing two body parts together. Crickets make a chirping sound by moving their wings against each other, with the **mole cricket** among the loudest because its underground burrow amplifies the sound. In contrast, grasshoppers rub their

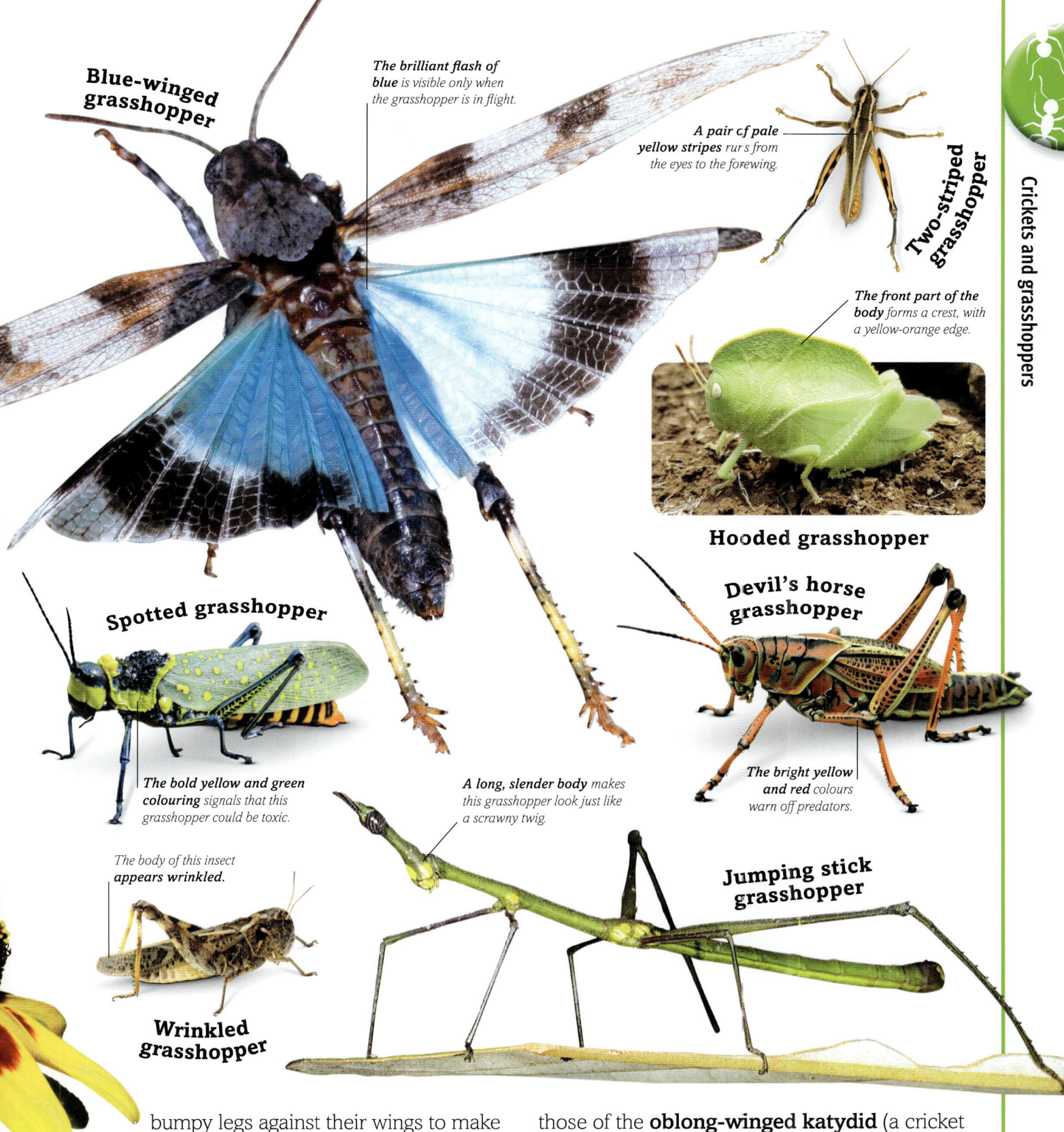

bumpy legs against their wings to make a buzzing noise. Most crickets and grasshoppers have wings, but a few species are wingless, such as the **barber pole grasshopper**. A physical difference between grasshoppers and crickets is the size of the antennae – the **wrinkled grasshopper's** antennae are shorter than those of the **oblong-winged katydid** (a cricket relative). Grasshoppers, such as the **horsehead grasshopper**, are usually active during the day, but crickets emerge mostly at night. While most grasshoppers and crickets prefer to eat plants, the **cave cricket** feeds on both dead insects and decaying plants.

FINDING FOOD

Hunting and feeding

Finding food

There are many different kinds of food on the menu for bugs to eat. Some may chomp through plants or animal remains, others might hunt smaller bugs, and others prefer specific kinds of plant pollen.

What bugs eat
Bug food includes plant matter, such as leaves, pollen, wood, and nectar, as well as a range of other organisms, including other insects, blood, or even rotting flesh. Most bugs don't eat the same thing their whole lives – they will often change their feeding habits once they grow from larvae into adults. The mouthparts of bugs are suited to the types of food they eat.

A ladybird may eat up to **5,000 bugs** in its lifetime.

A spongelike tongue helps suck up liquid food.

Hairy tongue of a green bottle fly

The hollow beak can pierce plant or animal parts.

Piercing beak of an assassin bug

The proboscis works like a straw, for sucking nectar out of flowers.

Coiled proboscis of a butterfly

Seven-spotted ladybird larva eating an aphid

Adult seven-spotted ladybird eating pollen

TOOLS FOR THE JOB
Insects have different types of mouthpart that suit their diets – some mouths are meant for chewing, others for sucking, piercing, and slicing.

FUSSY EATERS
Many bugs change what they eat as they grow, especially if they undergo metamorphosis. For example, the larvae of the seven-spotted ladybird feed on aphids, while the adults can also eat pollen and nectar.

On the hunt

Many bugs must work for their dinner – this may mean catching other bugs. Bugs use a range of different hunting tactics – some stay quiet, waiting to pounce on their next meal, while others take a more active role, chasing down their prey.

AMBUSH PREDATORS
Bugs that lie in wait for prey are known as ambush predators. They stay completely still, then strike with lightning speed once prey is within reach.

1 Patiently waiting › A praying mantis is a master of camouflage. Its colours and patterns match the plant life around it, which makes the mantis very hard to spot when it sits still among leaves or flowers. This predator waits, nearly motionless, until a prey walks or flies into sight.

The prey perches close by as the camouflaged mantis goes unnoticed.

2 Attack and grab › The mantis swiftly darts forward and grabs its prey. It pins the creature between its strong, spiky forelegs. The spikes make it difficult for its prey to wriggle free once it has been caught.

3 Meal secured › The mantis pulls its prey towards its mouth, which has sharp, slicing parts that are able to cut through a bug's tough exterior (exoskeleton). The mantis eats its prey right away.

*The fly cannot escape from between the **mantis's vice-like forearms**.*

ACTIVE HUNTERS
Bugs that catch their prey in pursuit are known as active hunters. Jumping spiders are fast and agile with excellent vision, which allows them to catch prey, such as hoverflies, by suddenly leaping on them.

Plant lovers

Tea mosquito bug

Long, **spindly legs** are suitable for crawling quickly between plants.

Lace-like brown wings

Oak lace bug

*This shiny beetle can **feed on more than 250 plants**.*

Japanese beetle

Chunky body

Box tree moth caterpillar

*The larva has a **pale yellow body**.*

Citrus leafminer larva

Thick white hairs can be released into the air to irritate attacking predators.

Many insects love feasting on plants, taking advantage of the plentiful vegetation in their natural habitats. This readily available food source is full of nutrients that help bugs to grow stronger and reproduce, while young larvae eat non-stop in preparation for adulthood.

Herbivore bugs can be very selective about what they eat. The **rose chafer** eats rose petals and leaves, the **red-striped leafhopper** likes fruit bushes, and the **Alpine longhorn beetle** enjoys beech trees. Insects such as the **tea mosquito bug** and **oak lace bug** have special mouthparts to pierce through plants and suck out the sugary sap. The larvae of these bugs have insatiable appetites.

Young larva has a soft body similar to a slug.

Rose sawfly larvae

The young wattle tick scale finds a feeding spot on the acacia tree and develops a ball-shaped body.

Wattle tick scale

Light brown body

Rose chafer

Red-striped leafhopper

Oak processionary caterpillars

Vivid stripes warn predators that this small insect is toxic.

Alpine longhorn beetle

Eye-catching blue colours help the beetle attract mates.

Plant lovers

The **oak processionary caterpillars** can strip plants bare of leaves as they prepare to transform into adult moths. Some insects even leave evidence of their movements. The **citrus leafminer larvae** leave behind a snakelike trail, while the **Japanese beetle** chews green leaves until they droop and fall off.

Finding food

True bugs

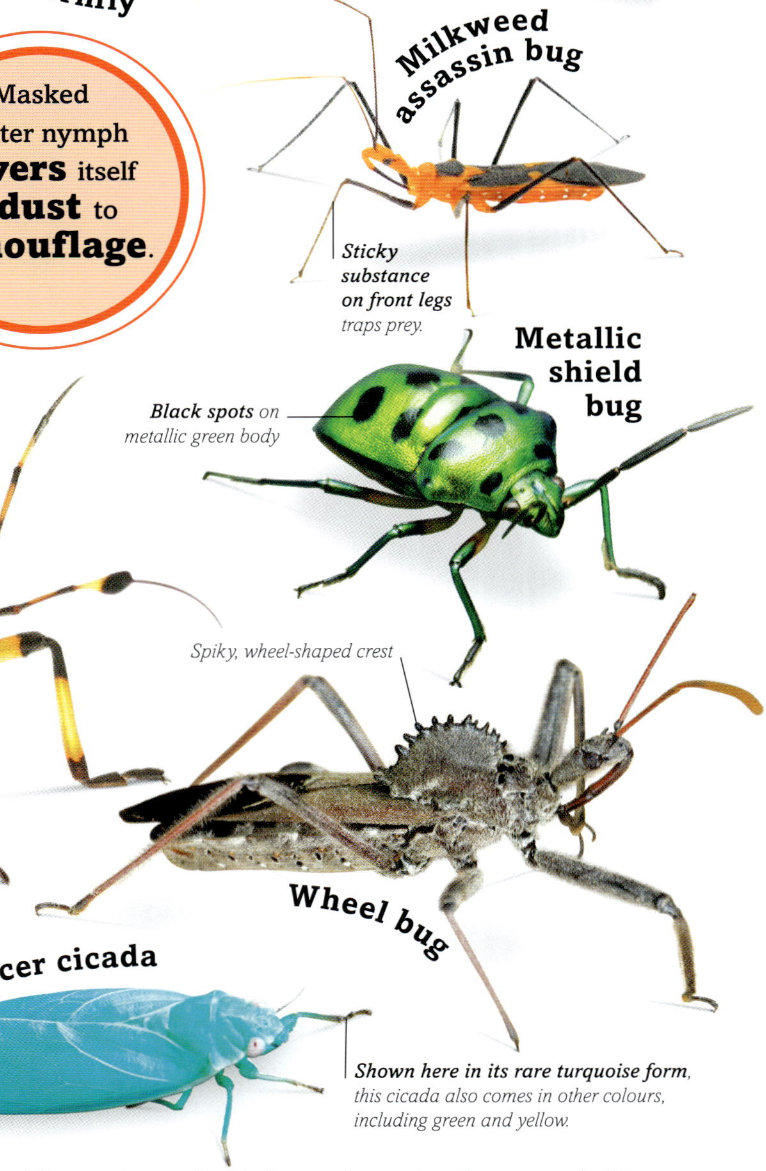

Eastern toe-biter — *Flat, wide hind legs help in swimming.*

Peanut-headed lanternfly — *Yellow and brown colours provide excellent camouflage on tree trunks.* *Head resembling a peanut shell*

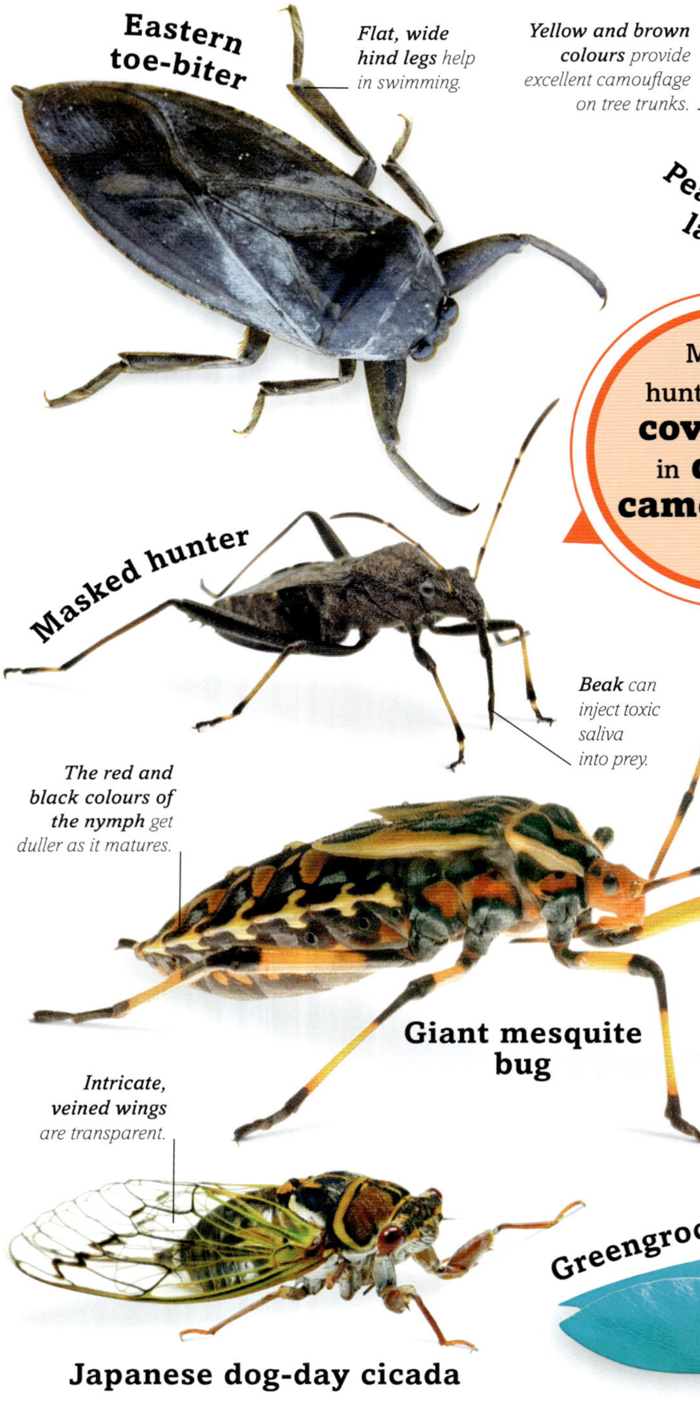

Milkweed assassin bug — *Sticky substance on front legs traps prey.*

> Masked hunter nymph **covers** itself in **dust** to **camouflage**.

Masked hunter — *Beak can inject toxic saliva into prey.*

Metallic shield bug — *Black spots on metallic green body*

Giant mesquite bug — *The red and black colours of the nymph get duller as it matures.*

Wheel bug — *Spiky, wheel-shaped crest*

Japanese dog-day cicada — *Intricate, veined wings are transparent.*

Greengrocer cicada — *Shown here in its rare turquoise form, this cicada also comes in other colours, including green and yellow.*

True bugs are insects that have a proboscis and grow by incomplete metamorphosis. Unlike those hatching as larvae and pupating (like caterpillars becoming butterflies), they emerge as nymphs. These nymphs are small versions of their adult forms and grow by moulting their exoskeleton.

All true bugs feed through a piercing, needlelike mouthpart called the proboscis, which they use as a straw. Some of them feed on tree sap – the **greengrocer cicada** loves to suck out the sap of the eucalyptus tree. Others, such as the **masked hunter** and **wheel bug**, pierce the skin of their prey with venomous saliva before slurping up the

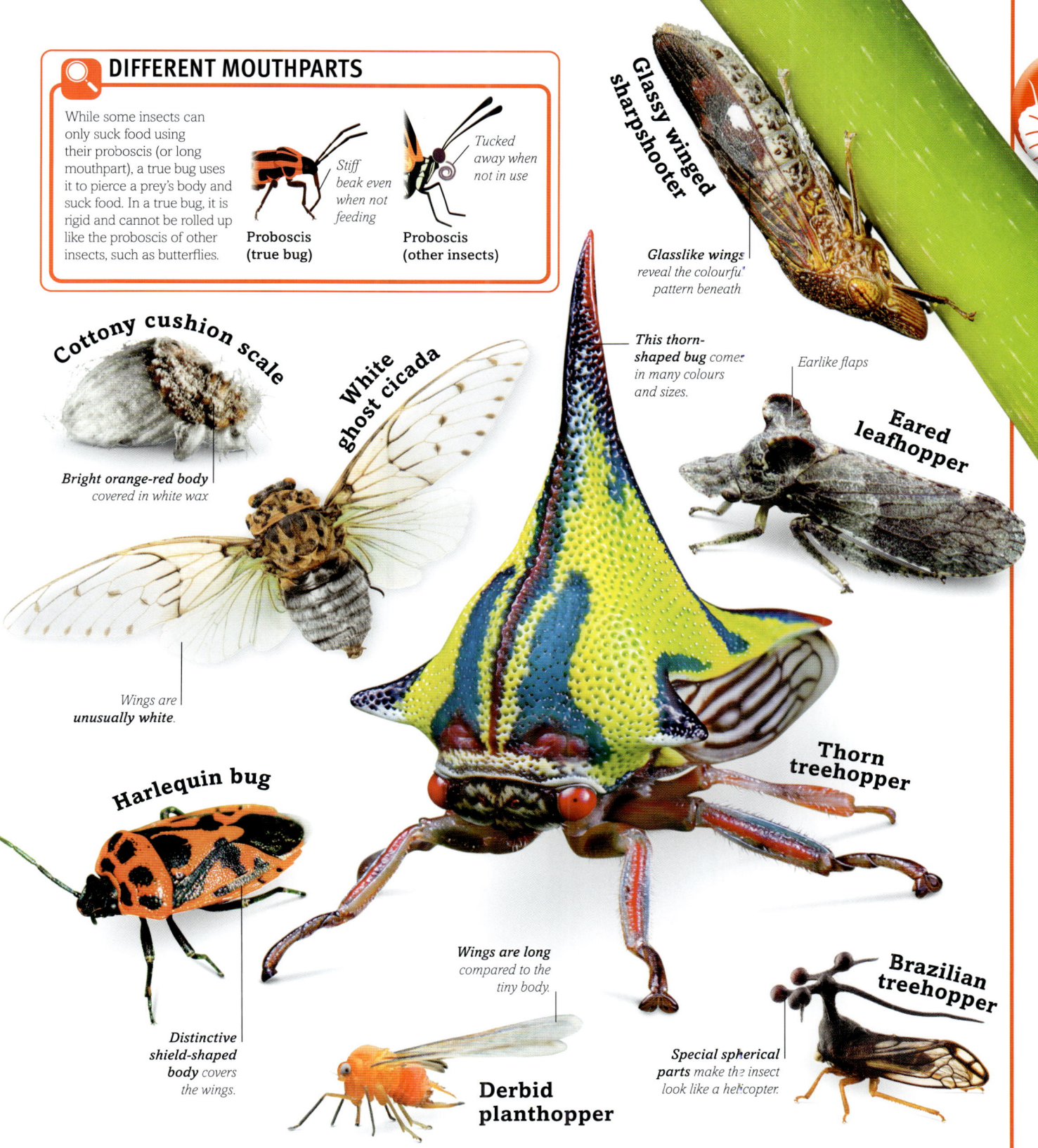

DIFFERENT MOUTHPARTS

While some insects can only suck food using their proboscis (or long mouthpart), a true bug uses it to pierce a prey's body and suck food. In a true bug, it is rigid and cannot be rolled up like the proboscis of other insects, such as butterflies.

Stiff beak even when not feeding
Proboscis (true bug)

Tucked away when not in use
Proboscis (other insects)

Glassy winged sharpshooter
Glasslike wings reveal the colourful pattern beneath

Cottony cushion scale
Bright orange-red body covered in white wax

White ghost cicada
Wings are unusually white.

This thorn-shaped bug comes in many colours and sizes.

Earlike flaps
Eared leafhopper

Thorn treehopper

Harlequin bug
Distinctive shield-shaped body covers the wings.

Wings are long compared to the tiny body.
Derbid planthopper

Brazilian treehopper
Special spherical parts make the insect look like a helicopter.

liquefied insides. The **eastern toe-biter** hunts and eats the same way, but under water, breathing through a snorkel-like structure on its abdomen. Some true bugs have evolved ingenious ways of warding off predators – the **harlequin bug** and the **giant mesquite bug** can give off a foul odour when threatened. True bugs can be visibly striking.

The shimmering **metallic shield bug** has a shiny gemlike body. The **thorn treehopper** has a pointed structure on its body, called a pronotum, which lets it hide in plain sight, while the **peanut-headed laternfly** is known for its bulging head and two huge eyespots on its hindwings.

Hungry hunters

Trapdoor spider
*The spider's deep tunnel has **a door made of silk, plant material, and dirt**.*

Rufous net-casting spider
*This hunter spins a silken net and **casts it over prey before trapping and eating it**.*

Yellow dung fly
***Strong front legs** are used to grab prey.*

Red-banded sand wasp
The wasp stings and paralyses the caterpillar before taking it to its underground nest to feed its larvae.

Crab spider
*The crab spider is ready to **devour the tiger beetle it has captured**.*

Common European scorpionfly
*Long beak is used to **feed on prey**.*

Many bugs are meat-eaters with insatiable appetites and they will stop at nothing to find their next meal. These creatures have a range of hunting techniques to capture prey to eat, and sometimes, to feed their offspring. And when food is scarce, some become scavengers or even eat their own.

Carnivorous bugs can use stealth, speed, or surprise tactics to target and take down prey. The **crab spider** blends in with foliage and hunts unsuspecting bugs. Both the **Chinese mantis** and **Hawaiian eupithecia caterpillar** use camouflage to mimic different plant parts and strike prey at lightning speed. Passing prey

Large compound eyes give the robber fly an excellent vision to spot prey.

Robber fly

Clawlike front legs of the caterpillar ruthlessly seize the fruitfly.

Hawaiian eupithecia caterpillar

Great diving beetle larva

Hungry larva feeds on tadpole underwater.

Spiny legs of the mantis extend swiftly to grab this Gray's Chinese gecko.

Chinese mantis

The Chinese mantis can strike prey in about **one-twentieth** of a second.

The bug pierces the entrapped fly to suck its body contents.

Ant damsel bug

The larvae create strands of sticky silk threads to lure and trap insects.

New Zealand glow-worm larva

This ladybird can devour many sap-sucking aphids.

Cream-spot ladybird

Hungry hunters

regularly fall victim to the **trapdoor spider** that waits inside its tunnel to grab insects that are close by. Other predators attract their prey with an irresistible lure. The **yellow dung fly** waits by mounds of dung – a popular spot for all kinds of insect visitors. The **New Zealand glow-worm larva** takes it further by glowing to capture the attention of insects that are attracted to light. Some bugs are not fussy eaters. The **common European scorpionfly** scavenges on dead or wounded prey, while the **great diving beetle larva** hunts underwater prey, including members of its own species sometimes.

SNEAKY SPIDER
Many spiders weave a web to snag prey out of the air. Some are active hunters that chase their prey down. Others wait patiently to ambush their prey with a lightning-fast attack. That's exactly what this female yellow crab spider is about to do. It has been hiding in plain sight, completely camouflaged against this flower, waiting patiently for this unsuspecting beetle to wander a little bit too close.

The spider sat perfectly still while waiting for dinner to arrive, and now it's time to strike! In the blink of an eye, the spider will grab the beetle with its huge front legs, which are already wide open and ready to attack. It will sink its fangs into its victim to paralyse it with venom. Although these spiders are only the size of a pea, their venom packs a punch. It is potent enough for the spider to take down prey much larger than itself, like bees or even butterflies and moths. Once the beetle is seized and subdued, the spider will inject its defenceless prey with digestive enzymes to liquefy its insides, which are then sucked out. What's left behind is the beetle's lifeless, hollow body, which might look completely unharmed.

Lacewings and relatives

EGGS ON STALKS

Green lacewings have a unique egg-laying method. The female produces silk threads to create stalks for each of her eggs to sit on top. This stops hungry young larvae from eating their siblings.

The lacewing family lives up to its name. It is a group of insects that have delicate, intricately veined wings resembling fine lace. These bugs are considered gardeners' friends because their young larvae – and in some species, the adults too – devour aphids and other bugs that damage plants.

The fragile, flapping wings of lacewings can be transparent as in the **green lacewing**, brown as in the **brown lacewing**, or shimmering as in the **Asian green lacewing**. Their colour patterns may also provide camouflage, as seen in the **spoonwing lacewing**, which flies almost unnoticed in forests and grasslands. Although

Lacewings and relatives

lacewings are not strong fliers, many can produce a nasty stink to protect themselves from predators. The relatives of lacewings include similar small flying insects, such as the **owlfly** that can dart and hunt down insects in mid-air. On the other hand, the **snakefly** and the **spotted snakefly** hunt by lifting their heads and catching prey between their powerful jaws in the blink of an eye. However, antlions such as the **European antlion** and the **pit-trapping antlion** don't hunt at all as adults. Instead, their larvae adopt clever hunting strategies and create traps in the soil, lying in wait for unsuspecting prey to accidentally fall in.

Deadly weapons

Large forelegs help this bug to catch fish and other larger prey.

This centipede uses its *modified claws* to inject venom.

Camel spider

Jagged ambush bug

Strong pincerlike limbs are used to hold and tear up prey, such as crickets.

Thick forelegs let this insect capture and subdue wasps and other bugs.

Tiger beetle larva

Giant water bug

Lurking in its burrow, the tiger beetle larva swiftly strikes an unsuspecting prey.

Scorpionfly

Long, beaklike mouthpart grabs dead or weakened insects before the bug can eat them.

Whether it's a needlelike tongue, venomous sting, or sawlike pincers, some bugs have the tools to deliver a devastating blow. Some even spray foul chemicals to injure attackers. They use their deadly body parts to stun and slay their victims, including predators, as staying out of reach doesn't always work.

Many bugs are ruthless hunters. The **giant water bug** and **jagged ambush bug** pierce their prey with pointed mouthparts before injecting a special saliva to dissolve their insides, which can then be consumed as a drink. The **camel spider** uses its very powerful fangs to subdue the prey. Some bugs attack in self-defence.

Deadly weapons

Pacific giant centipede

Parasitoid wasp

Bombardier beetle

Great golden digger wasp
The digger wasp captures and paralyses grasshoppers and other prey.

The hot, toxic chemical spray can paralyse an attacker.

Golden-haired robber fly

Assassin bug

The robberfly uses its stout, spiny legs to hold onto insects.

Needlelike rostrum pierces easily through moths and other prey.

The bombardier beetle's spray can reach temperatures of **100°C (212°F)**.

When threatened, **bombardier beetles** blast predators with acidlike chemicals. An even worse fate awaits the victims of some bug mothers. The female **great golden digger wasp** immobilizes its prey, lays an egg on it, and then buries the paralysed victim with the egg. When the egg hatches the larva eats the prey. The female **parasitoid wasp** injects her eggs directly into a caterpillar. As the larvae hatch, they devour the caterpillar.

Mighty mantises

Finding food

This mantis looks like a shrivelled petal.

Devil's praying mantis

Striking spines look like flower petals.

It holds a "praying" posture similar to other praying mantises.

Spiny flower mantis

Shield mantis

European mantis

Golden mantis

The small, shiny golden mantis catches flies and spiders.

Usually white, this mantis can change its colour to pink.

Orchid mantis

Delicate hindwings are shaped like a fan.

Small, sturdy body

African bark mantis

There are about 2,500 varieties of mantis around the world. They are expert hunters, highly skilled in catching and eating live prey. Mantises strike without warning, launching a surprise attack to trap passing prey. They're not picky eaters either, so anything from tiny bugs and beetles to big frogs and even small birds can end up as their dinner.

Mantises are masters of disguise. Some, such as the **orchid mantis**, impersonate beautiful flowers. Insects land on these mantises hoping for sweet nectar. But what seemed like pretty petals are actually deadly legs that grab them tight before they are devoured whole by the hunter. Similarly, some mantises, such as the **shield mantis**, pretend to be lush green leaves. Others, such as the **giant dead leaf mantis**, look more like dry, dead leaves. They lie low on the forest floor, appearing to be harmless just before they strike!

FORMIDABLE FLY
This bumblebee is having a bad day – it's been attacked by a predator! The robber fly is one of the largest flies and a highly efficient killer, seizing any opportunity it gets to tackle its prey. Its hunting strategy of aerial ambush attack has an almost faultless success rate. The robber fly stays out of sight, waiting for passing prey before catching them in mid-air and carrying them off to meet their inevitable doom.

The robber fly is an unstoppable predator because its entire body is built to overpower prey. After targeting its prey with its large compound eyes, the robber fly uses its strong, spiky legs to seize it in the air. The victims can never fight back as the robber fly's piercing proboscis (hollow feeding mouthparts) delivers a poison to paralyse them. Once inside the body, this potent chemical gets to work turning prey to liquid, making it easier for the robber fly to feed on it. By the time the robber fly lands in a safe space, the prey's insides are ready to be slurped. These flies will kill at least once, if not twice, a day.

Wonderful webs

The prey-trapping design of the orb webs resembles a bicycle's wheel.

Orb web

*The egg sac is made of spider's silk and may have **hundreds of eggs**.*

Tangle web

The mother spider guards its spiderlings as they hatch out of the egg.

Nursery web

The twisted network of silk has helped the spiders trap a beetle.

Communal sheet web

Communal tangle web

*These tiny tangle-web social spiders make a large **basket-shaped communal web**.*

*The triangle spider holds the web tight at one end, **and lets it collapse on prey**.*

Triangle web

Spiders are the extraordinary weavers of the natural world, spinning spectacular webs from their own silk supply. Their bodies have special organs, called spinnerets, through which they can produce silk. They weave webs to catch prey, raise their babies, or bridge gaps between branches.

Spider silk is an adaptable material that produces a staggering diversity of webs. These designs range from the simple, functional **orb web**, to the messy, irregular **tangle web**. Some spiders live in vast colonies and weave large, interconnected webs, such as the **communal sheet webs** woven by the Indian cooperative spiders. These

Bugs drop into this tentlike web for the dome web spider to devour.

Tent web

The legs of this net-casting spider hold the rectangular web to cast over prey.

Net-casting web

This criss-cross mass of thick silk threads can last for a long time.

Sheet web

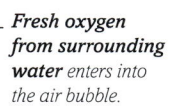

Funnel-shaped web surrounds the entrance to the Sydney funnel-web spider's burrow.

The spider throws silk thread with sticky droplets to catch prey mid-air.

Bolas web

Funnel web

A tubelike structure is constructed from the base of a tree by the spider.

Fresh oxygen from surrounding water enters into the air bubble.

Purse web

*The purse-web spider waits inside its web to **ambush prey**.*

Underwater silk web

🔍 MAKING A WEB

Most garden spiders follow the same orb web structure. The spider weaves a basic framework followed by an outer frame. The inner frame is attached by strong threads and multiple sticky lines to trap prey.

A Y-shaped frame is created.

The outer frame is being made.

Strong threads are added to the inner frame.

Sticky lines are woven.

colossal webs are perfect for trapping bigger prey. Other spiders stick to a clear shape for a reason. One corner of the **triangle web** is held by the spider, and as soon as a prey comes, it releases the stretchy web to trap the food. The rectangular **net-casting web** works like a fishing net to catch prey. Sometimes, webs are a matter of life and death. The aquatic diving-bell spider breathes by making an **underwater silk web**, which it uses as an air tank. The European nursery web spider weaves a **nursery web** as a protective cover to keep its egg sac, and later its spiderlings, hidden from hungry predators and sheltered from extreme weather.

Stinging scorpions

Finding food

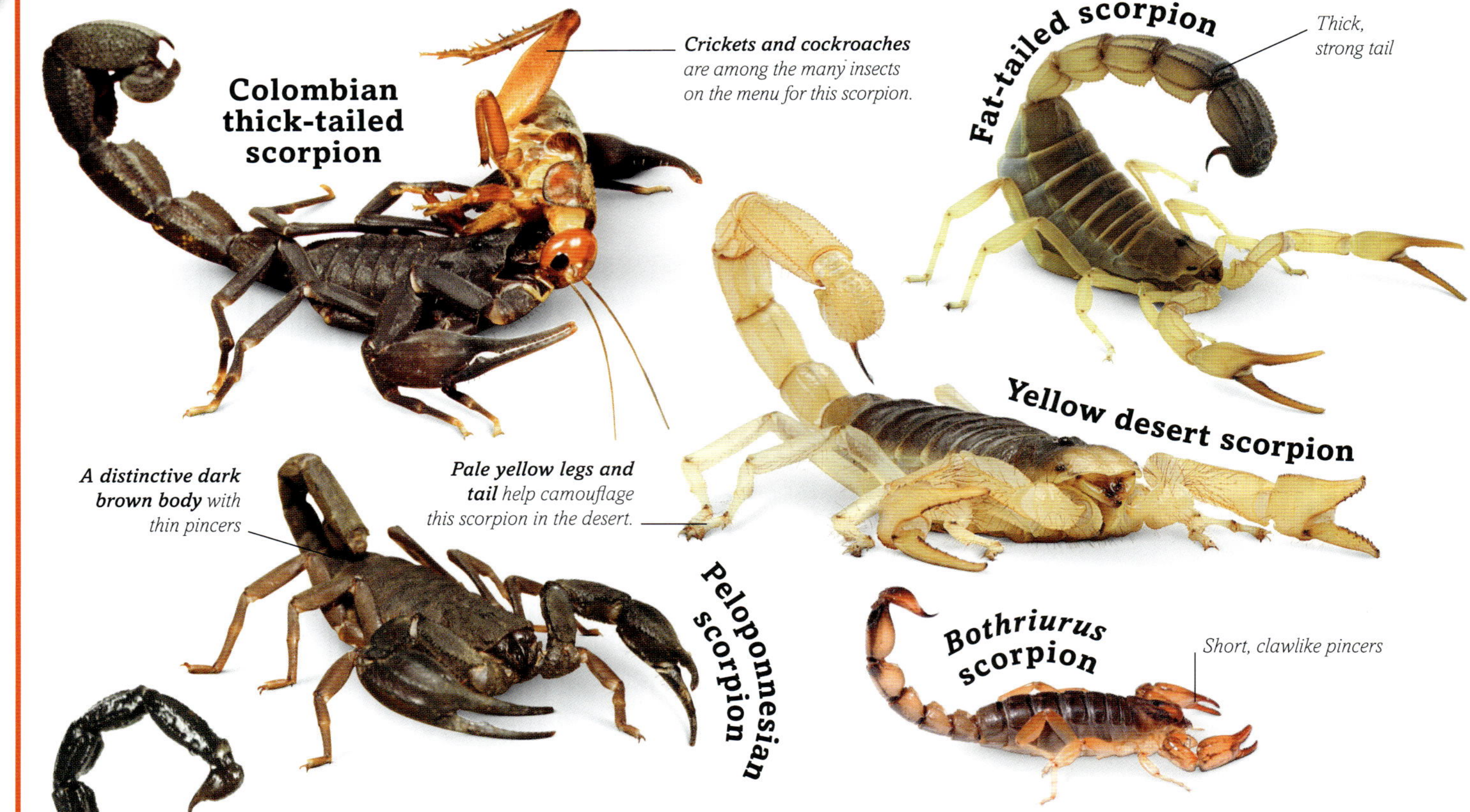

Colombian thick-tailed scorpion

Crickets and cockroaches are among the many insects on the menu for this scorpion.

Fat-tailed scorpion

Thick, strong tail

A distinctive dark brown body with thin pincers

Pale yellow legs and tail help camouflage this scorpion in the desert.

Peloponnesian scorpion

Yellow desert scorpion

Bothriurus scorpion

Short, clawlike pincers

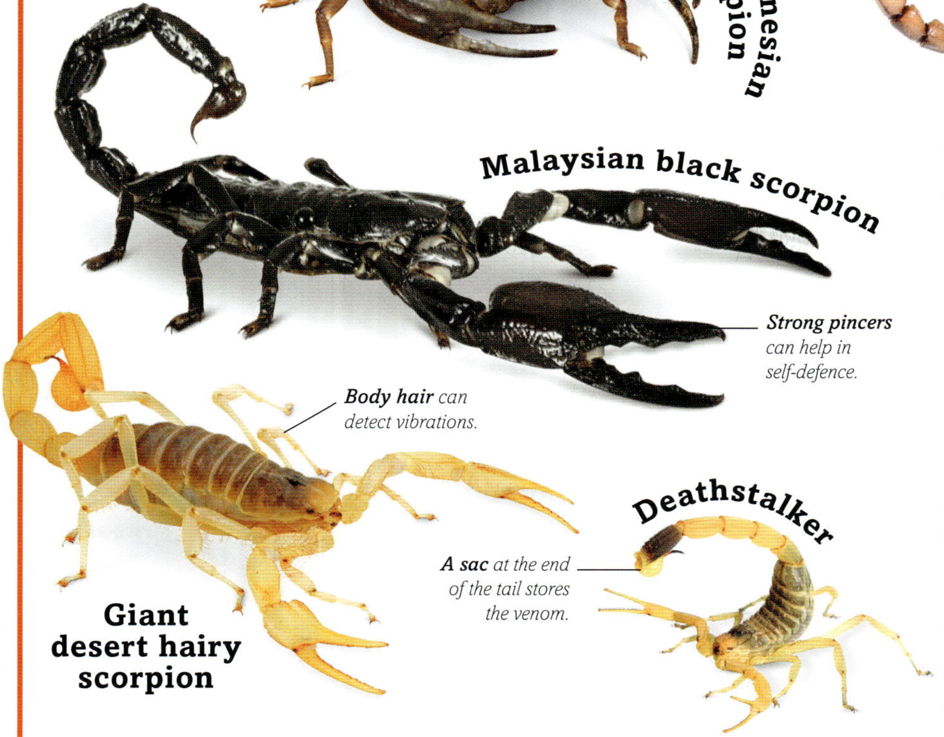

Malaysian black scorpion

Strong pincers can help in self-defence.

Body hair can detect vibrations.

Giant desert hairy scorpion

A sac at the end of the tail stores the venom.

Deathstalker

GLOW-IN-THE-DARK

All scorpions glow blue-green under ultraviolet (UV) light. Their exoskeleton (hard outer covering) contains a substance that is responsible for this, but scientists are not sure why.

Emperor scorpion under UV light

Under the cover of darkness, scorpions emerge to take down prey. These stealth hunters are equipped with powerful pincers, full body armour, and a venomous sting in their tail. Like spiders, scorpions are arachnids, and there are more than 2,360 species worldwide.

Scorpions have lived on Earth for more than 400 million years. Many live in hot habitats, such as deserts. The *Bothriurus* **scorpion** escapes the heat by tunnelling underground to keep cool. Other scorpions, such as the **Asian forest scorpion**, live in forests and can climb trees. Like most scorpions, the **giant desert hairy scorpion**

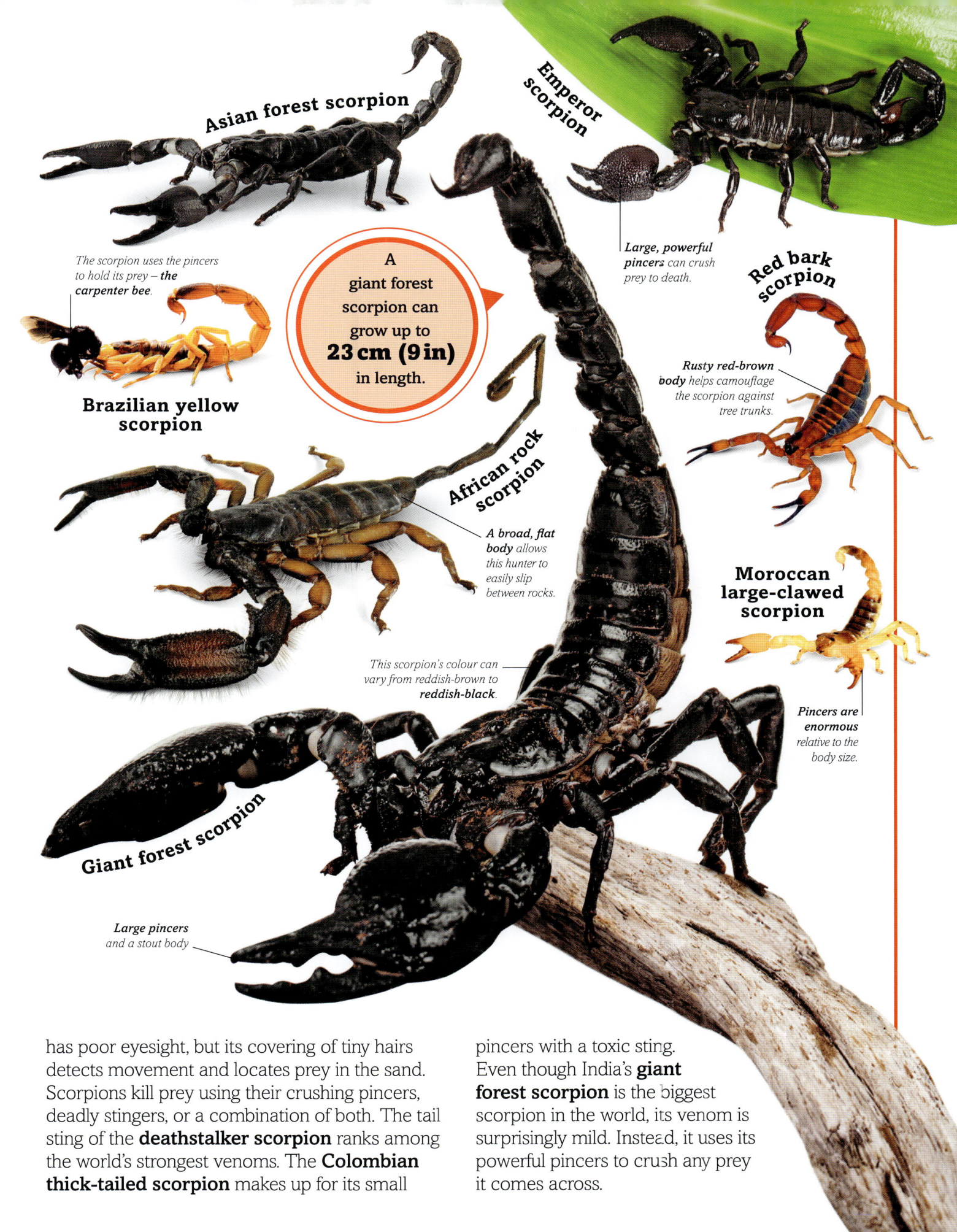

has poor eyesight, but its covering of tiny hairs detects movement and locates prey in the sand. Scorpions kill prey using their crushing pincers, deadly stingers, or a combination of both. The tail sting of the **deathstalker scorpion** ranks among the world's strongest venoms. The **Colombian thick-tailed scorpion** makes up for its small pincers with a toxic sting. Even though India's **giant forest scorpion** is the biggest scorpion in the world, its venom is surprisingly mild. Instead, it uses its powerful pincers to crush any prey it comes across.

Venomous insects

*The sting of the executioner wasp is among the **most painful** of any insect.*

The first pair of clear wings is larger than the second pair.

European wasp

Carpenter bee

Fuzzy legs help collect pollen from flowers.

Executioner wasp

Vibrant yellow body warns predators it is dangerous.

Common carder bee

Clear, membranous wings have a network of veins that provide support, stability, and flexibility in the air.

A chemical injected through the stinger (hidden behind this outer shell) paralyses tarantula spiders.

Tarantula hawk wasp

Smooth stinger can be used in self-defence multiple times.

Many bugs have earned a bad reputation for delivering a painful dose of venom through their specialized stingers. However, almost all of them – including ants, bees, wasps, and caterpillars – only sting in self-defence when provoked or threatened by other creatures.

Insects pass their venom by biting or stinging, but different species cause varying degrees of harm. The **European wasp** has a mild sting that produces redness and swelling when injected through human skin. However, the sting of the

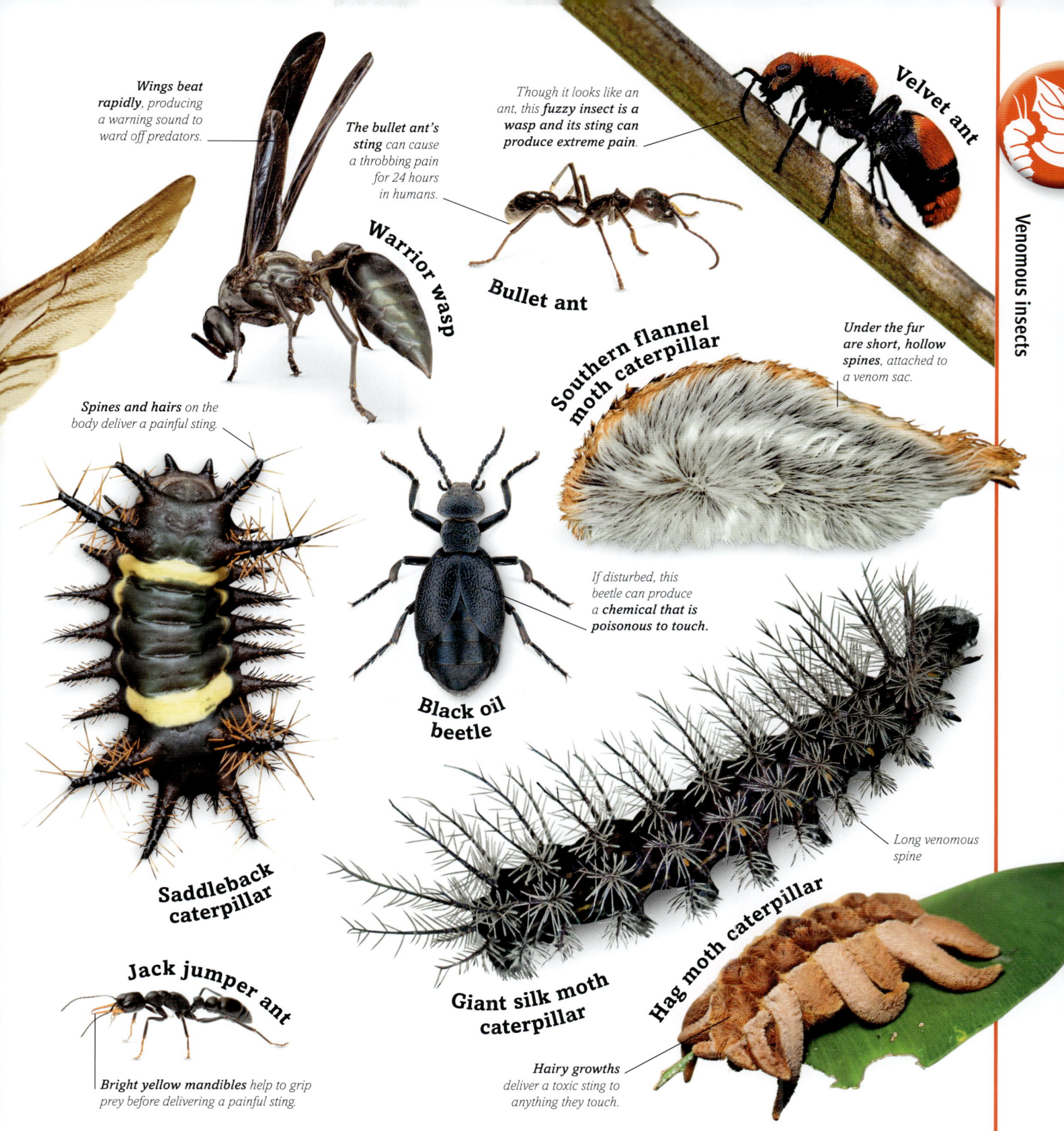

Venomous insects

Wings beat rapidly, producing a warning sound to ward off predators.

The bullet ant's sting can cause a throbbing pain for 24 hours in humans.

Though it looks like an ant, this **fuzzy insect is a wasp and its sting can produce extreme pain.**

Warrior wasp

Bullet ant

Velvet ant

Southern flannel moth caterpillar

Under the fur are short, hollow **spines**, attached to a venom sac.

Spines and hairs on the body deliver a painful sting.

If disturbed, this beetle can produce a **chemical that is poisonous to touch.**

Black oil beetle

Long venomous spine

Saddleback caterpillar

Jack jumper ant

Giant silk moth caterpillar

Hag moth caterpillar

Bright yellow mandibles help to grip prey before delivering a painful sting.

Hairy growths deliver a toxic sting to anything they touch.

bullet ant is extremely painful, making it highly dangerous because it can paralyse and kill other bugs. Not all venomous insects have visible stingers. Caterpillars can look deceptively soft and sweet. The **southern flannel moth caterpillar** may look like a cuddly toy, but within the fur are venomous spines that cause instant pain if touched by a predator. When it comes to bees, wasps, and ants, only the females are armed with stingers. In social species, like the **warrior wasp** and the **common carder bee**, one sting might soon turn into many as nestmates are never too far away to come and help defend the colony.

143

ANT ATTACK On the forest floors of coniferous, broad-leaved, or mixed woodlands, European red wood ants build massive nests from twigs, bark, and soil. These nests can be home to more than a million ants. When a predator approaches their nest, worker ants mobilize to launch a defensive strike. Tearing out of the nest in swarms, each ant fires a chemical called formic acid out of its rear end to try and harm the attacker.

Worker ants, which are wingless females, produce this acid. They secrete it from the venom gland in their abdomen and then store it in a venom sac by their stinger. The sac has a chemical lining that stops the acid from harming the ant itself. When the ants are under attack, the workers take up a defensive position with their jaws wide open and abdomen curled, and contract their venom sac to release the acid from the rear end of their body. Once sprayed into the air, it acts like an alarm, alerting the rest of the colony. This acid is useful for more than just defence. It helps disinfect ant nests and prevent the growth of harmful microbes.

Incredible interactions

Ants move aphids to healthier parts of the plant.

Ants tend to the caterpillar in return for honeydew.

Common imperial blue caterpillar and ant

These caterpillars release **chemicals** to trick the ants to protect them.

This fungus infects bugs, forcing them to climb up to a higher place where it can release its spores.

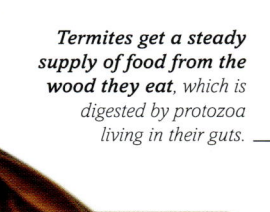

Spider and Cordyceps fungus

Aphid and ant

The adult wasp emerges from the dead cockroach it has fed on through the larval stage.

Termites get a steady supply of food from the wood they eat, which is digested by protozoa living in their guts.

Emerald cockroach wasp and cockroach

Termite and protozoa

Animal interactions vary and include more than just predator-prey relationships. Some creatures live closely with other species, including microbes and plants. These relationships can be mutually beneficial, or they can help one creature while harming or even killing the other.

Ants are fond of honeydew, a sweet liquid secreted by the bodies of bugs such as **aphids** and **common imperial blue caterpillars**. To make sure they have a constant supply of honeydew, the ants watch over those bugs, protecting them from predators. Some species of wasps form parasitic relationships with other bugs to make sure that

Stylops live as parasites inside a bee – only the male emerges, to mate with a female whose body sticks out of its host.

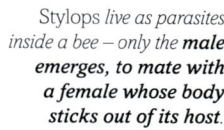

The beetle gives mites a ride to the carcasses of animals, where the mites will eat the fly eggs and maggots that are competing for food with the beetle's young.

Sexton beetle and mite

***Stylops* insect and bee**

Female fig wasps burrow inside figs to lay their eggs.

Mosquito larvae inside pitcher plants feed on microbes trapped there and break them down for the plant to absorb.

Leafcutter ants chew leaves into a pulp, which they use to grow the fungus they eat.

Fig wasp and fig tree

Yucca moths pollinate yucca plants, while laying their eggs inside the flowers.

Leafcutter ant and fungus

Mosquito larva and pitcher plant

The Telenomus wasp lays eggs inside the moth's eggs, and later, the wasp's larvae will eat all moth's eggs.

A cuckoo wasp lays its eggs in another bug's nest, and the host's young become food for the wasp's larvae.

Yucca moth and yucca plant

***Telenomus* wasp and autumn gum moth**

Cuckoo wasp and host

their young are fed – the **emerald cockroach wasp** stings a **cockroach** and takes control of its brain. The zombie insect doesn't try to escape even when the wasp's larvae are feeding on its body. On the other hand, **fig wasps** take a more mutually beneficial approach, by laying their eggs inside figs, and helping pollinate the **fig flowers** along the way. Similarly, **leafcutter ants** use the plant clippings they collect to grow **fungus** and feed their colony. The fungus, in return, gets access to food and a clean home. But, not all fungi are good, such as the ***Cordyceps* fungus**. The killer fungus gets into the body of a **spider** and takes control, eventually killing its host.

Unique diets

Many bugs feed on a fairly normal diet of plants, meat, or both. However, there are a wide range of insects that have developed a taste for much more unusual diets. These bugs are very particular about what they eat and opt for a specific food source, or live as parasites on just one animal. To some insects, rotting plants and flesh are a welcome feast.

Wood is one of the sources of cellulose that the termite eats.

Termite

Beetle larvae climb on the bee while it's feeding on nectar.

Black oil beetle larvae

These larvae feed on dry wood, damaging furniture and buildings.

Furniture beetle larvae

Males of the species use their mouthparts to feed on mammal blood.

Clothes moth caterpillar

Vampire moth

This caterpillar feeds on wool, feathers, and fur.

Termites eat only one type of carbohydrate – cellulose. Similarly, **clothes moths** are able to feed on keratin (the protein in hair, nails, and wool), as well as other fibres in our clothes. Some bugs prefer to get their nourishment from blood, including ours. **Human lice** are parasites that are only found on humans. They hide in our hair and jump from one head to another in search of food. **Human botflies** are less picky. They feed on the body fluids and tissue of humans as well as other mammals. **Dung beetles** specialize in drinking a smelly liquid found in poo. They collect fresh animal droppings, which they feed on and lay eggs into. **Black oil beetle larvae** lie inside flowers, waiting for bees to visit. Once a bee appears, the larvae jump aboard and are carried back to the bee's nest to feed on pollen stores or even bee larvae. **Thrips** eat leaves, fruits, and the seed-producing parts of plants, which makes them a common pest.

Unique diets

*When biting the host human for food, **this louse causes itchiness**.*

Human louse

*Thrip nymphs' food includes **fungus spores**.*

Thrip nymphs

*The head of the larva has **hardened mouth hooks**.*

Human botfly larva

*Gut bacteria inside this vulture bee help it to **digest rotting meat**.*

*Antennae are used to locate **dung**, which the beetle then rolls into a ball.*

Dung beetle

Vulture bee

Parasitic bugs

Leafminer parasitoid wasp

The parasitoid wasp lays eggs on or near leafminer larvae, where they hatch and feed on the host.

Feather-legged fly

Unique featherlike hairs on hind legs

A feather-legged fly lays several eggs on a host's body, but only **one survives**.

Norwegian cuckoo bumblebee

The cuckoo bumblebee lacks a pollen basket on its hind legs and cannot feed its young.

Varroa mite

The mites feed on the honeybee body tissue.

Red poultry mite

The mite turns red after feeding on blood.

Leptus mite larvae

The bright red larvae feed on a grasshopper and use it for transport.

A parasitic bug may live on or inside another living creature – its host – using it as a food source. Most parasites are smaller than their hosts and harm them indirectly. But some bugs, known as parasitoids, are deadly. They lay their eggs on or inside a host animal, which the young bugs feed on until it dies.

Some insects are ectoparasites, meaning they live on their hosts' bodies. The **red poultry mite**, **cat flea**, and **bat louse fly** all cling to the animal they're named after and suck their blood to survive. Their victims are better off than those that become infested by endoparasites – bugs that get inside the host's body. **Blowfly larvae** burrow into

Parasitic bugs

Blowfly larvae — The larvae are also called screwworms due to their **ringed, screwlike appearance**.

Tick — The tick attaches itself to humans and animals, swelling as it feeds on their blood.

Cat flea — Brown, wingless insect with **piercing and sucking mouthparts**.

Nose botfly — Adults have no mouthparts as they only feed as parasitic larvae.

Braconid wasp larvae — After cutting holes and coming out of the caterpillar's body, **each larva builds a cocoon and pupates inside it**.

Bat louse fly — Strong claws allow these flies to cling to their host bat even in flight.

the skin of livestock after hatching from eggs laid in their open wounds. They feast on flesh, causing severe disease that can kill the host. Similarly, **braconid wasp larvae** hatch from eggs laid by the mother wasp inside a caterpillar. They grow by feeding on the caterpillar's organs, eventually killing it. Unlike other parasitic bugs, the female **Norwegian cuckoo bumblebee** is a social parasite – it takes over a bumblebee colony, kills the queen, and forces the worker bees to look after its offspring.

LIVING WITH BUGS

Living with bugs

Why we need bugs

Bugs live all around us. They fly through the air, swim in the water, and live among plants and trees. Some can even be found on our bodies! Small, buzzing insects can be annoying, particularly if they bite and sting. But without them, our world would look very different. Insects are a key part of the world's ecosystems – the communities of plants and animals that live and interact with each other in an area.

Maintaining a healthy ecosystem
Bugs eat and are eaten in turn, which makes them a key part of many ecosystems. Here are three examples: near water, on a farm, and in grassland.

AROUND THE LAKE
Bugs play an important role in the water. They eat up dead and rotting plant matter, keeping the water clean. Without them, rivers and lakes would be congested with leaves and algae. Some bugs prey on others that may spread infections to humans.

A FARMER'S ASSISTANTS
Farmers rely on bugs for a number of different jobs: they help decompose dead material, improve soil fertility, and eat weeds and other bugs that damage the crops.

OUT IN THE FIELD
In woodlands and fields, animals such as birds rely on bugs for food. Bugs also bury dead animals, and keep the numbers of other bugs under control, by eating them.

Friend or foe

Bugs share different types of relationships with other creatures. Some of them help other creatures by spreading seeds, feeding fungus, pollinating flowers, and being a source of food for all sorts of animals. Others are more harmful – they bite or sting, or carry viruses, bacteria, and parasites that spread diseases.

Spreading seeds
Some ants carry seeds far away from the parent plant, which allows the seedling to grow in a new environment. These bugs aren't deliberate gardeners – the seeds are their food, and the bugs carry them away in order to store them.

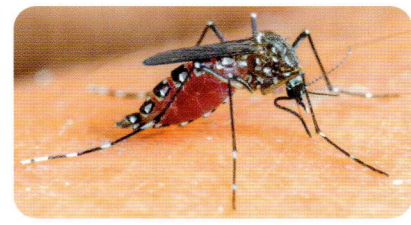

Spreading disease
Mosquitoes spread many diseases, such as malaria and dengue fever. These diseases are spread from human to human through mosquito bites. If a mosquito drinks the blood of an infected person, it carries that infection on to its next victim.

Dragonflies are predators that hunt many disease-carrying insects such as some mosquitoes.
Some mosquitoes drink nectar and pollinate flowers.
Adult caddisflies serve as food for fish, birds, and other predators.
The giant casemaker caddisfly larva eats rotting plant matter.

Bees, butterflies, and flies carry pollen from plant to plant, which allows the plants to reproduce and make seeds.
Ants eat some plant-eating insects, keeping their population in check.
Dung beetles feed on animal waste. They also break it down and bury it, helping to reduce the release of greenhouse gases like methane, create air pockets in the soil, and help plants grow.

Many animals feed on bugs. This includes birds, mammals, reptiles, amphibians, and other bugs.
Ants make tunnels for their nest that bring air into the soil and help recycle dead matter.
Burying beetles bury the bodies of dead rodents for their larvae to eat. This helps the bodies rot, preventing the spread of disease.
Tarantula hawk wasps hunt and drag spiders to their nest for their larvae to feed on.

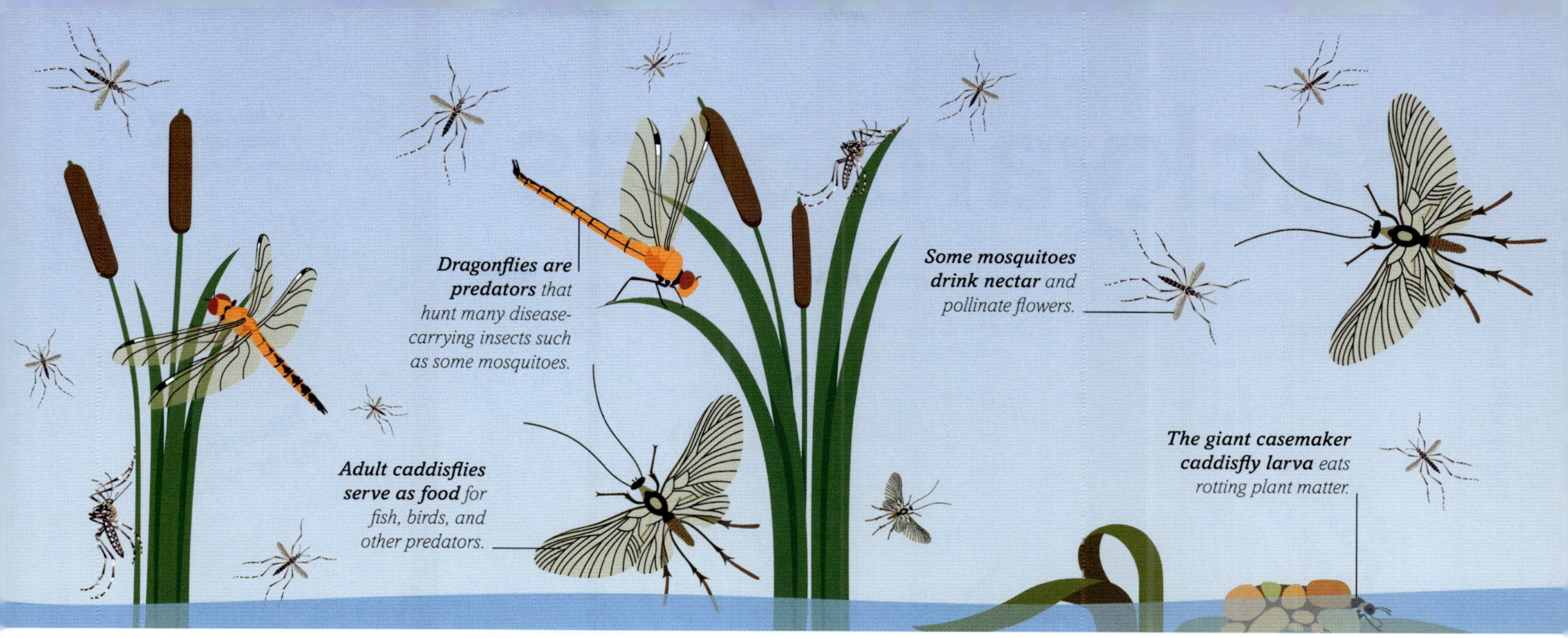

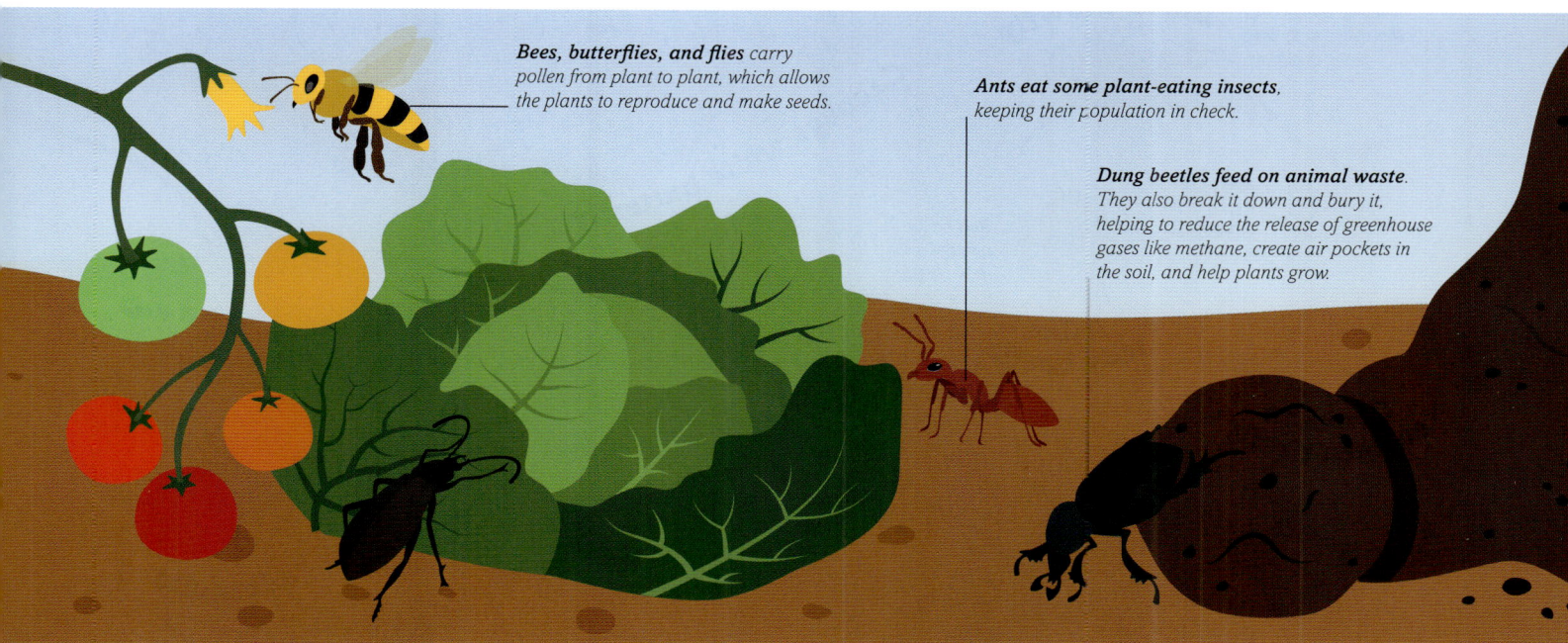

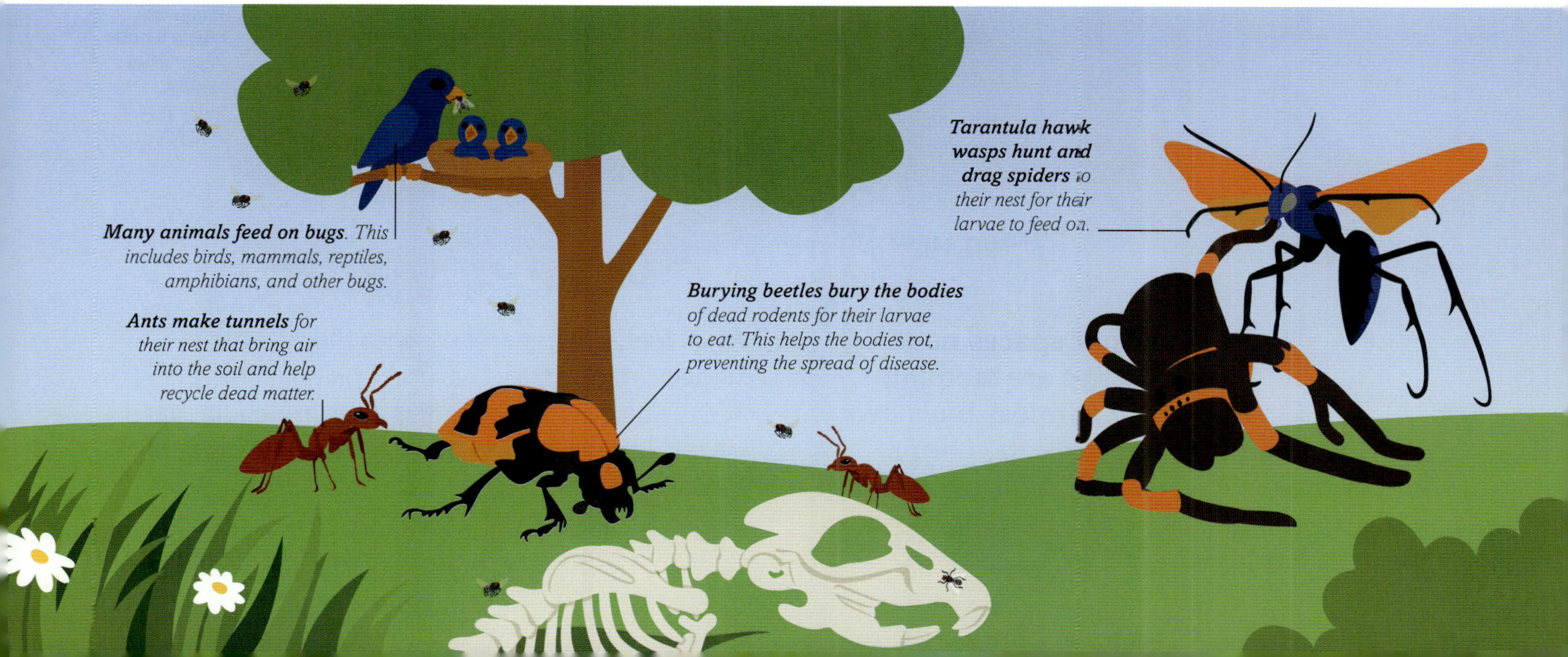

Backyard bugs

Outdoor spaces near our homes are teeming with life. Countless bugs live in balconies, courtyards, patios, and gardens. These spots offer everything a bug needs to thrive: food, shelter, and room to explore.

Bugs feel safe in gardens, with their leafy hedges, thick grass, flowering plants, and hideaway crevices. Some of them, such as the **green lacewing** and the **pill bug**, use colours as camouflage to blend into their surroundings. Bugs can also find a variety of food in outdoor spaces. While the **Asian lady beetle** mostly

feasts on aphids, the **black blowfly** feeds on nectar as well as decaying plants and animals. Backyard bugs sometimes have a bad reputation, but very few are problematic to people and some are even helpful. Arachnids, such as the **black-and-yellow garden spider** and **red-legged golden orb-web weaver**, may look dangerous, but they aren't aggressive to people. They help control garden pests and disease-carrying insects by trapping them in their webs. Similarly, the **northern plushback hoverfly** only mimics a wasp or bee, without having the power to really sting. It helps to pollinate plants and its larvae prey on garden pests.

House bugs

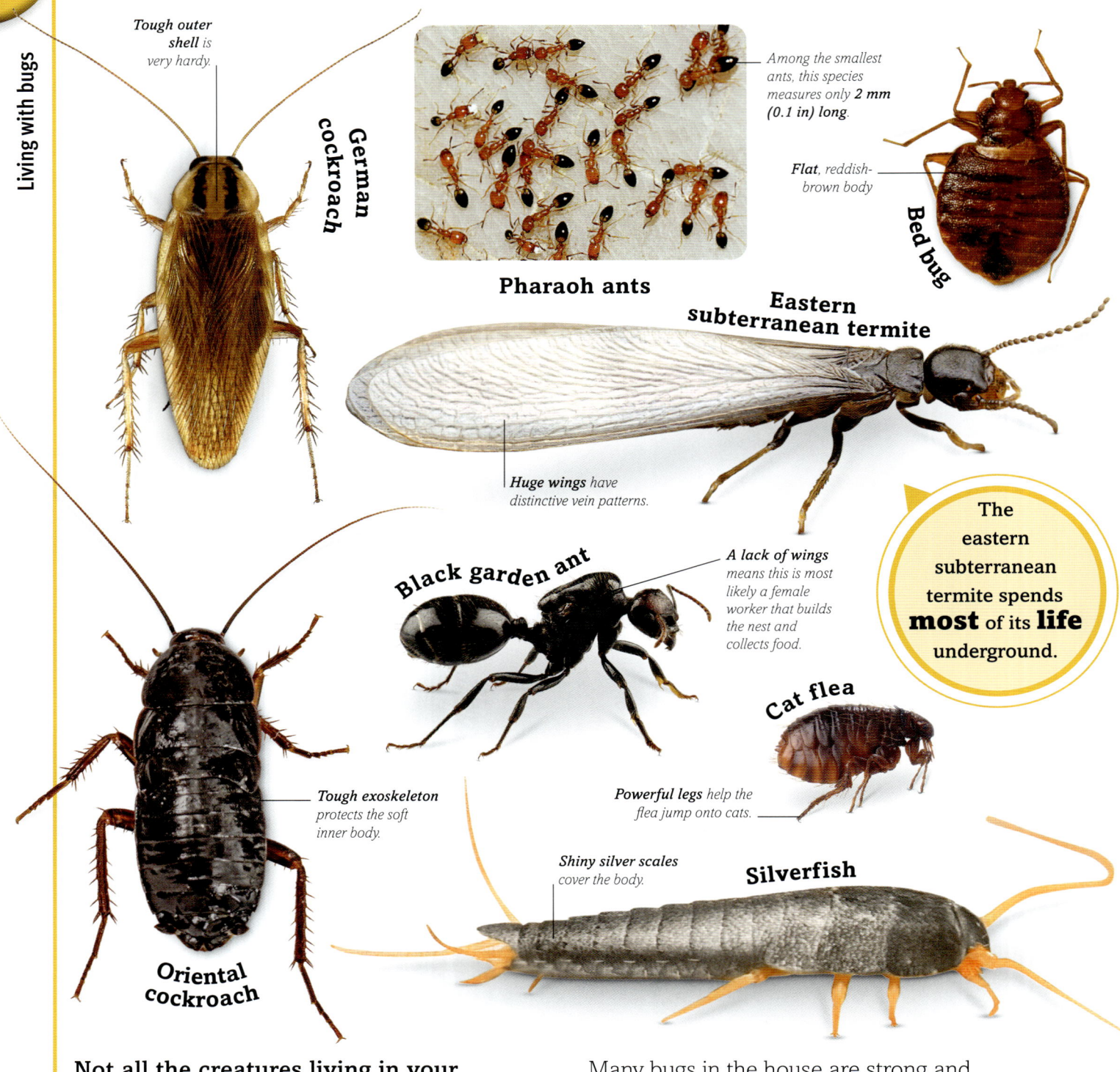

Not all the creatures living in your home were invited guests. Many small bugs create their own homes in human households. They take advantage of the plentiful shelter, space, food, and water. Your own home may be host to hundreds or even thousands of small creatures.

Many bugs in the house are strong and resilient with well-protected bodies. The **German cockroach** can survive under many outdoor conditions, but it prefers the comfort and warmth of a human home. Similarly, **pharaoh ants**, which live in large colonies, enjoy the warmth of central heating.

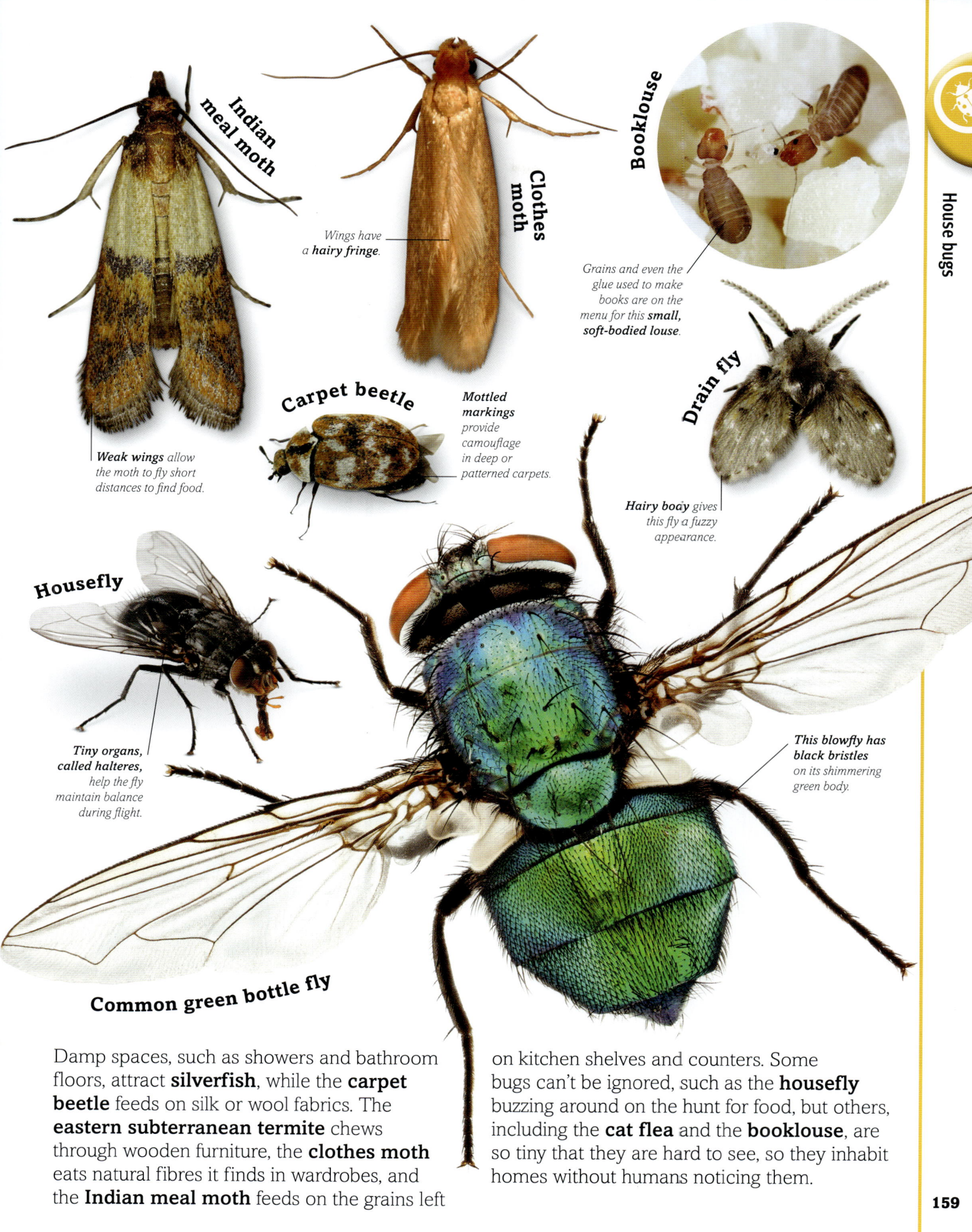

House bugs

Indian meal moth — *Weak wings* allow the moth to fly short distances to find food.

Clothes moth — Wings have a **hairy fringe**.

Booklouse — Grains and even the glue used to make books are on the menu for this **small, soft-bodied louse**.

Carpet beetle — *Mottled markings* provide camouflage in deep or patterned carpets.

Drain fly — *Hairy body* gives this fly a fuzzy appearance.

Housefly — *Tiny organs, called halteres,* help the fly maintain balance during flight.

Common green bottle fly — This blowfly has black bristles on its shimmering green body.

Damp spaces, such as showers and bathroom floors, attract **silverfish**, while the **carpet beetle** feeds on silk or wool fabrics. The **eastern subterranean termite** chews through wooden furniture, the **clothes moth** eats natural fibres it finds in wardrobes, and the **Indian meal moth** feeds on the grains left on kitchen shelves and counters. Some bugs can't be ignored, such as the **housefly** buzzing around on the hunt for food, but others, including the **cat flea** and the **booklouse**, are so tiny that they are hard to see, so they inhabit homes without humans noticing them.

159

SWARMING MAYFLIES What at first seems like snowfall is actually millions of pale burrower mayflies swarming on a late summer evening. Having spent most of their lives as flightless nymphs in the water, they have emerged as airborne adults to flutter above the river's surface and mate. But the amber glow of this bridge's lampposts has led these mayflies off course, which could spell disaster for the next generation.

Adult males swarm near the water, attracting females and mating with them mid-air. Mayflies navigate the river by following the moonlight reflecting off the water's surface. Artificial light can easily mislead them and bring them near human settlements, disrupting their reproductive cycle. To make matters worse, the asphalt on this bridge, lit by the lampposts, makes the road look just like water to these insects. This causes many female mayflies to mistakenly lay their eggs on the road, wasting their chance of reproducing. Unfortunately, this is just one of many examples of how human activities are impacting the life cycles of insects, spurring declines in their population.

Little helpers

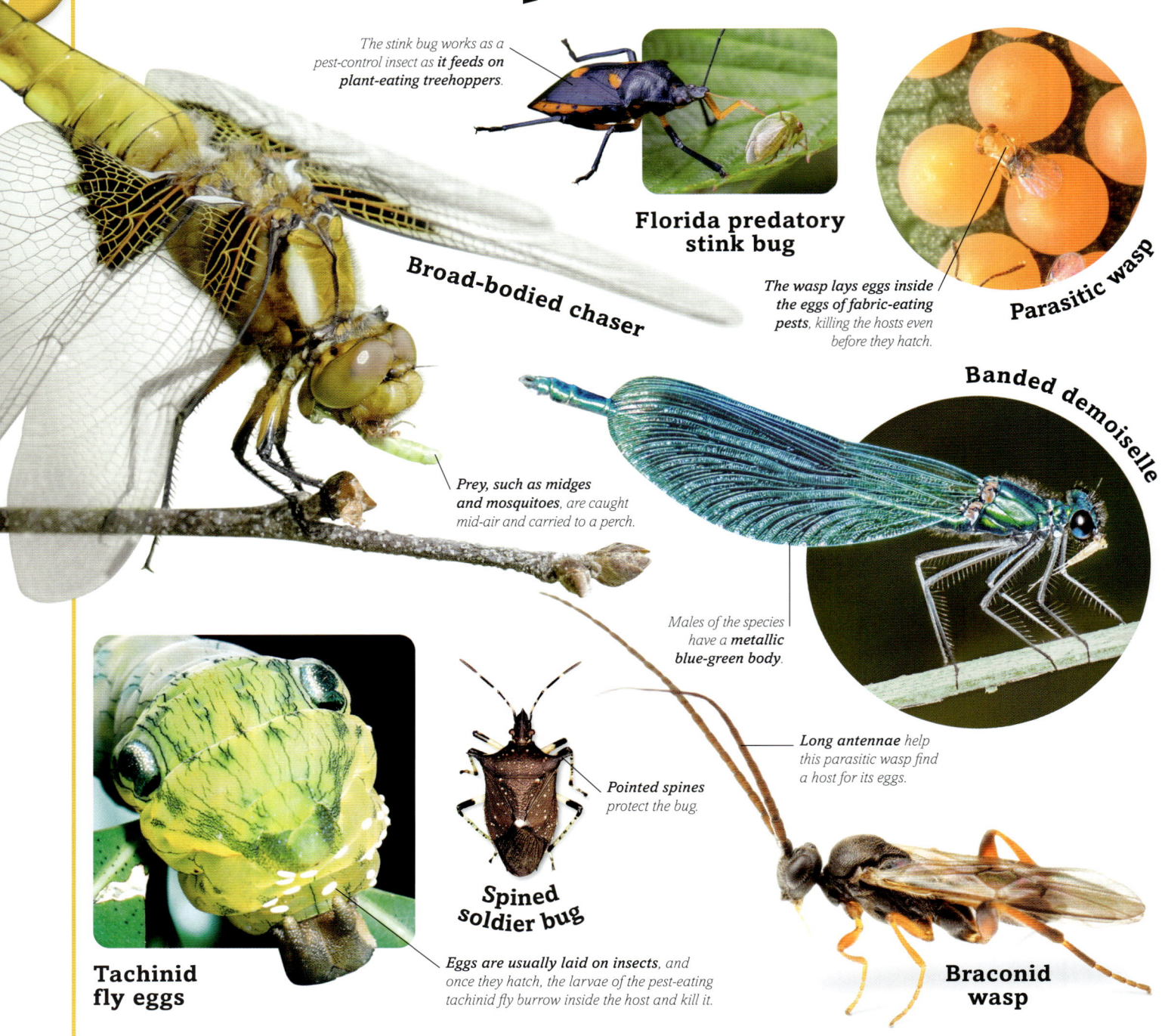

*The stink bug works as a pest-control insect as **it feeds on plant-eating treehoppers**.*

Florida predatory stink bug

*The wasp lays eggs inside the eggs of fabric-eating **pests**, killing the hosts even before they hatch.*

Parasitic wasp

Broad-bodied chaser

Prey, such as midges and mosquitoes, are caught mid-air and carried to a perch.

Banded demoiselle

*Males of the species have a **metallic blue-green body**.*

Pointed spines protect the bug.

Spined soldier bug

Long antennae help this parasitic wasp find a host for its eggs.

Tachinid fly eggs

Eggs are usually laid on insects, and once they hatch, the larvae of the pest-eating tachinid fly burrow inside the host and kill it.

Braconid wasp

Bugs and their offspring can benefit diverse ecosystems and support various human activities. Many feed on other bugs, stopping them from becoming pests as well as transmitting or carrying diseases. Others help in pollination and spreading seeds, consuming waste, and recycling nutrients in the soil.

Some bugs play a key role in reducing the number of pests for farmers and gardeners alike. The **minute pirate bug** and the **spined soldier bug** are insatiable eaters of small insects that cause lasting damage to plants. The hungry larvae of parasitic wasps, including the **braconid wasp**, feast on host aphids and caterpillars, removing the need for chemical pesticides that harm the environment. The **ground beetle**

Little helpers

Soil centipede — This centipede feeds on plant-eating insects, such as the slug moth caterpillar.

Cellar spider — The silk web traps *house pests*, and sometimes, other spiders.

Minute pirate bug — Brown-black body

Harvestman — The garden- and home-friendly harvestman has **long, slender legs**.

Ground beetle — Grasshoppers, often disease-carrying, are included in this **beetle's diet**.

Cross orbweaver spider — The insect uses its curved mouthparts to inject a venom, which liquefies the insides of pests, and suck it all out. The sticky web of the spider also **collects pollen that the spider eats**.

Assassin bug — The assassin bug can carry up to **20 dead ants at once**. Dead ants carried on the bug's back provide a unique camouflage.

burrows in soil, allowing air to reach the roots of plants and helping them grow. The presence of some bugs can also be an indication of the health of a habitat. Both the **broad-bodied chaser** and the **banded demoiselle** need a clean water supply to lay eggs, so sightings are a sign that local wetland habitats are thriving.

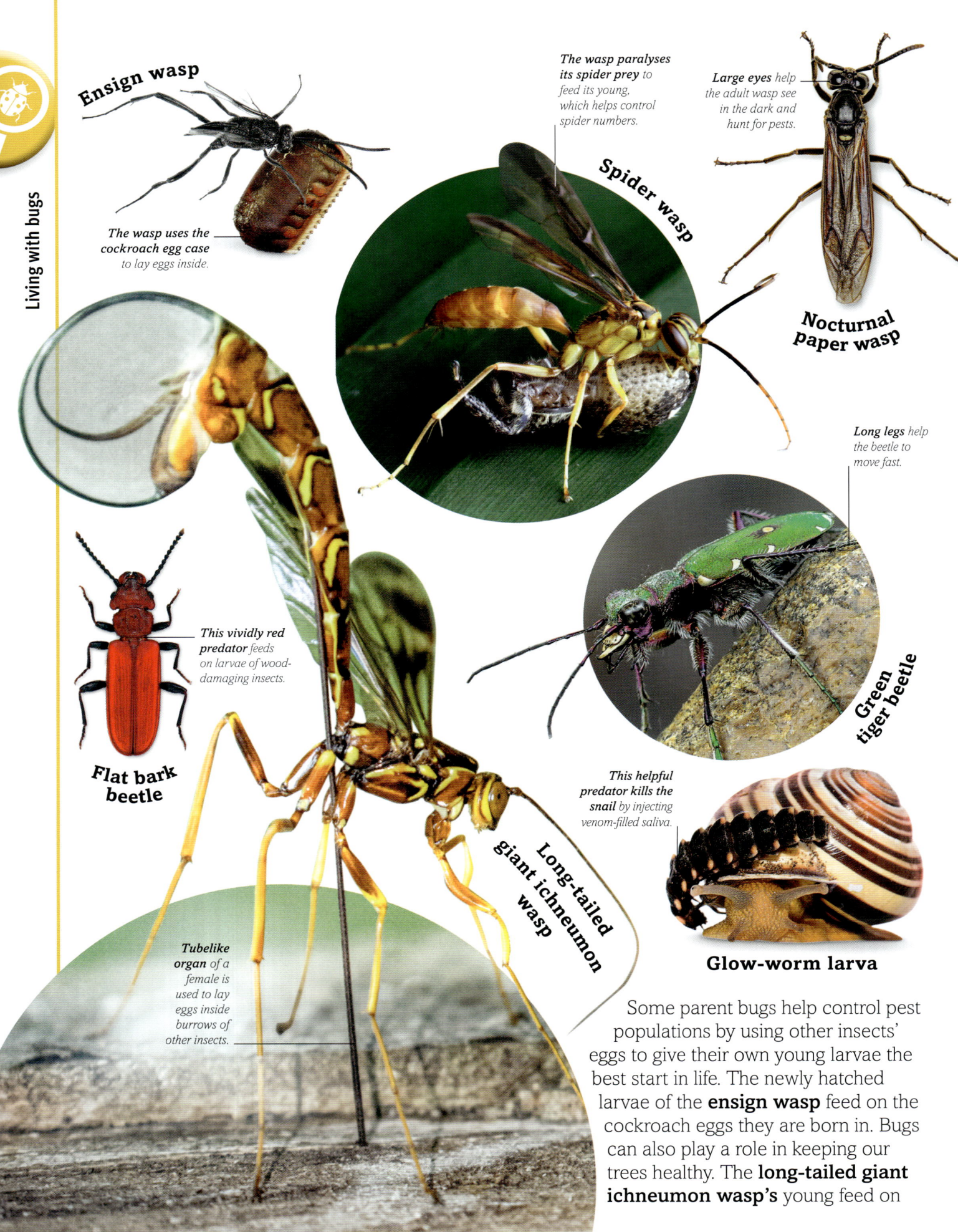

Living with bugs

Ensign wasp
The wasp uses the cockroach egg case to lay eggs inside.

The wasp paralyses its spider prey to feed its young, which helps control spider numbers.

Spider wasp

Large eyes help the adult wasp see in the dark and hunt for pests.

Nocturnal paper wasp

Long legs help the beetle to move fast.

This vividly red predator feeds on larvae of wood-damaging insects.

Flat bark beetle

Green tiger beetle

This helpful predator kills the snail by injecting venom-filled saliva.

Long-tailed giant ichneumon wasp

Glow-worm larva

Tubelike organ of a female is used to lay eggs inside burrows of other insects.

Some parent bugs help control pest populations by using other insects' eggs to give their own young larvae the best start in life. The newly hatched larvae of the **ensign wasp** feed on the cockroach eggs they are born in. Bugs can also play a role in keeping our trees healthy. The **long-tailed giant ichneumon wasp's** young feed on

Sharp, beaklike mouthpart is used to stab pests.

Big-eyed bug

Sweat bee

The black, flat beetle helps control fly population by hunting their larvae.

Underground ant nest lets air into the soil.

This metallic green bee feeds on nectar as well as human sweat.

Devil's coach horse rove beetle

A harvester ant nest can be **1 m (3 ft)** deep and **3.6 m (12 ft)** wide.

Harvester ants

African giant millipede

This millipede can grow up to 30 cm (12 in) in length.

Antennae help sense the smell of decaying animal flesh from afar.

Common sexton beetle

Pale white larvae devour decaying matter, from rotten food to animal waste.

Black soldier fly larvae

the tree-damaging horntail wasp larvae. Similarly, the **flat bark beetle** preys on wood-boring beetle larvae that tunnel into trees. On the other hand, the predatory **green tiger beetle** and its larvae devour bugs that are harmful to plants. Other insects clean up the natural habitat by breaking down waste and restore nutrients to the soil. The **common sexton beetle** buries the remains of small dead animals underground and lay eggs on them. Once they hatch, the beetle's larvae feed on the carcasses. The **African giant millipede** clears the forest floor by eating dead and decaying plants. **Harvester ants** gather seeds and take them on long journeys back to their nests. As seeds are spread along the way, plants grow far and wide. The **sweat bee** and the **nocturnal paper wasp** both carry pollen and help pollinate plants.

Bugs in danger

Crotch's bumble bee — The head of the female is black. EN

American burying beetle — Strong legs allow this beetle to dig into soil and leaf litter. CR

Japanese emperor butterfly — Distinctive bright purple iridescence (shine) on wings is present only in males. NT

Cook Strait giant wētā — At nearly 27 g (1 oz), this bug is one of New Zealand's heaviest insects. VU

Lord Howe Island stick insect — This huge stick insect can grow to the length of an adult human's hand. CR

Kaiser-i-Hind butterfly — The males of this Himalayan butterfly species display a striking yellow patch on each hindwing. NT

The bug population has been on a decline in recent years. A serious threat is habitat loss – when a habitat is damaged or destroyed and can no longer support life. Humans threaten bugs more directly – by keeping them as pets, displaying them on walls, or using chemicals to control pests that end up killing other bugs as well.

As cities are replacing forests and wetlands, many insects are losing their habitats. The population of the **Japanese emperor butterfly** is plummeting due to its habitat loss. Similarly, the **bog fritillary butterfly** and **false ringlet butterfly** all live in wetlands, but many of these landscapes have been drained for human activities. Introducing non-native species of

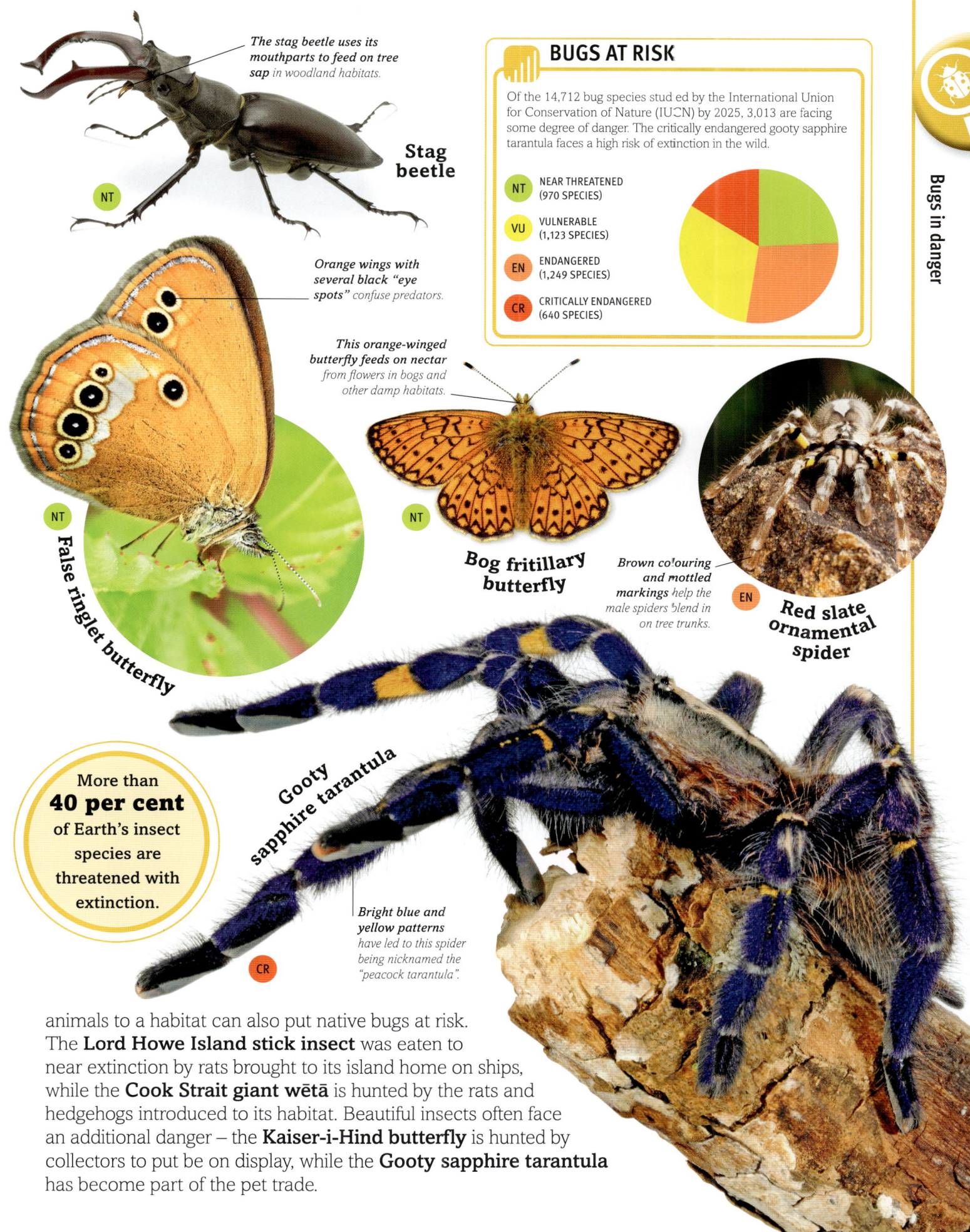

Bugs in danger

The stag beetle uses its mouthparts to feed on tree sap in woodland habitats.

Stag beetle NT

BUGS AT RISK

Of the 14,712 bug species studied by the International Union for Conservation of Nature (IUCN) by 2025, 3,013 are facing some degree of danger. The critically endangered gooty sapphire tarantula faces a high risk of extinction in the wild.

- **NT** NEAR THREATENED (970 SPECIES)
- **VU** VULNERABLE (1,123 SPECIES)
- **EN** ENDANGERED (1,249 SPECIES)
- **CR** CRITICALLY ENDANGERED (640 SPECIES)

Orange wings with several black "eye spots" confuse predators.

False ringlet butterfly NT

This orange-winged butterfly feeds on nectar from flowers in bogs and other damp habitats.

Bog fritillary butterfly NT

Brown colouring and mottled markings help the male spiders blend in on tree trunks.

Red slate ornamental spider EN

More than **40 per cent** of Earth's insect species are threatened with extinction.

Gooty sapphire tarantula CR

Bright blue and yellow patterns have led to this spider being nicknamed the "peacock tarantula".

animals to a habitat can also put native bugs at risk. The **Lord Howe Island stick insect** was eaten to near extinction by rats brought to its island home on ships, while the **Cook Strait giant wētā** is hunted by the rats and hedgehogs introduced to its habitat. Beautiful insects often face an additional danger – the **Kaiser-i-Hind butterfly** is hunted by collectors to put be on display, while the **Gooty sapphire tarantula** has become part of the pet trade.

Living with bugs

Helping bugs

Ecosystems are the communities of living things that interact with each other and their environment. Bugs play important roles in every ecosystem. They pollinate plants and keep pests under control. Gardens can be difficult environments for bugs, as people often like to keep them tidy in a way that would never happen in nature. But you can help them in different ways.

Avoid pesticides ❯ Insects such as wasps and ladybirds, which prey on plant-eating bugs, protect your garden. Avoid using pesticides as the chemicals in them will kill the bugs and damage the plants.

Flowering shrubs ❯ When choosing what to plant in your garden, try to pick flowering plants and shrubs. Flowers provide pollen and nectar, which are important food sources for a wide range of bugs.

Create water stations ❯ Bugs need water just like any other animal. Create a water station to give the bugs in your garden a place to drink. It doesn't have to be big – a shallow pond lined with stones is enough.

REWILDING
Returning areas of land to a more natural state is known as rewilding. Some farmers are now rewilding their land and adopting farming techniques that are less harmful for bugs and other animals. Rewilding can work in smaller spaces too – even small changes to your garden can make it a much better habitat for bugs.

Make compost › Don't throw away your vegetable peelings and plant waste in the bin, but instead use them to make compost in your garden. Adding compost to the soil makes it richer in nutrients. Compost heaps provide shelter and food for many different bugs, which eat the waste and break it down.

Grow native flowers › Try to choose plants and flowers that grow naturally in your area – these are native to the region. They are already part of the local ecosystem, and will feed the bugs better than exotic ones.

More ways to help

There are a number of simple things you can do to help the bugs around you. Some of these examples can work even if your garden is very small, if the adults in your home like to keep their outdoor space tidy, or if you only have a window ledge to grow plants on.

TURN OFF THE LIGHTS
Unnatural light can confuse nocturnal bugs, distracting them from their tasks. Try to make sure to turn off any outdoor lights that are not needed after sunset.

GARDEN IN A POT
Even in a small courtyard garden or a window box, you can grow plants that attract and nourish bugs.

MOW LESS
Grass is an important bug habitat. Cutting it less often means they have more food to eat and more shelter.

PROVIDE SHADE
Bugs need somewhere to hide from the heat of the Sun. You could create shade boxes, or cover an area with cloth to create shade.

CREATE A SAFE SPACE
Many bugs nest underneath wood and rocks. Lay pieces of wood or stone flat on the ground, and make resting spaces by adding dead plants and dried grass.

Logs and litter › Don't keep your garden too tidy! Let leaves and any fallen pieces of wood stay on the ground around your plants, to provide shelter and food for all sorts of bugs.

Glossary

Arachnid
An animal with a pincer-like mouth and four pairs of legs, such as spiders and scorpions.

Arthropod
An animal with a hard outer skeleton, no backbone, and jointed legs, including insects, spiders, and myriapods.

Breeding
The biological process by which living things reproduce.

Brood
A family of newborn bugs that hatched at the same time.

Carcass
The dead body of an animal.

Cellulose
The strong material that keeps the stems of plants upright.

Cerci
A pair of sensory structures sticking out from the rear end of some bugs.

Chrysalis
The protective outer layer that covers a butterfly pupa during metamorphosis.

Colony
A group of bugs or other creatures that live together.

Compound eye
A type of eye in adult bugs, made up of hundreds of tiny lenses to give excellent vision.

Dimorphism
The differences between males and females of the same species, such as size and colouring.

Ecosystem
A shared environment where all living and non-living things exist naturally together in a specific area.

Elytra
A set of hardened wings that protect the delicate flight wings of beetles.

Endangered
A plant or animal species that is at risk of going extinct.

Enzyme
A natural protein substance that speeds up chemical reactions inside the body.

Exoskeleton
The protective external skeleton of an arthropod.

Extinct
Plants or animals that have died out, leaving no members of the species alive on Earth.

Foliage
The leaves of a tree or other plant.

Forcipules
The pincer-like front legs that centipedes use to inject venom into prey.

Forewings
An insect's front set of wings.

Fungus
A living thing that produces spores to spread itself around, such as a mushroom or yeast.

Gill
The breathing organ of some aquatic insects that lets them take oxygen from the water.

Gland
A small organ in the body that produces substances such as saliva or silk.

Habitat
The environment where a species usually lives, such as a desert or forest.

Hindwings
An insect's back set of wings.

Infestation
A large number of species that take over an area where they are not wanted, for example, cockroaches in a kitchen.

Infrared
A type of energy that cannot be seen, but is felt in the form of heat.

Invertebrate
An animal that does not have a backbone.

Iridescence
A rainbow effect seen in many bugs when light bends as it hits their bodies.

Life cycle
The different stages through which a species passes, from the beginning of its life until it reaches adulthood, reproduces, and dies.

Mandible
The sharp jaw of a bug used to bite prey and chew food.

Metamorphosis
A biological process in which an insect undergoes a dramatic physical change after hatching.

Microbe
A tiny living thing, such as bacteria and viruses, that cannot be seen with the naked eye. Microbes can only be seen with a microscope.

Migration
The movement of a population from one location to another. The journey is typically taken to find warmer weather, food, or suitable breeding conditions.

Mimicry
When one species takes on the appearance of another in order to appear more threatening. This deters predators and helps them survive.

Moulting
The process of shedding a layer of skin so a bug can grow bigger.

Mutualism
A relationship between two living things in which both species benefit from each other. For example, ants protect aphids against hungry prey in exchange for their sweet honeydew.

Myriapod
An arthropod with many pairs of legs, such as a centipede or millipede.

Nutrient
A useful substance taken from food that living things need for energy and growth.

Nymph
The young, wingless form of an insect.

Ocellus
A simple eye in many bugs that can detect light but not form images. Also refers to eyelike markings on butterfly wings to deter predators.

Ommatidium
Each tiny individual unit that makes up an insect's compound eye.

Ovipositor
A hollow tube-like organ used by some insects to lay eggs.

Palp
The limb-like extension by the mouth of some insects used to touch and taste food.

Paralyse
The effect of making prey immovable and powerless by injecting venom.

Parasitic
The process by which one organism lives on or close to another organism to feed off it, but usually without actually killing it.

Parasitoid
A parasite that uses the body of another living thing as a host to grow its young larvae inside. This process eventually kills the host.

Pest
A type of bug that farmers and gardeners consider harmful because it eats crops, damages plants, or spreads diseases.

Pesticide
A harmful chemical that humans use to kill bugs.

Pheromone
The special scent given off by members of the same species to each other. This can be used to mark a territory or attract a mate.

Poisonous
When something contains a toxic substance that can harm or kill a living creature that eats it.

Pollen
Tiny grains produced by flowers that contain the male cells necessary to make seeds.

Pollinate
The process of delivering pollen to the female cells of a flower to help the plant reproduce.

Predator
An animal that kills other animals for food.

Proboscis
The long mouthparts of many insects used for feeding.

Pronotum
The protective plate that covers the upper part of the thorax of some insects.

Pupa
A stage during the life cycle of some insects when the young larva turns into an adult.

Range
The surrounding area within which a bug travels and feeds.

Reproduction
The natural process by which adults of a species produce offspring.

Scavenger
A species that searches for any leftovers, waste, or animal remains to feed on.

Segmented
A body of a bug that is divided into multiple separate sections.

Seta
One of the bristly hairs that some bugs use to catch prey, move around, or detect changes in their environment.

Species
A scientific grouping of animals that all look alike and mate with one another to create offspring.

Spinneret
A special organ of some bugs that produces silk.

Spiracle
The hole in a bug's outer skeleton that allows it to breathe.

Stimulus
The surrounding smells, sounds, and sights detected by a creature.

Stinger
The sharp extension on some bugs that can deliver a poisonous and painful injury.

Stridulation
The rubbing together of a bug's body parts to create a loud noise. It is common in crickets and grasshoppers.

Subterranean
Refers to a species that exists underground.

Synchronous
Refers to an action or activity that happens between different members of the same species at the same time, such as fireflies flashing their lights.

Thorax
The central part of an insect's body to which its legs and wings are attached.

Ultraviolet (UV)
A type of light that bugs can detect and use to travel in the dark and find food.

Venomous
Refers to a species that produces a poisonous bite or sting.

Wingspan
The measurement of a winged creature, from the tip of one wing to the tip of the other.

Index

Main topics are shown in **bold** page numbers.

A

abdomens 12
acrobat ants 92–93
African giant millipedes 14–15, 165
African jewel beetles 12–13
African termites 59
alderflies 131
alkali bees 86, 87
Alpine bumblebees 66
Alpine longhorn beetles 122, 123
altitudes 67
American bumblebees 87
American cockroaches 25, 31
ant-mimicking treehoppers 98, 99
antennae 13, 16, **24–25**
antlions 58, 59, 130, 131
ants **90–91**, 146, 147, 165
    anatomy 31, 115
    behaviour 80–81, 92–93, 102
    colonies 60, 61, 88
    habitats 65, 66, 69, 74, 158
    venomous 143, 144–145
aphids 120, 127, 146
aquatic bugs 51, 76–77, 154–155
Arabian fat-tailed scorpions 64
arachnids 7, 12
    see also mites; scorpions; spiders; ticks
architectural nests **60–61**
arthropods 7, **8–9**, 12
Asian ant mantises 98, 99
Asian forest scorpions 140, 141
Asian giant hornets 88, 89
Asian green lacewings 130
Asian honeybees 89
Asian lady beetles 156
assassin bugs 68, 69, 124, 163
    feeding 103, 120, 133
Atlas moth 42
Australian giant burrowing cockroaches 15
azure damselflies 48, 49

B

bald-faced hornets 60, 61
banded demoiselle damselflies 48, 49, 162, 163
barber pole grasshoppers 116, 117
bark beetles 47, 60–61, 164, 165
bark scorpions 96–97
barking spiders 70, 71
bat louse flies 150, 151
Batman hoverflies 82, 83
bed bugs 158
bee beetles 83
bees **86–87**, 142, 147, 165
    anatomy 17, 24
    feeding 149
    habitats 56, 66–67, 75
    pollination 82–83
    see also bumblebees; honeybees
beetles **44–47**, 143, 162–165, 166–167
    anatomy 12–13, 14–15, 30–31, 32–33, 52–53

beetles *cont.*
    aquatic 76, 77, 127
    behaviour 83, 96, 102–103, 105, 147
    feeding 84–85, 122, 123, 148–149
    habitats 59, 64–65, 66, 68, 74–75, 159
    nests 60–61
    predators and prey 128–129, 132, 133
    senses 17, 18, 24–25
    see also ladybirds
bioluminescence 106–107, 114
birch sawflies 94, 95
bird cherry ermine moths 62–63
biscuit beetles 74–75
black beauty stick insects 103
black blowflies 156, 157
black oil beetles 143, 148, 149
black widow spiders 71
black-and-yellow garden spiders 157
blowflies 150–151, 156, 157, 159
blue carpenter bees 86, 87
blue death-feigning beetles 64, 65
blue emperor dragonflies 48
blue jewel damselflies 48
blue tiger butterflies 82, 83
blue-winged eurybia butterflies 39
body language 115
Boehm's burrowing scorpions 58, 59
bog fritillary butterflies 166, 167
bombardier beetles 45, 133
booklice 14, 159
bothriurus scorpions 140
braconid wasps 151, 162
Brazilian wandering spiders 30, 31, 71
bristly millipedes 28, 29
broad-bodied chaser dragonflies 162, 163
broad-leaved willow sawflies 94
brown lacewings 130
brown marmorated stink bugs 105
buckeye butterflies 110, 111
buff-tailed bumblebees 30, 31
buffalo treehoppers 99
bug hunting 7
bugs (arthropods) 7, **8–9**, 12
bugs, true *see* true bugs
bulldog ants 91
bullet ants 90, 91, 143
bumblebee millipedes 29
bumblebees 66, 82, 87, 166
    anatomy 17, 30, 150
    nests 60, 151
    as prey 136–137
burrowing wolf spiders 58–59
butterflies **36–39**, 40–41, 166–167
    anatomy 19, 30, 32, 120
    behaviour 23, 82–83, 98
    habitats 57, 66–67, 68, 156
    migration 110, 111, 112–113

C

caddisflies 76, 77, 105
camel spiders 65, 132
camouflage 100–101, 128–129
    mimicry 80, 98–99, 135
carder bees 82–83, 87, 142–143
carnivorous bugs **126–127**, 128–129, 132–133, 136–137

carpenter ants 90, 91
carpenter bees 66–67, 83, 86–87, 142
carpet beetles 46, 47, 159
caterpillars 40–41, 143, 146, 162
    behaviour 22–23, 99
    feeding 74–75, 122–123, 126–127, 148
    nests 61, 62–63
cat fleas 150, 151, 158, 159
cathedral termites 60, 61, 88–89
cave beetles 59
cave crickets 116, 117
cave harvestman 58, 59
centipedes **28–29**, 31, 96, 97
    feeding 132–133, 163
    habitats 58, 65, 157
Central European bicoloured ants 74, 75
cerci 17
chafers 45, 105, 122, 123
Chan's megasticks 15
chemical signals (pheromones) 25, 115
Chinese mantises 126, 127
Chinese red-headed centipedes 28, 29
cicadas 66, 108, 124, 125
    anatomy 18, 19, 22–23
cinnabar moths 43
citrus leafminers 123
classification **8–9**
clothes moths 74–75, 148–149, 159
cockchafers 105
cockroaches 102, 103, 146, 147
    anatomy 15, 22, 23, 31
    habitats 58, 65, 158
    prehistoric 26, 27
    senses 17, 25
Colombian thick-tailed scorpions 140, 141
colonies 80–81, **88–89**, 144–145
colours **32–33**, 34–35
communication 22–23, **114–115**
compost heaps 168
convergent ladybugs 111
Cook Strait giant wētās 166, 167
crab spiders 32–33, 70, 126, 128–129
crane flies 104
crickets 13, 58, 102, **116–117**
    prehistoric 27
    sounds 22, 23, 114
crimson speckled footmen moths 32, 33
cross orbweaver spiders 70, 71, 163
"cuckoo spit" 72–73

D

damselflies 20–21, **48–49**, 162
    see also dragonflies
dance flies 16
deathstalker scorpions 140, 141
desert centipedes 28–29, 65
desert cockroaches 65
desert habitats 57, **64–65**
desert locusts 109
desert millipedes 64
desert scorpions 31, 140
diets 120–121, 122–123, **148–149**
    see also carnivorous bugs
diseases 7, 154, 162

diving bell spiders 76, 77, 139
Douglas fir glow-worm 25
dragonflies 26, **48–49**, 50–51, 162
    anatomy 18, 30
    behaviour 7, 111
    see also damselflies
dragon millipedes 28, 29
dragon-headed katydids 102
dung beetles 7, 64, 65, 149
    behaviour 96, 104, 105

EF

earwigs 96, 97, 156
eastern subterranean termites 158, 159
eastern toe-biter bugs 124, 125
ebony jewelwing damselflies 48, 49
ecosystems 56, 154–155, 168–169
eggs 80, 92–93, **96–97**, 130
    in lifecycles 40, 50
eight-spotted crab spiders 32, 33
elephant beetles 14, 68, 69
elephant hawk-moths 24, 42
emerald ash borer beetles 46
emerald cockroach wasps 69, 146, 147
emperor dragonflies 18, 30, 48
endangered species 167
ensign wasps 164
European antlions 131
European glow-worms 53, 102–103
European June beetles 105
European mole crickets 22, 58
European red wood ants 144–145
European scorpionflies 126, 127
European wasps 142
European wool carder bees 82, 83
extreme climates 64
extreme sizes **14–15**
eyes 16, 17, **18–19**, 20–21
fabulous longhorn beetles 24, 25
fairyfly wasps 15
false ringlet butterflies 166, 167
farming ecosystems 154–155
feather-horned beetles 24, 25
feet 17
females **52–53**
field crickets 23
fig wasps 83, 147
fire ants 91
fire beetles 17
firebrats 74
fireflies 104–105, 106–107, 114, 156
fishflies 131
flat bark beetles 47, 165
flat-backed millipedes 29
fleas 67
    cat fleas 150, 151, 158, 159
flies
    anatomy 53, 99, 120, 132
    behaviour 82, 97, 99, 104–105
    eggs and larvae 149, 162, 165
    habitats 75, 111, 156, 159
    hunting techniques 126, 127, 136–137
    parasitic 150, 151
    senses 16, 18–19
fog-basking darkling beetles 64, 65
forest scorpions 140, 141
forests 56–57, 68–69

formic acid 144
four-spotted chaser dragonflies 49, 111
four-spotted palpita moths 42, 43
fruit flies 16, 75
fungi 61, 146, 147

G

garden bugs **156–157**
German cockroach 158
giant African millipede 14–15
giant dead leaf mantises 135
giant desert hairy scorpions 140
giant forest scorpions 141
giant honeybees 60, 89
giant Malayan stick insects 69
giant mesquite bugs 124, 125
giant owl butterflies 68, 98, 99
giant scoliid wasps 94, 95
giant turtle ants 90, 91
giant water bugs 77, 80, 97, 132
giant wood spider 70, 71
giraffe weevils 24, 25, 52
glacier midges 66
glow-worms 59, 102–103, 127, 164
  anatomy 25, 53
gnats 27
golden silk orb-weaver spiders 69
Goliath beetles 15, 44, 68
Goliath birdeater spiders 15
gooty sapphire tarantulas 167
grass yellow butterflies 36, 110, 111
grasshoppers 13, 67, **116–117**
great diving beetles 76, 77, 127
great golden digger wasps 133
great orange tip butterflies 36, 37
green huntsman spiders 71
green lacewings 105, 130, 156, 157
green longhorn moths 25
green metallic sweat bees 87
green peacock swallowtail butterflies 36–37
green tiger beetles 164, 165
greengrocer cicadas 124
Grote's bertholdia moths 22, 23
ground beetles 162–163
gypsy moths 104

HI

hairs 17
halteres 16
harlequin bugs 125
harvester ants 90, 91, 165
harvestmen 58, 59, 96, 163
Hawaiian eupithecia caterpillars 126, 127
hawk-moths 22, 24, 42
heads 13
herbivores **122–123**
Hercules moths 52, 53
Himalayan jumping spiders 67
honeybees 17, 86–87, 115
  nests 56, 60, 88, 89
  swarms 108, 109
honeycomb structure 87
hornets 19, 95, 105
  nests 60, 61, 88, 89
horrid king assassin bugs 68, 69
horseflies 18, 19, 30
horsehead grasshoppers 116, 117
house bugs **158–159**
houseflies 159
hoverflies 82–83, 99, 111, 156
human lice 149
humans, and bugs 154–155, 162–165
  habitats 74–75, 156–159, 160–161
  helping bugs 168–169

hunting techniques **120–121**, 126–127, 136–137
huntsman spiders 71
ice crawlers 66, 67
ichneumon wasps 164
imperial blue caterpillars 146
imperial hairstreak butterflies 38, 39
imperial moths **100–101**
imperial orchid bees 83
Indian domino cockroaches 102, 103
Indian honeybees 86, 87
Indian meal moths 159
Indian sunbeam butterflies 38
insects 7, 8, **12–13**
interactions **146–147**
  see also carnivorous bugs
iron cross blister beetles 44, 45

JKL

jack jumper ants 90–91, 143
jagged ambush bugs 132
Japanese beetles 122, 123
Japanese emperor butterflies 166
Japanese giant hornets 95
Japanese orbweaver spiders 70, 71
Joro spiders 71
jumping spiders 67, 121, 157
  anatomy 17, 19, 32
jungle nymphs 14, 52–53
Kaiser-i-Hind butterflies 166, 167
katydids 116, 117
  behaviour 23, 102
  prehistoric 27
kissing bugs 103
lacewings 105, **130–131**, 156, 157
ladybird mimic spiders 99
ladybirds 45–47, 111, 156
  feeding 120, 127
lantern bugs 57, 69
lanternflies 33, 124
larvae 16, 80, 147, 164–165
  aquatic 76, 77, 127
  feeding 122–123, 127, 132, 148–149
  habitats 58, 59
  lifecycles 40, 50
  parasitic 149, 150–151
leaf insects 98, 99
leaf nests 60
leafcutter ants 88, 102, 147
leafcutter bees 86, 87
leafhoppers 122, 123, 125
legs 13
lice 14, 149, 159
lifecycles **40–41**, **50–51**
lights 106–107, 114
lobed Argiope spiders 53
locusts 109, 110
long-legged ants 90
long-tailed giant ichneumon wasps 164
long-tailed skipper butterflies 38, 39
longhorn beetles 24, 25, 46, 123
Lord Howe Island stick insects 166, 167
luna moths 104

M

Madagascan moon moths 43
Madagascan sunset moths 68, 69
Madagascar hissing cockroaches 22, 23
Malayan jungle nymphs 52–53, 69
Malaysian leaf insects 98, 99
males **52–53**

mantises 98, 99, **134–135**
  anatomy 13, 18, 33, 53
  hunting techniques 121, 126, 127
marble gall wasps 60, 61
Maricopa harvester ants 90, 91
marmalade hoverflies 111
masked devil cicadas 22, 23
masked hunter bugs 124
mayflies 19, 104, 160–161
metallic shield bugs 124, 125
metalmark butterflies 38, 39
metamorphosis 40–41, 50–51, 63, 120
Mexican redknee tarantulas 70
Mexican treehoppers 69
midges 66, 76
migrant hoverflies 99
migration **110–111**, 112–113
milkweed bugs 110, 111
millipedes 14–15, **28–29**, 30, 165
  habitats 57, 58, 64–65
  prehistoric 26, 27
mimicry 80, **98–99**, 100–101, 135
minute pirate bugs 14, 162, 163
mites 147, 150, 157
  anatomy 12, 14, 15
mole crickets 13, 22, 58, 116
monarch butterflies 37, 112–113
moon moths 25, 43
mosquito bugs 122
mosquitoes 16, 105, 108–109, 147
  habitats 77, 156
moths **42–43**, 147
  anatomy 22–23, 30, 32–33, 52
  antennae 16, 24, 25
  behaviour 98–99, 100–101, 102–103, 104
  caterpillars 61, 62–63, 122, 143, 148
  habitats 68, 69, 75, 156, 159
mountain habitats **66–67**
mountain ringlet butterflies 66, 67
mouthparts 13, 120
  see also proboscises
mud pots 60
mutually beneficial relationships 146–147, 162–165
myriapods 7, 9, 28
  see also centipedes; millipedes

NO

nests 56, **60–61**, 88–89, 144
  see also webs
New Guinea stag beetles 52
New Zealand glow-worms 59, 127
nocturnal insects **102–103**, 104–105, 106–107
noises **22–23**, 114
northern plushback hoverflies 156, 157
Norwegian cuckoo bumblebees 150, 151
nursery web spiders 70, 71, 138, 139
nymphs 50, 76, 149
  stick insects 14, 52–53
  true bugs 34–35, 72–73, 124
oak lace bugs 122
oak processionary caterpillars 123
oblong-winged katydids 116, 117
ocelli 18
Old World swallowtail butterflies 37
ommatidia 18
orb-weaver spiders 69, 70–71, 157, 163
orchid bees 83, 87
orchid mantises 18, 134, 135
organ pipe mud dauber wasps 96, 97
owlflies 131

P

Pacific giant centipedes 96, 97, 133
painted lady butterflies 19, 111
palps 16
Pandora sphinx moths 30, 31
paper wasps 89, 94–95, 164, 165
parasitic wasps 146–147, 149, **150–151**
parasitoid wasps 133, 162
parental care 80, **96–97**
patterns **32–33**
peacock butterflies 22, 23, 36–37
peacock spiders 32
peanut-headed lanternflies 124, 125
periander metalmark butterflies 38, 39
periodical cicadas 22, 23, 108
pesticides 168
pharaoh ants 158
pheromones 115
pill bugs 156, 157
pill millipedes 29
pink toe tarantulas 68, 69
pit-trapping antlions 131
planthoppers 33, 99, 125
plants 62–63, 72–73, 98, 147
  bug-friendly 168–169
plume moths 98, 99
pollen 83
pollinators 6, 81, **82–83**, 84–85
pond skaters 76, 77
pond wolf spiders 77
predators 126–127, 128–129, **132–133**, 136–137
prehistoric bugs **26–27**
proboscises 16, 120, 125
procession ants 91
ptiliid beetles 14, 15
pupa 40, 81
purple emperor butterflies 32

QR

Queen Alexandra's birdwing butterflies 36, 37
queen ants 81
queen butterflies 110, 111
Queen of Spain fritillary butterflies 67
rainbow scarab beetles 47
rainbow stag beetles 44, 45
rainforest habitats 56–57, **68–69**
red cracker butterflies 37
red dwarf honeybees 88, 89
red flat bark beetles 47
red milkweed beetles 46
red net winged beetles 44, 45
red poultry mites 150
red speckled jewel beetles 47
red wood ants 88, 91, 144–145
red-legged golden orb-web weaver spiders 157
red-striped leafhoppers 122, 123
regal jumping spiders 19, 157
regal purple tip butterflies 36, 37
resh cicadas 23
rewilding 168–169
rhinoceros beetles 68, 105
robber flies 127, 133, 136–137
rose chafers 45, 122, 123
rusty spider wasps 94, 95

S

sacred scarab dung beetles 64, 65
saucer bugs 77
savannahs 57
sawflies **94–95**, 123

Index

scales 123, 125
scarab beetles 47, 64, 65, 103
scarlet tiger moths 43
scorpionflies 52, 126, 127, 132
scorpions 26, **140–141**
 behaviour 31, 96–97
 habitats 58, 59, 64, 77
seed dispersal 154
senses **16–17**, 58
 antennae 13, 16, **24–25**
 eyes and sight **18–19**, 20–21
sensors 17
setae 17, 82
seventeen-year periodical cicadas 22, 23
sexton beetles 46, 96–97, 147, 165
sexual dimorphism 52
shield bugs 34–35, 124, 125
shield mantises 53, 134, 135
Sierra luminous millipedes 28, 29
Sierra Nevada ice crawlers 66, 67
silk 62–63, 138–139
silkworms 16, 17
silver-spotted skipper butterflies 38
silverfish 74, 158, 159
six-spot burnet moths 43
size, extremes **14–15**
skimmer dragonflies 49
skipper butterflies 38, 39
small elephant hawk-moth 24
snakeflies 131
snow fleas 67
social insects **88–89**, 143, 151
soil centipede 58, 163
soil health 6, 169
soldier ants 81
soldier bugs 162
sounds **22–23**, 114, 116
southern flannel moths 143
Spanish fly beetles 44, 45
Spanish moon moths 43
speed 30–31
spider mites 14, 15
spiders **70–71**, 163, 167
 anatomy 12, 15, 30–31, 32, 53
 behaviour 96–97, 99
 habitats 59, 65, 67, 68–69, 76–77, 157
 hunting techniques 121, 126–127, 128–129, 132
 and parasites 146, 147
 prehistoric 27
 senses 17, 19, 115
 webs 138–139
spider wasps 94, 95, 164
spinybacked orbweaver spiders 70, 71
spittlebugs 72–73
splay-footed carpenter bees 66, 67
spoonwing lacewings 130
spotted lanternflies 33
spotted maize beetles 84–85
spotted snakeflies 131
spotted tortoise beetles 46
spring dumbledor beetles 44, 45
stag beetles 25, 44–45, 52, 167
stalk-eyed flies 18–19
steel blue cricket hunter wasps 94, 95
stick insects 99, 103, 166
 anatomy 14, 52–53
 habitats 69, 76, 77
stink bugs 105, 162
stoneflies 76, 77
Sudanese gossamerwing damselflies 49
sunburst diving beetles 33
swallowtail butterflies 37
swarms **108–109**, 160–161
sweat bees 87, 165
swift river cruiser dragonflies 49
symbiosis 146–147, 162–165

T

tailed jay butterflies 40–41
tarantula hawk spider wasps 95, 142
tarantulas 68, 69, 70, 167
Tasmanian peacock spiders 32
tawny mining bees 82
tea mosquito bugs 122
termites
 behaviour 97, 146
 colonies 88–89, 60–61
 feeding 148, 149
 habitats 56, 59, 67, 158–159
 swarms 108, 109
thoraxes 12
thorn bugs 98
thorn treehoppers 125
threatened species 167
thrips 14, 15, 149
ticks 151
tiger beetles 45, 105, 164, 165
 anatomy 18, 30, 132
tiger moths 43, 103, 156
tit butterflies 38
titan beetles 15, 105
tobacco hornworm caterpillars 22, 23
trapdoor spiders 126, 127
treehoppers 69, 98, 99, 125
tropical rainforest habitats 56–57, **68–69**
true bugs 122, **124–125**, 162, 163
 anatomy 14, 32, 98
 aquatic 77, 132
 behaviour 96, 103, 105, 110
 habitats 57, 68, 69, 158
tsetse flies 97
tundra 57
twenty-two-spot ladybird 46, 47

UVWY

ultraviolet (UV) light 140
underground dwellers **58–59**
urban dwellers **74–75**
venomous bugs 132, **142–143**, 145
vine weevils 75
vulnerable species 167
Wallace's giant bees 86, 87
warrior wasps 143
wasps 15, 19, **94–95**, 146–147
 behaviour 83, 96–97, 105, 165
 colonies 60, 61, 88, 89
 habitats 64, 69, 156
 hunting techniques 126, 133, 142–143, 164
 parasitic 150, 151, 162
water boatmen 23, 77
water measurers 76, 77
water scorpions 77
water stations 168
water stick insects 77
water striders 17
webs 62–63, 115, **138–139**
weevils 46, 47, 75
 anatomy 24, 25, 52
western honeybees 86, 108, 109
wētās 116, 166
wheel bugs 124
white-barred emperor butterflies 37
white-M hairstreak butterflies 38, 39
white-tailed bumblebees 82
wings 13, 51
wolf spiders 30, 96, 97, 157
 habitats 59, 77
woodlands 154–155
worker ants 81, 144–145
wrinkled grasshoppers 117
yellow dung flies 126, 127
Yellow Monday cicadas 18, 19
yellow-spotted millipedes 28, 29

ACKNOWLEDGMENTS

Dorling Kindersley would like to thank the following people for their help with making the book: Bharti Bedi and Abhijit Dutta for editing; Geetika Bhandari and Rahul Paarcha for picture research; Manpreet Kaur and Samrajkumar S for picture credit work; Jagtar Singh for hires work; Pawan Kumar, Rakesh Kumar, and Dheeraj Singh for DTP work; Hazel Beynon for proofreading; and Elizabeth Wise for indexing.

The publisher would like to thank the following for their kind permission to reproduce their photographs:
(Key: a-above; b-below/bottom; c-centre; f-far; l-left; r-right; t-top)

1 Adobe Stock: Rolf Müller. **2 Getty Images / iStock:** Liliboas (tl, tc). **2–3 Shutterstock.com:** Conscarsch (c). **3 Alamy Stock Photo:** Blickwinkel / B. Trapp (bl); Jonathan Tichon (c); George Grall (bc); Nature Picture Library / Gabriel Rojo (br). **Dreamstime.com:** Argenlant (tr); Paul Reeves (tl). **4 Adobe Stock:** Alessandro Grandini (br). **Dreamstime.com:** Floriankittemann (tc). **5 Alamy Stock Photo:** Blickwinkel / F. Hecker (br). **Depositphotos Inc** Cheattha (c). **Dreamstime.com:** Amwu (bc); Catocala7 (tr); Faunuslsd (cr). **Getty Images / iStock:** Antagain (cra); JUN2 (bl). **6 Dreamstime.com:** Vladvitek (cb). **Getty Images / iStock:** Aleksey Karpenko (crb). **7 Adobe Stock:** Liubov Kartashova (cr); Sandris Veveris (cla); Wayhome.studio (c/ Tab). **Alamy Stock Photo:** Eng Wah Teo (cra); Jim Corwin (cl). **Dreamstime.com:** Musat Christian (c); Tatiana Kulagina (ca); Duncan Noakes (crb). **Getty Images / iStock:** Pavol Klimek (cb); Yurikr (cb). **8 Alamy Stock Photo:** Blickwinkel / B. Trapp (crb). **Annual Reviews:** Vol. 63:31-45 (Volume publication date January 2018) https://doi.org/10.1146/annurev-ento-020117-043348 (c) (Insect Pie Chart). **Dreamstime.com:** Artushfoto (cb); Nymphalyda (bl); Sailorr (bc); Gordzam (bc/Mosquito); Daniel Prudek (br). **9 Adobe Stock:** Macronatura.es (cla, bc/Aphid). **Alamy Stock Photo:** Piotr Naskrecki / Minden Pictures (crb). **Dreamstime.com:** Chrisp543 (br); Melinda Fawver (cr); Danut Vieru (cb); Rudmer Zwerver (cb); Henrikhl (bl); Domiciano Pablo Romero Franco (bc). **10–11 Shutterstock.com:** Fendercapture. **12–13 Alamy Stock Photo:** Nature Picture Library / Chris Mattison (c). **14–15 Alamy Stock Photo:** Anka Agency International (b). **14 Alamy Stock Photo:** Dorling Kindersley ltd (cr); The History Collection (fcl); Piemags / Nature (clb/Psocid). **Dreamstime.com:** Palex66 (clb); Yael Weiss (fclb). **Getty Images / iStock:** Tomasz Klejdysz (cl). **Shutterstock. com:** Talia Maldonado (cla); Protasov AN (cb). **15 Alamy Stock Photo:** Blickwinkel (cra). **Dreamstime.com:** Alslutsky (crb); Vasyl Helevachuk (r); Amwu (cla). **16 Alamy Stock Photo:** Apurv Jadhav (ca); Ed Brown Wildlife (cb). **Dreamstime.com:** Isselee (tl); Roblan (clb). **Getty Images:** David Spears FRPS FRMS (cra). **Science Photo Library:** Eye Of Science (c); Hakan Kvarnstrom (cl); Wim Van Egmond (crb). **Shutterstock.com:** Cosmin Manci (cr); Ozgur Kerem Bulur (ca). **16–17 Science Photo Library:** Eye Of Science (t). **17 Adobe Stock:** Macronatura.es (c). **Alamy Stock Photo:** Andrè Skonieczny / F1online Digitale Bildagentur Gmbh (crb/Bee); Piemags / Nature (ca). **Dreamstime.com:** C Sphillipson (br); Dmitry Knorre (tc); Isselee (clb). **Getty Images:** David Spears FRPS FRMS (cl). **naturepl.com:** Barry Mansell (cr). **Science Photo Library:** Anne Weston, Em Stp, The Francis Crick Institute (cb); Dennis Kunkel Microscopy (tr); Eye Of Science (cra); Leonard Lessin (crb). **18 Alamy Stock Photo:** Denis Crawford (crb). **Dreamstime.com:** Lkpro555 (cra). **Getty Images / iStock:** RasmusAllesoee (clb). **Science Photo Library:** Steve Gschmeissner (ca). **Shutterstock.com:** Ireneusz Waledzik (cla). **18–19 Dreamstime.com:** Parkpoom4 (tc). **Shutterstock.com:** TuanTranPG (b). **19 Adobe Stock:** Gerry (cl). **Alamy Stock Photo:** imageBROKER.com / Matthias Lenke (tr); Steve Taylor ARPS (cr); Papilio / Robert Pickett (crb). **20–21 Alamy Stock Photo:** Biosphoto / Alberto Ghizzi Panizza. **22 Alamy Stock Photo:** John Abott / Nature Picture Library (ca); John Abbott (ca); Maximilian Weinzierl (cl); Malcolm Schuyl (cr); MYN / Lily Kumpe (clb). **22–23 Adobe Stock:** Panosud360 (c). **Dreamstime. com:** Melinda Fawver (cb). **23 Alamy Stock Photo:** Blickwinkel / Hecker (crb); MYN / Lily Kumpe (cl); MYN / JP Lawrence (cr). **Alamy Stock Photo:** Brett Hondow (cra); Gradts (tl); Viter8 (tr); Zhbampton (cla). **24 Adobe Stock:** Andre (cb); Wrightouthere (cl); Imagebroker (tr). **Dreamstime.com:** Javarman (cr). **naturepl.com:** Thomas Marent (crb). **25 Adobe Stock:** Denis (cr). **Alamy Stock Photo:** Alex Hyde (cl); Phil Degginger (tr); Malcolm Schuyl (cra). **Dreamstime. com:** South12th (crb). **Getty Images / iStock:** Dragi52 (tl). **26 123RF.com:** Corey A Ford (cr). **Alamy Stock Photo:** Corbin17 (cra); The Natural History Museum (cla, crb); Minden Pictures / Albert Lleal (tr); Science Photo Library / Mark Garlick (cb). **27 Alamy Stock Photo:** John Cancalosi (clb); Martin Shields (tl). **Getty Images:** Marc Deville (cb). **Science Photo Library:** Pascal Goetgheluck (cla). **Paul A. Selden:** (r). **28 123RF.com:** Yothinpi (t). **Alamy Stock Photo:** Blickwinkel / B. Trapp (cb); Tim Zurowski (cla). **Dreamstime.com:** Danolsen (cl). **Science Photo Library:** Dant Fenolio (ca). **Shutterstock.com:**

Skippy666 (c). **28–29 Alamy Stock Photo:** Danitadelimont.com (c). **29 Alamy Stock Photo:** Blickwinkel / R. Sturm (cla); Oliver Thompson-Holmes (ca); Clarence Holmes Wildlife (cr); Blickwinkel / B. Trapp (clb); Chris Howes / Wild Places Photography (crb). **Dreamstime.com:** Isselee (cra); Jason Ondreicka (tl). **30 Adobe Stock:** Erhard Nerger / Imagebroker (cb); Henrik Larsson (cla); Ondreicka (ca). **Alamy Stock Photo:** Gerry Pearce (cr). **Dreamstime.com:** Isselee (cl); Michal Fuglevic (clb). **31 Adobe Stock:** Macronatura.es (cla); Wayan Sumatika (tr). **Alamy Stock Photo:** Jack Milchanowski (cl); Konrad Wothe / Minden Pictures (cr). **Depositphotos Inc:** Ifeonwhite (tl). **Dreamstime.com:** Adogslifephoto (clb); Kingmaphotos (clb/Ant). **Getty Images / iStock:** Danut Vieru (cb). **32 Alamy Stock Photo:** Charles Melton (cr); Stuart Wilson / Biosphoto (cl); Lessydoang (clb); Jonathan Tichon (tr); Piemags / Nature (cra). **Dreamstime.com:** Catocala7 (tl); Oleksii Kriachko (crb). **Shutterstock.com:** Simon Mustoe (c). **33 Adobe Stock:** Macronatura.es (cr). **Alamy Stock Photo:** Colin Marshall (cra); Zssd / Minden Pictures (crb). **Dreamstime.com:** Argenlant (tr); Catocala7 (l). **34–35 naturepl.com:** Alex Hyde. **36 Dreamstime.com:** Shubhrojyoti Datta (cla); Photowitch (tr); Domiciano Pablo Romero Franco (c). **Getty Images / iStock:** JUN2 (clb); Richwai777 (ca). **Getty Images:** The Image Bank / Darrell Gulin (crb). **Science Photo Library:** Pascal Goetgheluck (cb). **Shutterstock.com:** Feathercollector (cra); Vitalii Hulai (cr). **37 Alamy Stock Photo:** Blickwinkel / Schmidbauer (crb); Nature Picture Library / Konrad Wothe (tl). **Dreamstime.com:** Filip Fuxa (cl); Rqs (ca); Fritz Rositzka (cla); Yodke67 (cra/Leopard lacewing); Vasyl Helevachuk (cr); Parvatti (clb); Pimmimemom (cb). **Getty Images / iStock:** Oleksii Kriachko (cra); Liliboas (tc, tc/Butterflies, tr). **38 Alamy Stock Photo:** Charles Melton (cb); Kevin Elsby (cla). **Dreamstime.com:** Brett Hondow (tl); Shubhrojyoti Datta (tc); Thawats (tr); Diego Cano Cabanes (cra); Sandra Standbridge (cr). **Getty Images / iStock:** Marcophotos (clb). **Shutterstock.com:** BMJ (br); Jim and Lynne Weber (c). **39 Alamy Stock Photo:** Malcolm Schuyl (crb); Minden Pictures / Thomas Marent (tr). **Dorling Kindersley:** Natural History Museum, London / Frank Greenaway (cla, clb). **Getty Images / iStock:** Marcophotos (tl). **Shutterstock.com:** Marcos Cesar Campis (cb); Michal Pesata (cl). **40–41 Dreamstime.com:** Matee Nuserm (1). **41 Dreamstime.com:** Geza Farkas (br); Sutisa Kangvansap (bl). **42–43 Dreamstime.com:** Denboma (ca). **42 Dreamstime.com:** Viktor Chekaramit (cb); Sarah2 (tr); Henk Wallays (cla); Filip Fuxa (cl); Tamer Yilmaz (bl). **43 Adobe Stock:** Marek R. Swadzba (tl). **Alamy Stock Photo:** Nature / Piemags (tc). **Dreamstime.com:** Brett Hondow (ca); Sander Meertins (tr); Dennis Jacobsen (cl); Cathy Keifer (cr); O2beat (clb); Faunuslsd (cb); Leslie Williams (cb/Rosy maple). **Getty Images / iStock:** Eileen Kumpf (cra). **Shutterstock.com:** DJTaylor (crb). **44 Adobe Stock:** Alessandro Grandini (clb). **Alamy Stock Photo:** Clarence Holmes Wildlife (crb); Piemags / Nature (cl). **Dreamstime.com:** Catocala7 (tl); Melinda Fawver (cla); Digitalimagined (cr); Chris Hill (cb). **Getty Images / iStock:** GlobalP (tr). **44–45 Getty Images / iStock:** Harukaze01 (c). **45 Alamy Stock Photo:** Nature Picture Library / John Abbott (tr); Botany Vision (cr); Frank Hecker (cb). **Dreamstime.com:** Natalya Aksenova (cla); Kclarksphotography (tl); Musat Christian (fcla); Viniciussouza06 (ca); Paul Reeves (c). **Getty Images / iStock:** Antagain (crb). **46 Adobe Stock:** Moneycue_Canada (crb). **Alamy Stock Photo:** Frank Hecker (fclb); Piemags / Nature (tc, c); B. Mete Uz (clb). **Dreamstime.com:** Digitalimagined (cla); Tomasz Klejdysz (tl); Surachai2 (tr); Paul Reeves (cra); EPhotocorp (cl). **47 Adobe Stock:** Stan (ca). **Alamy Stock Photo:** Marco McGinty (cl); Minden Pictures / Paul van Hoof / Buiten-beeld (cr). **Depositphotos Inc:** Cheattha (tl). **Dreamstime.com:** Jason Ondreicka (crb); Toxotes (cla). **naturepl.com:** John Abbott (clb). **Shutterstock.com:** Muddy Knees (tr). **48 Alamy Stock Photo:** Ivan Kuzmin (ca); mauritius images GmbH / Luis Castaneda (clb); Nature Picture Library / Robert Thompson (br). **Dreamstime.com:** Isselee (cra/Azure); Shan-lian Mo (cla); Ilona Tymchenko (cr). **Getty Images / iStock:** Ookawaphoto (cra). **49 Alamy Stock Photo:** Sabena Jane Blackbird (cra); imageBROKER.com / Horst Jegen (tl); Danita Delimont (cb); Nature Picture Library / MYN / Edwin Brosens (cl); Dembinsky Photo Associates / Skip Moody (clb). **Dreamstime.com:** Alslutsky (cla); Frank Cornelissen (tr). **Shutterstock.com:** Alslutsky (crb); Dr.NC (cr). **50 Shutterstock.com:** Patrick Rolands (tl). **50–51 Dreamstime.com:** Johnny Lye (Stalk). **Shutterstock.com:** Michal Hykel. **51 Alamy Stock Photo:** Avalon.red / Stephen Dalton (br). **Shutterstock.com:** Alslutsky (cr). **52 Adobe Stock:** Marek R. Swadzba (clb). **Alamy Stock Photo:** Hemis.fr / Dozier Marc (cra). **Dreamstime.com:** Rafael Ben Ari (ca); Suwat Sirivutcharungchit (cl); Isselee (crb). **Getty Images:** Paul Taylor (cr). **53 Adobe Stock:** Distracted_by_Bugs (tr); imageBROKER (crb). **Alamy Stock Photo:** Avalon / Picture Nature / Photoshot (fcrb); Nature Picture Library / MYN / Gil Wizen (tl, tc). **Dreamstime.com:** Isselee (cra, clb). **Getty Images / iStock:** Difydave (ca); Henrik_L (cr). **Dr. Andrew Mitchell (Unseen Universe):** (cla). **54–55 Alamy Stock Photo:** Michiel Vaartjes. **56 Alamy Stock Photo:** Ch'ien Lee / Minden Pictures (clb); Imagebroker / Parameswaran Pillai Karunakaran (cl). **Dreamstime.com:** Matee Nuserm (cla). **56–57 Getty Images:** Peter Adams (c). **57 Alamy Stock Photo:** Adam Seward (crb); Loetscher Chlaus (tr). **Depositphotos Inc:** CherylRamalho (tc). **Dreamstime.com:** Agami Photo Agency (cra); Maciej Czekajewski (tl). **Shutterstock.com:** Sifrx90 Photography (cr). **58 Alamy Stock Photo:** Wildlife Gmbh (cla). **Alexander Hyde:** © Alex Hyde (cl). **Getty Images:** AFP / Torsten Blackwood (clb); Stone / Paul Starosta (cra). **Getty Images / iStock:** FrankRamspott (crb). **Science Photo Library:** Dante Fenolio (c). **59 Adobe Stock:** Shoma81 (cl). **Alamy Stock Photo:** Hemis / Blanchot Philippe (cb); Nature Picture Library / Solvin Zankl (tl); Premaphotos (cla); Nature Picture Library / Alex Hyde (clb); Scott Camazine (crb). **Shutterstock.com:** Charlene Manet (tr). **60 Alamy Stock Photo:** Cothron Photography (cla); M@rcel (cra); Nature Photographers Ltd / Paul R. Sterry (cr); imageBROKER / Farina Grassmann (cl); Gillian Pullinger (c). **Dreamstime.com:** Cherdchai Chaivimol (crb). **61 Alamy Stock Photo:** Blickwinkel / Hecker (tc); Andrew Michael (r). **Dreamstime.com:** Randy Fletcher (clb); Hguerrio (tl); Michael Siluk (c). **62–63 Alamy Stock Photo:** Blickwinkel / Fieber. **64 Alamy Stock Photo:** Blickwinkel / A. Hartl (ca); Piemags / Nature (cla); Michael & Patricia Fogden / Minden Pictures (cl). **Dreamstime.com:** Ernest Cooper (crb); Vaclav Vitovec (tr). **Getty Images / iStock:** Morven Marsh (c). **64–65 Alamy Stock Photo:** John Abbott (cb); Piemags / Nature (ca). **65 Alamy Stock Photo:** Mark Moffett / Minden Pictures (c); Scott Camazine (cra). **Dreamstime.com:** Khaled Ladjimi (crb). **66 Adobe Stock:** Anton (ca). **Alamy Stock Photo:** Richard Becker (cr); Piemags / Nature (cla); Minden Pictures / Piotr Naskrecki (clb). **Dreamstime.com:** Alslutsky (crb); Marcouliana (cl); Claudiodivizia (cb). **66–67 naturepl.com:** Gavin Maxwell (tc). **67 Alamy Stock Photo:** Biosphoto / Marie Aymerez (clb/Grasshopper). **Dreamstime.com:** Jason Ondreicka (c); (null) (null) (cr); Sandra Standbridge (cl); Oleksii Kriachko (crb). **68 Alamy Stock Photo:** Avalon / Bruce Coleman Inc / Jean Claude Carton (cl). **Dreamstime.com:** (c); Aleksey Popov (tr); Yauheni Labanau (ca); Dreamer82 (cb); Konstantin Grigorev (crb). **Shutterstock.com:** Milan Zygmunt (clb). **68–69 Alamy Stock Photo:** Minden Pictures / Paul Bertner (tc). **69 Adobe Stock:** Keith (cra). **Dreamstime.com:** Amwu (cr); Herlinde Noppe (tc); Isselee (clb); Lukaschaloupka (br). **Shutterstock.com:** Patrick K. Campbell (c). **70 Adobe Stock:** Alex Coan (ca). **Alamy Stock Photo:** Blickwinkel / H. Bellmann / F. Hecker (tr); Nature Picture Library / Paul Harcourt Davies (tl); Judith (tc); Phil Degginger (clb). **Dreamstime.com:** Yuri Arcurs (cb); Danolsen (cl); Rudmer Zwerver (c); Isselee (cr). **70–71 Alamy Stock Photo:** EDU Vision (c). **Dreamstime.com:** David Hansche (tc). **71 123RF.com:** Danrieck (tc). **Adobe Stock:** GuillermoOssa (cra); Milkovasa (tr); Macronatura.es (cb). **Alamy Stock Photo:** Nature Picture Library / Gabriel Rojo (br); Andy Newman's Tarantulas (clb). **Dreamstime.com:** Dwiputra18 (cr). **naturepl.com:** Edwin Giesbers (ca). **72–73 © Kephra Beckett.** **74 Adobe Stock:** Ondreicka (cr). **Alamy Stock Photo:** Hakan Soderholm (cl, clb); Piemags / Nature (cra); WildPictures (crb). **Dreamstime.com:** Tomasz Klejdysz (cla). **75 Adobe Stock:** Nechaevkon (cl). **Alamy Stock Photo:** Alan Williams (cb); DP Wildlife Invertebrates (tl); Robert Slade (cra); Blickwinkel / H. Bellmann / F. Hecker (clb). **Dreamstime.com:** Whiskybottle (crb). **Getty Images / iStock:** Karlis Kukainis (tr); Tomasz Klejdysz (cla). **76 Adobe Stock:** Anton (cla). **Alamy Stock Photo:** Blickwinkel / A. Hartl (cb); Blickwinkel / H. Bellmann / F. Hecker (bl); Stephen Dalton (crb). **Dreamstime.com:** Digitalimagined (br); Slowmotiongli (cl). **76–77 Dreamstime.com:** Mr.noppadol Buaroey (cb). **naturepl.com:** Andy Sands (c). **77 Adobe Stock:** Witsawat (c). **Alamy Stock Photo:** Blickwinkel / Bellmann (cra); Paul R. Sterry (ca); Hakan Soderholm (cb); Imagebroker / Matthias Lenke (cr); Myn / Dirk Funhoff (r). **Dreamstime.com:** Earnesttse (cla); Martin Pelanek (cl); Wirestock (clb); Lukas Blazek (bl). **78–79 Getty Images / iStock:** Tramont_Ana. **80 Dreamstime.com:** Alexander Kuzovlev (bl); Abdul Latif (cl). **82 Adobe Stock:** Thijs de Graaf (tr). **Dreamstime.com:** Digitalimagined (cra, cb); Henk Wallays (tc, bc); Alexander Korovin (cla); Ritam777 (clb); Ondrej Prosicky (crb). **Getty Images / iStock:** Wirestock (ca). **83 Alamy Stock Photo:** MichaelGrantWildlife (tc); Zoonar GmbH / Manfred Ruckszio (cla); Nature Picture Library / MYN / Clay Bolt (cl). **Dreamstime.com:** 7active Studio (cra); Bimserd (cr); Vladimir Blinov (clb). **naturepl.com:** Piotr Naskrecki (tl). **84–85 Alamy Stock Photo:** AfriPics.com. **86 Adobe Stock:** Chase DAnimulls (cla). **Alamy Stock Photo:** Joe Dlugo (cra); Premaphotos (tl); Nicolas Vereecken (ca); Elizabeth Nunn (b). **Dreamstime.com:** Alslutsky (cl, cr); Catocala7 (clb); Manoranjan Mishra (crb). **87 Adobe Stock:** Yod67 (c). **Alamy Stock Photo:** George Grall (cra); Nature Picture Library / MYN / Clay Bolt (cla); The Natural History Museum, London (cl). **Depositphotos Inc:** Spineback (cb). **Dreamstime.com:** Danut Vieru (ca). **Getty Images / iStock:** Emer1940 (c/bumblebee). **naturepl.com:** Thomas Marent (br). **Shutterstock.com:** Alslutsky (crb). **88 123RF.com:** Aukid (clb). **Alamy Stock Photo:** Ingo Arndt / Minden Pictures (crb); Juniors Bildarchiv / F356 (cra); Scott Camazine (cr). **Dreamstime.com:** Kidsada Manchinda (cla); Wirestock (tr); Nuwat Phansuwan (cl); Salparadis (crb/Leaf). **89 Adobe Stock:** Ted17 / Wirestock Creators (clb). **Alamy Stock Photo:** Pascal Pittorino (crb); Robert Kennett (tl); Ramki (cr). **Dreamstime.com:** Anant Kasetsinsombut (tr); Arisa Thepbanchornchai (cra); Rafal Rutkowski (cla). **90 Alamy Stock Photo:** Blickwinkel / Hecker (tr); Anton Sorokin (tl); Nature Picture Library / Martin Dohrn (cra); MYN / Lily Kumpe (crb). **Dreamstime.com:** Poravute Siriphiroon (cl); Viniciussouza06 (c). **naturepl.com:** Piotr Naskrecki (clb); Nature Production (cr). **91 Adobe Stock:** AK ST (tc); Elharo (cl); Muhammad (c). **Alamy Stock Photo:** Denis Crawford (tr). **Dreamstime.com:** EPhotocorp (ca); Isselee (cra). **92–93 Alamy Stock Photo:** Minden Pictures / Mark Moffett. **94 Adobe Stock:** imageBROKER (tc). **Alamy Stock Photo:** Biosphoto / Stephane Vitzthum (cra); imageBROKER.com / Andre Skonieczny (tr); Nature / Piemags (cr). **Dreamstime.com:** Alslutsky (ca); Wirestock (tl); Isselee (ca); Yoga Apriliant o (crb). **naturepl.com:** Rolf Nussbaumer (c). **94–95 naturepl.com:** Nick Upton (tc). **95 Adobe Stock:** Wirestock Creators / Reinier Blok (cla). **Alamy Stock Photo:** Nature Picture Library / MYN / Lily Kumpe (tc); Dembinsky Photo Associates / Skip Moody (tr); The Natural History Museum, London (ca); Minden Pictures / Michael Durham (c). **Depositphotos Inc:** Wirestock (bc). **Dreamstime.com:** Alslutsky (cr); Dwiputra18 (cra); Jameskho (clb); Fotogigi85 (cb); Björn Wylezich (crb). **Getty Images / iStock:** ConstantinCorel (cl). **96 Alamy Stock Photo:** Blickwinkel / H. Bellmann / F. Hecker (tl); Nature Photographers Ltd / Richard Revels (clb). **Dreamstime.com:** Cathy Keifer (cr). **Getty Images:** Andrew M. Snyder (tr). **naturepl.com:** Nature Production (cl). **97 Alamy Stock Photo:** Michael D. Kern (crb); Nature Picture Library / Doug Wechsler (cr); Nature Picture Library / Michael D. Kern (cb). **Dreamstime.com:** Ernest Cooper (tl). **naturepl.com:** Nature Production (cl). **Shutterstock.com:** Frauenversand Cleopatra (clb). **98 Alamy Stock Photo:** Martin Shields (l). **Dreamstime.com:** Chris Moncrieff (cb); Viniciussouza06 (ca); Nataliavo (c). **Getty Images / iStock:** Feathercollector (cr). **naturepl.com:** Rolf Nussbaumer (cra). **Shutterstock.com:** Kawin Jiaranaisakul (crb). **99 Alamy Stock Photo:** Nature Photographers Ltd / Paul R. Sterry (cl); John Richmond (tl); Andrew Newman Nature Pictures (tc); Nigel Cattlin (crb). **Dreamstime.com:** Ines Carrara (c); Paul Reeves (cla). **naturepl.com:** Mark Bowler (tr). **Science Photo Library:** Melvyn Yeo (clb). **100–101 naturepl.com:** Nick Garbutt. **102 Alamy Stock Photo:** Minden Pictures / Ch'ien Lee (tl). **Dreamstime.com:** Isselee (cla); Olga Ovchinnikova (cl); I Wayan Sumatika (cr); Palex66 (crb). **Getty Images / iStock:** Henrik_L (tr). **naturepl.com:** Bence Mate (c). **102–103 Dreamstime.com:** Toby Gibson (ca). **103 Alamy Stock Photo:** David Chapman (tr); Helmut Göthel Symbiosis (tl); Anton Sorokin (clb). **Dreamstime.com:** Fotogigi85 (cl); Iuliia Morozova (cra); Wirestock (cr). **104 Adobe Stock:** Pedro (tr/White Ermine); Yoderphotography (bl). **Alamy Stock Photo:** Moth (tc); Nature Picture Library / Nick Hawkins (cra). **Dreamstime.com:** Tony Bosse (tl); Dero2084 (tr); Henk Wallays (cla); Susan Hodgson (ca); Zagorskid (cr). **105 Adobe Stock:** Elharo (cl); Marco Uliana (cr). **Alamy Stock Photo:** Phil Degginger (clb); SBS Eclectic Images (cla). **Dreamstime.com:** Grafvision (tc/Cockchafer); Viter8 (tl); Björn Wylezich (tc); Danut Vieru (tr); Apurv Jadhav (cra); Marcouliana (ca); Alexander Hasenkampf (c); Isselee (cl/Hornet); Vasyl Helevachuk (cb); Jaroslav Noska (crb). **106–107 Alamy Stock Photo:**

Acknowledgments

Nature Picture Library / Tony Wu. **108 Alamy Stock Photo:** Emanuel Tanjala (b). **naturepl.com:** Ingo Arndt (tr); Doug Wechsler (tl). **109 Alamy Stock Photo:** Imago (t). **Getty Images:** AFP / Yasuyoshi Chiba (b). **110 Alamy Stock Photo:** Ivan Kuzmin (ca); Tim Fitzharris / Minden Pictures (cla); Premaphotos (cr). **Dreamstime.com:** Wrangel (cl). **110–111 Alamy Stock Photo:** Charles Marden Fitch (b). **Dreamstime.com:** Andreistanescu (ca). **111 Alamy Stock Photo:** Blickwinkel / Hecker (c); Terrance Klassen (cb); Malcolm Schuyl (cr). **112–113 Getty Images:** Gamma-Rapho / Sylvain Cordier. **114 Alamy Stock Photo:** Dave Rimes (cla). **Dreamstime.com:** Fernando Gregory (cra). **115 Alamy Stock Photo:** Nature Picture Library / Rod Williams (tr). **Dreamstime.com:** Dave Massey (cra). **Shutterstock.com:** Orapin Joonkhajohn (cla). **116 Alamy Stock Photo:** Ephotocorp / Apurv Jadhav (tl); Minden Pictures / Ingrid Visser / Hedgehog House (cla); Tammy Wolfe (ca); Nature Picture Library / Alex Hyde (cra). **Dreamstime.com:** Isselee (tr); Urospoteko (cl); Kaido Rummel (clb); Apisit Wilaijit (cb). **116–117 Alamy Stock Photo:** Rolf Nussbaumer Photography / Bill Draker / Rolfnp (bc). **117 Alamy Stock Photo:** Blickwinkel / F. Hecker (tl). **Dreamstime.com:** Gerald Deboer (tr); Mailmeviju (cra); Yodke67 (cl); Kaye Oberstar (cr); Melinda Fawver (cb). **Shutterstock.com:** Dr Morley Read (crb). **118–119 Alamy Stock Photo:** Nature Picture Library / Stephen Dalton. **120 Alamy Stock Photo:** Richard Becker (crb); Jürgen Kottmann (cr). **Dreamstime.com:** Musat Christian (cb). **Getty Images / iStock:** Kickers (clb). **Shutterstock.com:** Russell Marshall (cl). **121 Alamy Stock Photo:** Nature Picture Library / Kim Taylor (bl). **122 Alamy Stock Photo:** Nigel Cattlin (cb). **Dreamstime.com:** Sander Meertins (ca). **Getty Images / iStock:** Constantincornel (cr); Lam Van Linh (cla). **naturepl.com:** Nature Production (c). **122–123 Alamy Stock Photo:** Dieter Hopf (c). **Dreamstime.com:** S Walker (t). **123 Adobe Stock:** Rolf Müller (cra). **Alamy Stock Photo:** Piemags / Nature (cla); Ray Kriner / Grant Heilman Photography (cra). **Dreamstime.com:** Paul Reeves (c). **124 Alamy Stock Photo:** FLPA (tl); Nature Picture Library / MYN / Andrew Snyder (cl). **Dreamstime.com:** EPhotocorp (cr); Maryann Preisinger (tr); Spineback (cra); Ernest Cooper (cla); Eyeblink (clb). **Getty Images / iStock:** BrianEKushner (crb). **Shutterstock.com:** Stacey-Lia (cb). **125 Adobe Stock:** Paul.E (cra). **Alamy Stock Photo:** George Grall (c). **Dreamstime.com:** Bertino8425 (cli); Jeff Jarrett (tr); Palex66 (tl); Rqs (cla). **Science Photo Library:** Pascal Goetgheluck (crb). **Shutterstock.com:** Hellomumu (cb). **126 Adobe Stock:** Federico (tl); Sue (cr). **Alamy Stock Photo:** Cbstockfoto (tc); Larry Doherty (cra). **Dreamstime.com:** Sandra Standbridge (ch); Harry Syahrizuan (cl). **127 Alamy Stock Photo:** Blickwinkel (tc); Photo Resource Hawaii / Steven Lee Montgomery (tr); Nature Picture Library / Shibai Xiao (cr); Nature Picture Library / Solvin Zankl (ch); David Norton (cb). **Dreamstime.com:** Ian Redding (crb); Slowmotiongli (c). **128–129 Alamy Stock Photo:** Itsik Marom. **130 Adobe Stock:** ihorhvozdetskiy (cb); Peter_Waters (cla). **Alamy Stock Photo:** Imagebroker / Dieter Mahlke (c). **Dreamstime.com:** Macrowildlife (ca); Iamtkb (cra); Spineback (cl). **Getty Images / iStock:** M Alan Mirza (cb). **Shutterstock.com:** Kungfu01 (crb). **131 123RF.com:** Mguntow (c). **Alamy Stock Photo:** Piemags / Nature (tl, clb). **Depositphotos Inc:** Christian (cr). **Dreamstime.com:** Agami Photo Agency (cl); Rudmer Zwerver (tr); O2beat (ca); Slavkosereda (cb). **naturepl.com:** MYN / Paul Harcourt Davies (crb). **132–133 Dreamstime.com:** Amwu (tc). **132 Adobe Stock:** Gerry (ca). **Alamy Stock Photo:** Blickwinkel / Hecker (cra). **Dreamstime.com:** Aaskolnick (tl); Roman Milert (clb). **Shutterstock.com:** Ondrej Michalek (cra). **133 Alamy Stock Photo:** Hum Images (cl). **Dreamstime.com:** Henk Wallays (clb); Oleg Kovtun (tr). **naturepl.com:** Nature Production (c); Paul Harcourt Davies (cr). **134–135 Shutterstock.com:** Conscarsch (c). **134 Adobe Stock:** Lessysebastian (cl). **Alamy Stock Photo:** Minden Pictures / Piotr Naskrecki (tr, ca, crb). **Dreamstime.com:** Kuritafsheen (bl). **Shutterstock.com:** Natalie Gagnon (cla). **135 Adobe Stock:** Agustin (c); Sebastian (cr). **Alamy Stock Photo:** Biosphoto / Frank Deschandol & Philippe Sabine (cl); Nature Picture Library / MYN / Emanuele Biggi (cb); Biosphoto / Tonci Maletic (bc). **Depositphotos Inc:** Lifeonwhite (tc). **Dreamstime.com:** Miroslaw Kijewski (ca). **naturepl.com:** Alex Hyde (tr). **136–137 Alamy Stock Photo:** Phil Degginger. **138 Alamy Stock Photo:** Minden Pictures / Claus Meyer (cr); Pix (tl); Nature Picture Library / Bernard Castelein (tr); Minden Pictures / Stephen Dalton (crb). **Dreamstime.com:** Jason Ondreicka (tc). **Getty Images / iStock:** ePhotocorp (cl). **139 Adobe Stock:** Sahara Frost (ca); Recep (tr). **Alamy Stock Photo:** Biosphoto / Frank Deschandol & Philippe Sabine (tc); Minden Pictures / Paul Bertner (ca); Blickwinkel / H. Bellmann / F. Hecker (clb); Piemags / Nature (cb, crb). **Shutterstock.com:** Ogijs4 (tll). **140 Alamy Stock Photo:** Biosphoto / Michel Gunther (cra); Minden Pictures / James Christensen (tl); Richard Garvey-Williams (ca); Minden Pictures / Agustin Esmoris (cr); Danita Delimont Creative / Adam Jones / DanitaDelimont.com (crb). **Depositphotos Inc:** EWTC (tr). **Dreamstime.com:** Cynoclub (c); Ernest Cooper (clb); Palex66 (cb). **141 Alamy Stock Photo:** Blickwinkel / B. Trapp (cra, cr); Blickwinkel (cl). **Dreamstime.com:** Alexey Kuznetsov (tr); Adilson Sochodolak (cla). **Getty Images / iStock:** Xesai (c). **Shutterstock.com:** Kurit Afshen (tl). **142–143 Alamy Stock Photo:** Imagebroker / Friedhelm Adam (c). **142 Adobe Stock:** Tonia (clb). **Dreamstime.com:** Domiciano Pablo Romero Franco (cra); Lingkon Serao (cla); Maciej Olszewski (crb). **Shutterstock.com:** Hopeby (ca). **143 Alamy Stock Photo:** MYN / Andrew Snyder (ca); MYN / Lily Kumpe (clb). **Depositphotos Inc:** Squarelens (c). **Dreamstime.com:** Brett Hondow (cr). **Getty Images / iStock:** Dustin Rhoades (cl); Vinisouza128 (cla). **naturepl.com:** Claudio Contreras (crb). **Shutterstock.com:** Fusco Davide (cb); Pixelworlds (tr). **144–145 naturepl.com:** Ingo Arndt. **146 Alamy Stock Photo:** FLPA (clb). **Dreamstime.com:** Floriankittemann (tr); Ken Griffiths (tl). **Getty Images / iStock:** Tevarak (crb). **naturepl.com:** Morley Read (c). **147 Alamy Stock Photo:** Denis Crawford (cb); Les Gibbon (tr); Gabbro (c); Mark Moffett / Minden Pictures (cr). **Alan Cressler:** Alan Cressler (clb). **Depositphotos Inc:** Ianredding (crb). **Getty Images / iStock:** Jojo Dexter (crb). **Science Photo Library:** Gregory Dimijian (cl). **148 Alamy Stock Photo:** Blickwinkel / H. Duty (cra); Nature / Piemags (bc). **Getty Images / iStock:** Victor Golmer (bl); Pawich Sattalerd (cla). **Shutterstock.com:** Gherzak (cl). **148–149 Dreamstime.com:** Henkbogaard (c). **149 Adobe Stock:** Henri Koskinen (cr). **Alamy Stock Photo:** Jonathan Mbu (Pura Vida Exotics) (br); Nature Picture Library / MYN / Gil Wizen (c). **Shutterstock.com:** Protasov AN (ca). **150 Adobe Stock:** Paul Tessier / Stocksy (c). **Alamy Stock Photo:** Blickwinkel (cb); Nigel Cattlin (cla); Mario Saccomano (ca). **Dreamstime.com:** Lillian Tveit (cl). **naturepl.com:** Stephen Dalton (cr).

150–151 Alamy Stock Photo: Science History Images (t). **151 Alamy Stock Photo:** Chronicle (ca); Ivan Kuzmin (clb); Diana Meister (cr). **Dreamstime.com:** Henrikhl (cl); Veremer (tr). **152–153 naturepl.com:** Etienne Littlefair. **154 Dreamstime.com:** Mr.Smith Chetanachan / Smuaya (bc). **Getty Images / iStock:** Imnature (bl). **156 Alamy Stock Photo:** Minden Pictures / Rob Blanken / NIS (b). **Depositphotos Inc:** Harmonia101 (cl). **Dreamstime.com:** Cherdchai Chaivimol (c); Danut Vieru (tl); Marigo20 (cra); Palex66 (c). **Getty Images / iStock:** Dimitris66 (cr); Andreas Häuslbetz (tc). **Shutterstock.com:** Luc Pouliot (tr). **156–157 Dreamstime.com:** Isselee (c). **157 Alamy Stock Photo:** Daniel Borzynski (crb/Mite). **Depositphotos Inc:** Vladvitek (crb). **Dreamstime.com:** Cathy Keifer (tr); Palex66 (tl); Danut Vieru (c); Wirestock (cb); Leerobin (cr). **Getty Images / iStock:** Brett_Hondow (clb); Moonstone Images (ca). **158 Alamy Stock Photo:** Clarence Holmes Wildlife (ca). **Dreamstime.com:** Domiciano Pablo Romero Franco (c); Palex66 (tl); Jason Ondreicka (tr); Oleksandr Kostiuchenko (ca); Pitris (cr). **Shutterstock.com:** AjayTvm (tc). **159 Alamy Stock Photo:** The Natural History Museum, London (b). **Dorling Kindersley:** Ashley Bradford (cra). **Dreamstime.com:** Bogdan Dumitru (c); Tomasz Klejdysz (tl); Zagorskid (tc); Armando Frazão (cl). **Getty Images / iStock:** Tomasz Klejdysz (tr). **160–161 naturepl.com:** Eduardo Blanco. **162 Adobe Stock:** Samuel (c). **Alamy Stock Photo:** Clarence Holmes Wildlife (crb); Michael & Patricia Fogden / Minden Pictures (clb). **Dreamstime.com:** KPixMining (cr). **naturepl.com:** Jussi Murtosaari (cla). **Shutterstock.com:** Bok David (cb); Chinahbzyg (cra). **163 Alamy Stock Photo:** Frank Deschandol & Philippe Sabine / Biosphoto (cl); Husni Che Ngah / Biosphoto (crb). **Depositphotos Inc:** Ppl1958 (cl). **Dreamstime.com:** Isselee (clb). **Getty Images / iStock:** Alexey Protasov (cra); Tomasz Klejdysz (ca); ViniSouza128 (cr). **164 Adobe Stock:** Imkerei Hablützel (cra). **Dreamstime.com:** Marcouliana (c); Palex66 (tr); Viniciussouza06 (tr); O2beat (tc). **naturepl.com:** Paul Bertner (ca); Doug Wechsler (bl). **165 Alamy Stock Photo:** Blickwinkel / H. Bellmann / F. Hecker (clb); Nature Picture Library / Alex Hyde (c). **Dreamstime.com:** Joseph Khoury (tl); Harms Scott (cr). **Getty Images / iStock:** Tomasz Klejdysz (tr); Luc Pouliot (tc). **Shutterstock.com:** Anjeliazola (crb). **166 Adobe Stock:** Danita Delimont (crb); Magic Hen (tr); CTK (clb); 2020 Images (tr). **Dorling Kindersley:** Natural History Museum, London / Frank Greenaway (tl); Natural History Museum, London / Colin Keates (c). **167 Alamy Stock Photo:** Nature Picture Library / Sandesh Kadur (cr); Blickwinkel / B. Trapp (br). **Dreamstime.com:** Roman Ivaschenko (cr); Rudmer Zwerver (c). **Getty Images / iStock:** Sh_Trail (cl). **IUCN 2025. The IUCN Red List of Threatened Species. Version 2025-1. https://www.iucnredlist.org:** Information on the threatened status of species obtained from IUCN. 2025. The IUCN Red List of Threatened Species. Version 2025-1. https://www.iucnredlist.org. Accessed on [25/11/2025]. (tr) (Bug at Risk Pie Chart).

Cover images: *Front:* **123RF.com:** Alekss / Alexandr Pakhnyushchyy crb; **Adobe Stock:** Yod67 ca/ (Bee); **Alamy Stock Photo:** George Grall bc; **Dreamstime.com:** Isselee tl/ (Scorpion), Marcouliana tl, cra, Pitris bl; **Getty Images / iStock:** Ale-ks cb, Mathisa_S tc/ (Moth), TomDeer tc; **Science Photo Library:** Dant Fenolio ca; **Shutterstock.com:** Anatol br, Anton Kozyrev clb; *Back:* **Dreamstime.com:** Catocala7 ca, Domiciano Pablo Romero Franco cra, crb, Jeff Johnson tr, Cosmin Manci clb, bl, Mattwatt, Spineback ca/ (Rosy Maple Moth), Takepicsforfun br, Thawats bc; **Getty Images / iStock:** Cyoginan tl; **Shutterstock.com:** Conscarsch cla; *Spine:* **Shutterstock.com:** Anatol

OUR WORLD IN PICTURES

BOOKS

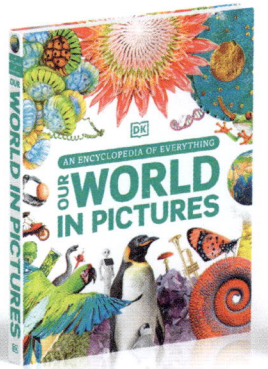 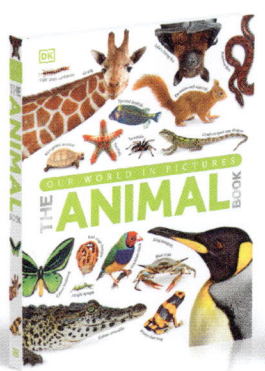 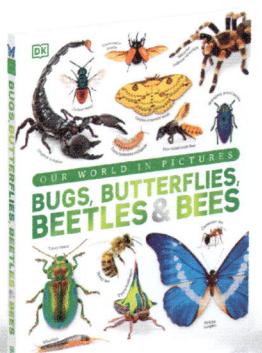 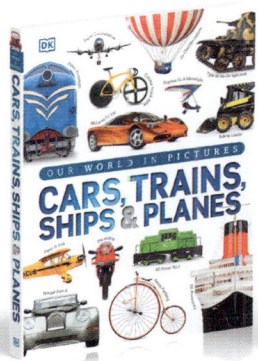 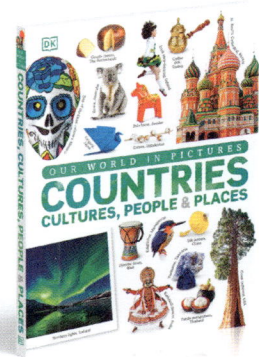

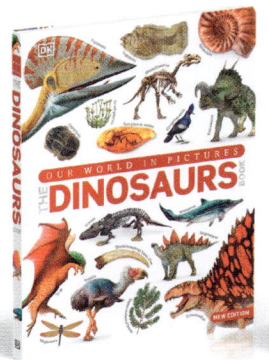 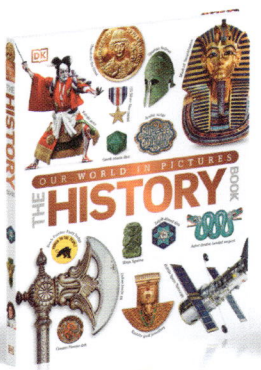 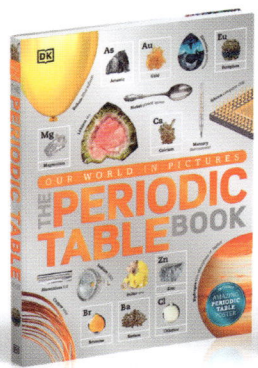 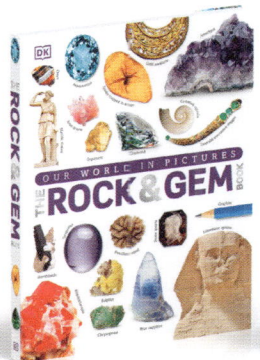 

FLASH CARDS

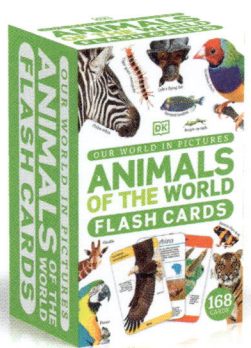 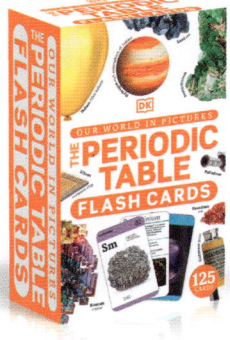 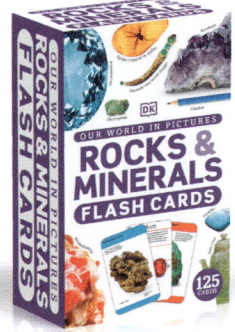 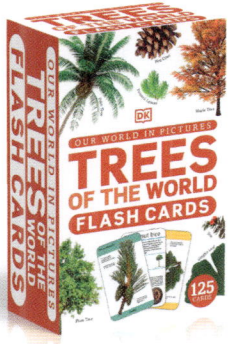